THE MORAN BROTHERS

THE MORAN BROTHERS

Brian Burford

TEMPUS

First published 2002

PUBLISHED IN THE UNITED KINGDOM BY:

Tempus Publishing Ltd
The Mill, Brimscombe Port
Stroud, Gloucestershire GL5 2QG

PUBLISHED IN THE UNITED STATES OF AMERICA BY:

Tempus Publishing Inc.
2A Cumberland Street
Charleston, SC 29401

Tempus books are available in France and Germany from the following addresses:

Tempus Publishing Group   Tempus Publishing Group
21 Avenue de la République   Hockheimer Strasse 59
37300 Joué-lès-Tours   D-99094 Erfurt
FRANCE   GERMANY

British Library Cataloguing in Publication Data.
A catalogue record for this book is available from the British Library.

ISBN 0 7524 2424 6

Typesetting and origination by Tempus Publishing.
PRINTED AND BOUND IN GREAT BRITAIN.

CONTENTS

Acknowledgements	6
Foreword by Billy Hamill	7
Introduction	8
1. Desert Brats	10
2. Rain and Roundabouts	25
3. Chasing Gold	63
4. Flying the Flag	105
5. Have Bike, Will Travel	138
6. An Ocean Apart	149
7. Pair-fect	171
Epilogue	219
Racing Records	220

ACKNOWLEDGEMENTS

I would like to express my thanks to the following people for all their help with this book:

All the riders, promoters and managers who have spared their time to contribute their thoughts and memories. Special thanks go to Billy Hamill and Craig Cummings, who were always ready to answer questions and offer opinions – thanks guys, you're a credit to the sport. A big thank you to John Chaplin for all of his help and guidance over the years, to Ken Carpenter for supplying the excellent cover shot, and to James Howarth and all at Tempus Publishing for their continued support and interest in speedway publications. I'd also like to express my gratitude to Nick Barber and Sean Wilson. Special thanks to Philip Handel for his technical expertise, and to Geoff Pennell for getting me started with the necessary technology. Thanks also to my good friend Gareth Owen for his support and interest, and for re-igniting my enthusiasm for this project without actually realising it! A special mention too, for my mother, who has always supported me and puts up with my ever-expanding archive.

This book would not have been quite the same without the interest and input from Kelly and Shawn – if you guys only knew how I nervous I was when I made that first call! – and I would like to pass on my thanks to them and to Kelly for his kind words.

This book is dedicated to the memory of my father, who was a big supporter of the Moran brothers and speedway racing. Without him, this would never ever have been possible. God Bless.

FOREWORD
BY BILLY HAMILL (1996 WORLD CHAMPION)

I first remember seeing Shawn and Kelly Moran as a little kid. They were two of the most talented speedway riders I've ever been privileged enough to watch and, of course, race against. They were unique and ahead of their time.

My first impression of them was that it didn't matter how tight their schedule was, they always had time for people and were very friendly. I remember going up to them as a child and they would talk to you on the same level, and not down to you as some would to a nine-year-old boy. Then, when I was starting out in junior speedway, Kelly was racing at home, and I was always bugging him for advice, but he was always helpful.

When I came over to England, I had the privilege of racing against them, and then alongside them in the American team. The USA had qualified for the World Team Cup at Pardubice, in the Czech Republic, and it was my first trip to the European continent. They were nothing but helpful to me. They were certainly there for me with whatever help I needed, or anything they could help with. It was a fantastic experience because we were victorious and I was lucky enough to go with those guys who were my heroes.

As racers they were phenomenal. You can't say enough about them – so much talent. Part of their talent came from their character. I believe if they didn't have that character, that charisma, they probably wouldn't have been so successful or so popular. Whether they would have been so talented; who can say?

They not only brought something to the Americans, they also brought something to the sport. They were very well respected and liked on and off the track as being the fairest riders in the world. You don't get many riders like that, even less so in these days of intense racing. Off the track, they were the life and soul of the party – always. If you were at Sheffield, Belle Vue, or wherever, it was always like, 'Hey, the party's at my place.' That was their spirit, they were fun-loving guys. They were the kind of people who would give you the shirt off their back, and they're still the same way.

There is no way you can ignore the Moran brothers. Not only with what they accomplished themselves, but they more or less paved the way for guys like Greg Hancock and myself. When I came to England to race, everybody had this picture of Americans as being charismatic, being showmen, and in one way it was hard to live up to that. But in another it opened up a lot of doors for me.

They will always be my favourites – the ones that shine on and off the track. They lived up to my expectations with the kind of genuine people they were and still are. The memories I have of watching them as a kid, racing against them, and then racing with them in the American team, are very fond memories.

INTRODUCTION

Many years ago, I had occasion to travel to Bexhill to interview the town's local celebrity, the charming Desmond Llewellyn – better known as 'Q' in the James Bond films. The interview went well, but when I climbed into my car to begin my journey home, the exhaust broke and I had to find a garage for a quick repair as I couldn't roar my way home for the next 200 miles, however tempting it might be.

Luckily it wasn't too late in the day and I found a garage to do the repairs. One of the fitters there noticed the 'Kelly Moran – Belle Vue Speedway' sticker on the back window, and he told me that Kelly was a real hero at Eastbourne and was always around to help the juniors. This fitter was one of those junior riders who had benefited from his help and advice, but never actually made the grade from junior status to being a full-time professional rider.

It was at this point that I decided to pursue, on a part-time basis, a book about the Moran brothers and their racing careers. Although it is eight years or so since Shawn Moran retired, they remain very popular and everyone has a particular memory of them.

I approached Shawn about a biography shortly after he retired in 1994. At first he wasn't too keen, but after using a few of my persuasive powers he began to come round to the idea. He said that he would have to discuss the matter with his brother Kelly and asked me to call back in a week. Unfortunately, when I called back he hadn't talked to Kelly and he had decided to sell his house in England and return to the USA. Therefore, I decided to drop the idea. But such is the interest in them that I chose to do a racing biography, told through the eyes of the people who raced and worked with them, and combine it with the many articles and clippings from my own private collection. I was sure that it would make entertaining reading.

It was during the research and preparation for this book that I came in to contact with former World Champion, Billy Hamill. Not only was he kind enough to write the foreword, but he also paved the way for me to make contact with the brothers again. Despite the years that have passed, they still remain as friendly and as helpful as they ever were. The Moran magic was still very much in evidence, and they have had a significant input into the book.

I first saw Kelly riding for Hull in 1979 at my local track, Swindon, when the Vikings looked like they were championship contenders. Their team also included Ivan Mauger – soon to be crowned World Champion for the sixth time – and another American star, Dennis Sigalos.

On this particular August day it rained and rained and rained! I was quite young at the time and full of enthusiasm for speedway racing. In June of that year, as a special treat, my father had taken me for my first taste and smell of a sport that I have followed with such enthusiasm ever since. I looked forward to every Saturday for my weekly fix of action and the elements outside did not bode well for this particular fixture. I remember asking my mother: 'When will it stop raining?' She replied: 'When you see a patch of blue sky big enough to make a pair of sailor's trousers, then it will clear up.' Sure enough, at around 4 p.m., the clouds parted like a scene from the Bible and it stopped raining!

My first impression of Kelly was that his Christian name was not one for a speedway rider. After all, the only 'Kelly' I knew of at that time was Jaclyn Smith's character in the 1970s television show *Charlie's Angels*. However, on a rain-soaked track he soon proved his talent by scoring a paid 11 points and beating Swindon's best – including Phil Crump, who was usually in top form in those days.

It was just under a year later at the same fixture when I first encountered Shawn. He caught my attention because of his long hair. He didn't make the same kind of impression as his brother (who had now left Hull), but it was obvious that he also had a lot of talent.

Both of them had bags of ability, but what endeared them to me and to the crowds all around the world was how friendly and approachable they were. They were stars, but they were not touched by their stardom, and came across as fun-loving Californians. It was no trouble to either of them to stop and sign autographs, pose for photographs or answer questions. Furthermore, neither of them were strangers to the many bars at the various tracks around the world, which made them even more popular and accessible to the public. They were two of the most colourful and exciting riders to grace the speedway tracks during the late 1970s, '80s, and early '90s. Belle Vue boss John Perrin, who had them both in his team at one point said of them: 'They put bums on seats.' Their exciting and entertaining style of racing meant that neither of them knew when they were beaten, and this attracted the crowds. At Eastbourne, such was Kelly's popularity in Sussex that on his way to the tapes for a race it was reported that he could be seen shaking hands with the fans as they hung over the safety fence to greet his arrival to the start line.

They were among the first wave of US riders who swamped the British League and for a time dominated the international arena. It began with the arrival of Scott Autrey at Exeter in 1973, and reached its height when Bruce Penhall became the first American since Jack Milne in 1937, to win the World Individual Championship with back-to-back wins in 1981 and 1982. The Morans were at the beginning of this domination, and continued to fly the flag when the USA's star had begun to dim during the mid- to late 1980s.

Both of them courted controversy during their careers, and their laid back approach to the life of a professional speedway rider did not please some critics. However, as you will read, success on a team or an individual level was no stranger to either of them.

1

DESERT BRATS

When Kelly Moran was born on 21 September 1960, speedway racing in the USA was almost dead. There were no Americans racing in Britain and their last World Finalist was Ernie Roccio in 1951. Tragically, Roccio was killed at West Ham before he could fulfil his potential. It seemed that speedway in the USA had all but died with him. For their last World Champion, historians had to go back to the pre-war years and 1937, when Jack Milne lifted the crown and the US riders filled the top three places. No men from this once proud speedway nation had even made the podium since the war, and but for Roccio and a few other racers, the sport was barely surviving. In speedway terms, this can only be described as the 'dark ages' for the USA.

Jack Milne and many others blamed the arrival of the new entertainment medium of television for the decline. This also affected speedway in Europe too, but the sport had a more secure footing here and, despite the hard times, it continued to progress, with riders like Ove Fundin, Peter Craven, Barry Briggs, Ivan Mauger and Ronnie Moore all thrilling the crowds.

Traditionally, speedway racing in America has made its home in California, although there has been racing in other parts of the country. Therefore, when the time came for a rebirth, it was not surprising that it was in the so-called Golden State, where the dying roots of speedway racing were revived from near extinction.

Jack Milne was almost the forgotten man as far as speedway racing was concerned. His achievements attracted more recognition in Europe than they did in his homeland. But motorcycles were always in his blood, and he ran a highly successful motorcycle shop in Pasedena, California, where he built up a solid reputation within the trade.

One day, Jack decided to take on a new employee by the name of Harry Oxley, who took on the role of his manager, dealing with sales, parts and service. A former commercial fisherman among other things, Oxley ran his own motorcycle shop in Northern California, but the business folded and he headed south. However, the brake-less speedway bikes in Milne's shop fascinated Oxley.

'I'd never seen a speedway bike in my life and he had his old world championship bike and his brother Cordy's old bike on the shop floor – and I was pretty fascinated by them,' said Oxley in the June 1995 edition of *5-One* magazine.

'He used to look at the speedway bikes and didn't know what the hell they were,' recalled Milne. 'He got very interested in them.'

When Milne took a bike to Costa Mesa and raced round the tiny horse show track, Oxley thought it was great. He also dabbled in bike racing as he used to ride in the TT dirt-track races that included jumps. More importantly, he enjoyed this so much that he also promoted some of these events too. Harry recognised the potential of this form of motorcycle racing that he had just discovered, so he asked Jack about getting a bunch of these old bikes together and running a few races. Milne agreed, and so began a revival.

With some financial help from the former World Champion, Oxley set about running his first speedway events in the San Fernando Valley in 1968. They had a newspaperman on hand to record the rebirth and announce to the world that speedway racing was back in the USA. It was a moderate success and caught the attention of the then recently crowned World Champion, Ivan Mauger.

The duo's enthusiasm for the sport rubbed off on Mauger and he agreed to come to the States and run a fortnight's training school at the Whiteman Stadium. But it wasn't quite what the Kiwi had expected, as he revealed in the 1972 *Webster's Speedway Annual*.

'I'll never forget my first sight of American speedway at Whiteman. All the riders wore old-fashioned leathers, and they had battered old bikes with the handlebars turned down. No one was sliding round the bends and if I hadn't just landed at Los Angeles Airport I would have thought I was back in the 1940s. It was just unbelievable.'

The ever-popular Scottish globetrotter Bert Harkins had beaten Mauger and his colleague from New Zealand, Barry Briggs, by one week to be the first Europe-based rider to visit America. His first sight of America's speedway revival surprised him too.

'They were Flat Tracking really, which was what Kenny Roberts (three times World 500cc Road Racing Champion) used to do. In Europe we had big handlebars, because we needed to be able to turn the bike because of the dirt, you see? But the Americans learnt very quickly.'

However, when Mauger and Briggs unloaded their machines and demonstrated the skills which had made them two of the sport's most successful riders, their keen students and other spectators couldn't believe it, as Oxley explained:

'We had never seen anyone who could ride a motorcycle like Ivan and Barry could. They would do a match race, and Barry could put his foot on Ivan's footrest and they'd run around side by side for four laps! No one had ever seen anyone do that in this country because our motorbikes weren't capable of it.'

Nonetheless, this only fuelled Oxley's enthusiasm to promote modern day speedway racing, and he planned to introduce it to the Orange County Fairgrounds and the tiny horse-show track at Costa Mesa. Top Swede Ove Fundin was shown this tiny arena, and he agreed with Milne that it had great potential for speedway racing.

Costa Mesa officially opened for business on 13 June 1969, and from this track, which was small by European standards, all of America's top riders of recent years began their careers.

'In that first season it was pretty good, so we ran in 1970 and 1971, and they were good too,' said Oxley. 'Then in 1972 it just exploded. In 1974, the first thirteen Friday nights of speedway were sold out, we had to lock the parking lot to keep the people out of the area because if we let them park their car, they got into the stadium.'

Naturally, other tracks began to spring up all over California, with racing taking place at Ascot Park, Bakersfield, Napa, San Bernardino and Ventura. Some of these only ran a short season, but it was clear that this was a sport whose popularity was increasing rapidly.

While America embraced the concept of modern day speedway, being the nation that it is, they had to stamp their own mark upon it. The main diet for the British speedway fan, and indeed many of the other European countries, is team racing. But in California all the tracks run a weekly dose of individual racing. The format for this is a combination of scratch and handicap racing. Scratch racing is the traditional format of four riders and four laps, which is run on a knockout basis that is similar to the modern Grand Prix series of today. Handicap racing involves a staggered start, with the best of the six riders starting off a handicap of 50 yards, and having to battle their way through to the front of the field. Kelly recalled that in the very early days the handicap for the best rider could as much as 100 yards – which meant starting on the back straight for some riders! Another major difference is that the referee watches the races from the centre green, whereas in Britain he is usually perched in a box high above the home straight with a bird's-eye view of the track.

Among the early track stars were Mike and Steve Bast, Rick Woods, Sonny Nutter, Bill Cody and Jeff Sexton. An American team shocked the world when they managed to win a test series in 1971 against a Rest of the World side that included such stars as Mauger, Briggs, Harkins and Australian Jim Airey.

'From that moment on we produced a tremendous amount of top riders,' said Oxley proudly. 'I think that little track produced 'em.'

Among the crowd during that boom year of 1972, were two motorcycle-mad brothers whose father had taken them to see this exciting new motor sport as a special treat. Kelly and his younger brother, Shawn, sat in the stands and were astounded.

'My father took Shawn and I to watch speedway for the first time in 1972 and we couldn't believe it,' said Kelly many years later. 'We were used to riding on bikes, but watching guys on 500cc machines with no brakes was something that really excited us. It was real neat and these guys were getting paid for it too. From that moment on, that's all we wanted to do.'

As Kelly said, the Moran brothers were no strangers to motorcycles, and they learnt their skills by participating in another motorcycle craze that was sweeping the nation – Mini Bikes. Its popularity was so big in California that *Life Magazine* ran a feature in its January 1971 edition.

Its author described this new phenomenon with a tag line that read: 'Little kids on noisy wheels are whizzing around like Hell's Angels from coast to coast.' This feature showed little kids with small bodies and large heads, racing enthusiastically

Tom Moran, flanked by his sons Shawn (left) and Kelly in the early 1980s.

on small motorcycles that could reach speeds of up to 40mph. While in the majority of the country this new craze was looked upon as another youthful menace which had resulted in two recorded deaths, it was in go-ahead sunny California where this new motorcycle craze was accepted.

It could be considered somewhat ironic that motorcycle racing should find such as foothold in California, when it could be argued that it was Hollywood who helped tarnish the image of motorcycles. Movies such as the James Dean classic *Rebel Without A Cause* and *The Wild One* starring Marlon Brando not only presented motorcycles as noisy and dangerous, but were often associated with trouble-making thugs who would roar their way onto the screen in black and terrorise the peaceful folk of Middle America. At best they would be portrayed as being owned by lazy, scruffy, beer-swilling wanderers who were happy to live life on the open road and not contribute to US society. Little wonder, then, that clean living Americans were horrified at the thought of their sons – or worse, daughters – speeding around on these two-wheeled beasts, with danger and crime seemingly waiting for them around the next corner.

But California, to the outside observer, always seems to be an area with its own liberal ideas and laid-back, free spirit. It was here that this article revealed the organised competition at the weekends for the kids to participate in. These events lasted all day and produced competitive racing for different ages and classes with trophies for the winners. Every weekend, Dry Lake Beds and desert areas around Los Angeles like Trojan, Corona, The Indian Dunes, and Carlsbad, would echo to the sounds of young boys and girls racing their Mini Bikes against each other.

With such enthusiasm and ambition on display from both the kids and their equally enthusiastic parents, it is not surprising that future stars developed their racing skills here. Kelly and Shawn Moran were among some distinguished names: the future World 500cc Champions Wayne Rainey and Eddie Lawson were regular visitors, and so too was Motocross star Jeff Ward – who now races cars in the Indy Racing League. It seems that those Mini Bikes have a lot to answer for …

In a correspondence with the author, Bill Cody recalled the Mini Bikes craze: 'I know Jeff Ward from birth, and I remember him on Mini Bikes at the age of four. Kelly and Shawn started the same way. I knew their father, Tom, and he was there for both the kids when they first started and pushed them along. They started at an early age and they did a bit of everything before settling in on junior speedway.'

In Michael Scott's excellent biography, *Wayne Rainey – His Own Story,* Rainey's father, Sandy, noted that the Morans were fast even at that early age.

'On a long track we just couldn't run 'em down. So I wondered what to do. I read the rulebook over and over,' he said.

However, places like Trojan and The Indian Dunes were not places solely for the youngsters and their parents to go and have fun. Motorcycling, and dirt-track racing in particular, was becoming a very popular pastime and adults and professionals alike would also use these areas as well.

By this time, Barry Briggs was a regular visitor to America, and he also raced at these venues. He met with other like-minded bikers like Bruce Brown, who

Little Shawn Moran shows his racing skills on board a Mini Bike.

produced the classic motorcycling film, *On Any Sunday*, starring Malcolm Smith and movie legend Steve McQueen. Briggs' two boys, Gary and Tony, and McQueen's son Chad, all dabbled in the Dunes. Incidentally, the makers of film and television shows like *M*A*S*H*, would also use the Dunes for location shooting.

Kelly and Shawn found themselves alongside these stars, and their friendly, outgoing nature soon endeared themselves to these famous people – as it would to everyone around the world in years to come. In interviews and profiles carried out on the two brothers, they would always acknowledge how lucky and privileged they were to get to know the McQueens. They got to stay with the McQueens for summer vacation and in one profile Kelly even noted that Steve's daughter, Terri, was among his first loves. Steve McQueen was an avid motorcyclist, and his enthusiasm for bikes was illustrated to the world by his now famous bike scene in the classic 1963 Second World War adventure movie, *The Great Escape*.

'We got along really well with Chad, and we had no idea who his father was. But when we found out it was real neat,' Kelly said. 'Steve used to run on the big track as we used to call it, and he was a good motorcyclist. My Mom was so thrilled that we were connected to Steve McQueen. On one particular occasion, it was Halloween, and she got what we call 'egged' by some kids. And Steve came out with hand towels and helped her to clean herself up. She was so thrilled; she would tell everyone that she knew Steve McQueen. She would get all dressed up and everything just to drop us off. We met and got to know a lot of the Hollywood stars. Gene Hackman was another, as his son Chris used to ride Mini Bikes too. When we see these people on TV, it's nice to look back and remember that we knew them.'

The riders emerging from the deserts of California were all-round motorcyclists, as Bert Harkins recalled:

'In Southern California they would race speedway and then go off into the desert and race other motorcycles. For example, Jeff Ward used to race at Costa Mesa and then you'd find him in the desert too.'

Tom Moran was keen to see his two boys develop their bike racing skills and he recognised the potential his two sons possessed. He would later refer to them as his 'pair of champions' and he guided and influenced them during their developing years. However, he was not a biker himself. It was something that he thought that his two sons would enjoy, and gave them something exciting to do as a family on the weekends. Shawn said that his father also enjoyed the camaraderie of the junior scene.

'My father first got us interested in motorbikes when Kelly and I were very young,' recalled Shawn. 'He bought us a couple of Mini Bikes and from there we progressed until the age of ten, when we were introduced to speedway at Costa Mesa. The night we went there, Gene Woods was riding a junior speedway bike and my father invested in a couple of these machines for us. It developed from there.'

The family's roots are in Ireland, and Kelly said that although they have never done a family tree, it is believed that the original Morans came from around the Dublin area. Their Irish roots were reflected in their early years through their leathers, which Kelly referred to as 'Team Shamrock.' Green and white in colour and adorned with the national emblem of the Emerald Isle, this was not only distinctive but was also their first sponsorship arrangement. Their father had made a deal with Cycle Town, a local cycle shop in the area, who supplied their leathers and with whom they had an agreement for some new machinery.

The Mini Bikes they had been racing on were 3-horsepower Powell Challengers, but the boys' skills soon progressed to Mini Cycles. They were mounted on an Indian machine from which they could have a choice of 50, 60, or 70cc, and they provided a little more comfort when compared to the basic lawnmower like Challenger.

'Mini Bikes had no suspension and boy they could be hard to ride. The Indian had a bit of suspension and it was like, why did we spend so long on Mini Bikes?' said Kelly.

These youngsters would provide the entertainment during the intervals at some of the tracks, while out in the deserts they would ride as often as they could. Their mother also supplied her two sons with a Honda XR75 mini motorcycles, which they both rode to help them to further enhance their all-round motorcycling skills – although they never used this bike in a racing environment. With different classes and levels available to them, Kelly said that they could appear in as many as ten races per day.

'We didn't know any better,' he said. 'Being small and light gave us an edge over some of the others, but thank God we were naturals.'

America, it seemed, was the place to be for aspiring racers, whether it was speedway or one of the other motorcycle disciplines. Tony Briggs, the younger of Barry's two boys, said in an interview that appeared in the 1974 book *Speedway with Briggo* that it was the 'place to go.'

Unfortunately, injuries are an occupational hazard in any form of motorcycle racing, and Kelly got acquainted quite early on in his life with the pain that is associated with broken bones. Shawn recalled in a feature in *Speedway Mail* in 1985, when asked about his favourite childhood memory, that his brother received a painful lesson in the dangers of two-wheeled transport.

'It's not really my favourite,' he said, 'but it stands out in my memory. It must have been when we were about eight or nine, and he tried to jump over 13 wagons on his bicycle! He landed on his front wheel, did a complete somersault and stayed on his bike, upright at the end! I guess it wasn't so funny because he broke his collarbone, but watching him was something else!'

Perhaps Kelly realised that stunt riding was not for him and best left for the likes of Evel Knievel and company. In another feature, Kelly said that he did not like the

Kelly (left) and Shawn on board their Indian motorcycles. Notice the 'team shamrock' leathers.

number thirteen, and one wonders if this stems from his failure to clear those thirteen wagons with disastrous consequences? Sadly, injuries to his collarbones would feature prominently in his career, and he said that he had broken them a total of nine times! However, his first injury came in 1968 when he fractured his left ankle while racing Mini Bikes.

Shawn Moran was born on 19 November 1961 – just over a year after Kelly. Both of them were born in Lakewood, California, and attended Huntington Beach High School. They both left before they were scheduled to as they were desperate to ride speedway. They tried other sports while they were there, including Little League Baseball, but their lack of stature meant that they were not best suited to American Football – although Kelly was once quoted as saying that he was happy in the running-back position.

'I wasn't there for very long,' admitted Shawn. 'I hated being at school and when I was there I either did something wrong or not at all! I preferred to go to the beach and surf. Kelly stayed on until the ninth grade and I stayed a year later. We weren't supposed to leave – we just didn't go! I remember when I was about seven, this other kid and I were always having fights, and we always had a crowd. Every day we would end up wrestling in this corner.'

During their formative years, the brothers both did different jobs to earn some pocket money. Kelly had a job as a gardener and Shawn worked in a car wash.

'I joined one of those Youth Employment programmes,' revealed Kelly. 'I used to have to go round schools and be the gardener. It only lasted a month because I hated getting up so early and all my friends were at the beach. In those times, it was quite easy to get a job for a little while. We would work and get some money and then quit and enjoy spending it. When it was gone, we'd just get another job because they always needed brats somewhere!'

When they were very young, they would sometimes quarrel and as Kelly was the elder, he nearly always came off best and occasionally leaving Shawn in tears. But their father was anxious that his two boys should be able to handle themselves, and would say: 'Stop crying – if it ain't bleeding, it don't hurt.' In another incident which Tom recalled in another edition of *Speedway Mail*, he returned one evening to find five-year-old Shawn at the top of a lamp post. When he asked him what he was doing up there, Shawn sobbed: 'Kelly told me to, Dad!' Shawn had been up there for some time and, needless to say, his brother was nowhere to be found.

Nevertheless, the two brothers were united when they were aboard a motor-cycle, and this shared interest built up a close bond that would grow and strengthen as their careers progressed. They were very close as brothers; one would support the other, and they shared in each other's success and disappointments. Shawn once said that his wish was that he and Kelly would have a run-off for the world title.

'There would be no love lost in the actual race,' he said. 'I'm sure whoever lost would be chuffed for the winner anyway.'

Craig Cummings was a mechanic to both of them during different times of their careers and went on to be a big influence in the career of Billy Hamill. He said of

Karen Miester, a friend of the Morans, is flanked by Kelly (left) and Shawn. Kelly was eleven years old, while Shawn and Karen were ten.

this close relationship: 'Kelly and Shawn are the closest brothers I've ever met. They would fight like cats and dogs. Kelly can slag off Shawn, and Shawn can slag off Kelly, but never slag off Shawn or Kelly in front of them because they'd defend each other to the hilt. They absolutely adore each other.'

The two brothers continued to make progress through the junior ranks and also developed a following. They both earned nicknames such as 'Slidin' Kelly' and 'Get it on, Shawn', and were fast earning a lot of recognition as well as trophies. They both won the World Mini Bikes Grand Prix Championship in the levels open to them.

As the Morans continued to learn their skills that would take them to the top, speedway in the USA was constantly developing. Barry Briggs and Ivan Mauger brought their World Champions' Troupe series over on a regular basis to provide the locals with much-needed top-class competition. The highlight of this enterprise was a match between the USA and the Rest of the World at the impressive indoor arena in Texas, the Houston Astrodome, which saw America lose 64-44. The Rest Of the World side, in addition to Briggs and Mauger, consisted of some of the world's top riders including the then reigning World Champion, Anders Michanek, Ole Olsen, Peter Collins and Ray Wilson. The US side led by Mike Bast and Jeff Sexton

Kelly (left) and Shawn sit on the wall in between races, with adoring fans in the background.

struggled to contain their opponents like they have done at tracks like Costa Mesa.

The British League was considered the best speedway set-up in the world, and the US riders had not really made the effort to race in this league. It was widely believed that if a rider was serious about winning a world championship or enjoying international success, then a few seasons in Britain was essential.

'Until America mix in a different class of competition, they can never hope to provide that World Champion,' wrote Mauger in his book published in 1972, *Ivan Mauger's Speedway Book.* 'It is no good one rider being attached to a British track – all the top riders must do the same.'

As of the defeat at Houston, only a handful had made the trek across the Atlantic Ocean, and only two had endured a full season. Rick Woods and Steve Bast were two of the Yanks' best riders, but they both returned to the US after just a few weeks of British racing.

Mauger offered this explanation for the apparent failure of the American riders to sacrifice their seemingly comfortable lifestyle for the tougher demands of BL racing.

'With America, there are bigger problems than with other countries. The standard of living on the other side of the pond is so much higher than in Britain, and to ride in this country an American must be prepared to make sacrifices.'

For Oxley, as much as he wanted his riders to do well in international competition, he was also keen to see his top stars remain in the US to keep his turnstiles clicking. This conflict would increase as a new batch of riders began to get more ambitious. It started when Mauger brought Scott Autrey to Exeter in 1973 and, not only did he complete a full season, but he proved that he had the potential to be a big star. Others would slowly follow; Steve Gresham and Mike Curoso started at Hull and branched out at other clubs.

1976 was an important year in American motorcycle racing. Pat Hennen became the first American to win a 500cc Grand Prix and pave the way for Kenny Roberts and other US racers. In speedway, Scott Autrey became the first American for twenty-five years to reach a World Final, which proved that regular British racing did have a positive outcome. While in domestic speedway it was decided to try team racing again in bid to prevent some of the more ambitious young stars from leaving home.

Bert Harkins was the only Europe-based star who gave up the BL for a taste of a full season in California.

'I raced for Bakersfield,' he said. 'The other tracks to take part were Irwindale, Costa Mesa, San Bernardino and Ventura. It was quite exciting to ride there. The Americans were so laid back and the weather was so good. The tracks were all small, tiny by European standards, but they were so wide. They used to move the white line out as the meeting progressed. That might seem odd, but it sort of made two tracks in one if you like.'

But team racing did not capture the interest of the public. Oxley described it as a 'horrible flop.' He explained in the American publication, *Speedway Magazine* in 1983: 'It cost us fans because all of a sudden we were taking Rick Woods, superstar,

Kelly (left) outside his brother, Shawn, displays their early team riding skills.

away from them for some weeks.'

But despite this, their attempt at team racing did provide a few things that would later surface in Britain.

'All the riders had team leathers to race in,' said Harkins, 'it was their own colours. That was unique in those days, but now they do it in the British Elite League all the time. Anyway, it was run along the same lines as the BL, but after the team event all the riders would change back into their own sponsored leathers for the individual event. It was a shame that the public never took to team racing.'

As the season was drawing to a close, Kelly turned sixteen and was eligible to turn out as a professional on a 500cc speedway monster. But as there were only few weeks remaining, his father put off purchasing a 500 until the start of the 1977 season.

Kelly was raring to go and he made an immediate impression. His exciting style of racing was a hit with the fans and Oxley dubbed him 'The Wizard of Balance'. It was a term that had already been used to describe another small racer, England's only double World Champion, Peter Craven.

'People say I look radical, or out of control when I ride,' said Kelly. 'But I lean off the bike to keep it as straight up and down as I can. Because for speedway racing you go faster when the bike is in a straight line, rather than leaned over, spinning the rear tyre.

'I had no problems adjusting to a 500 machine. In many ways it was easier to race than what I had been riding. And I loved to slide the bike and turn left. That's what I liked and I never really considered doing any other kind of motorcycle racing.'

His talent attracted the attention of Ken McGoldricks, better known as 'KK'. He had been around the junior speedway scene and got to know the brothers' father and a relationship developed from there. Others also helped to establish them in their early years, like Peter Rovazzini – who sponsored Kelly in his early days – and Kenny Best.

In America, the riders are graded by division. At first, Kelly would have started in the Third Division as he was a novice at professional level. The first requirement of a novice is to prove that he can lay down his bike when necessary. A rider would be racing around the track, and an official would be present in the centre. He would usually stand on the apex of one of the turns with an arm raised, and when he dropped his arm, the rider would be expected to lay down his machine safely. If it was done to the official's satisfaction, then that rider was free to compete. The Second Division is for riders who have proved too good for the lower ranks, but not yet at a sufficient standard for the First Division. The top rider in the US at that time was Mike Bast, who went on to win the US National Championship seven times. Other top riders were his brother, Steve, Dubb Ferrell, Bruce Penhall, Bill Cody, Larry Shaw and Jim 'the Animal' Fishback.

Kelly made rapid progress through the different ranks and his approachable, happy-go-lucky nature went down well with the race fans. He was named 'Rookie of the Year' for 1977 and reached the US Nationals in his first professional season. If that was not a remarkable feat in itself, he didn't go there to make up the numbers as he finished in a very promising sixth place. He also finished fifth in the California State Championship at San Bernardino. Kelly had a great time and enjoyed every minute of it.

'It wasn't the money – that was nice – it was the racing,' he said. 'Racing against the other riders, riders that I had watched and admired, hanging around with older guys who were more experienced than me. It was cool, and to a seventeen year old like me it was real neat. I enjoyed it, and I think I was the first rider in his debut season to make the Nationals.'

In a book published in 1986 entitled *The Inside Line*, Kelly recounted a tale of his early off-track antics during these early racing days.

'I gave my friend Dale a lift from my house to his house on the back of my speedway bike. It was about half a mile, and I was trying to pop wheelies on the street. Dale was really scared and was trying to stop the bike with his feet. When we got to his place he was shaking and the soles of his shoes were worn out. Dale's never been on a bike with me since!'

For Shawn it was slightly different. As he was a little younger, he had his first taste of 500cc machines in 1977 at Barry Briggs' training school at Elsinore. It was a 180-yard track, and he crashed in his first race. In spite of this inauspicious start, Briggs could see that he had a lot of natural talent.

About this time, Hull boss Ian Thomas was keeping an eye on developments in the USA and this ambitious promoter was looking for another American.

'I had a contact in America in the '70s and they, a man and a woman, provided me with the tips on all the American riders. I had a lot of them over the years, and that's basically how I got to hear about Kelly.'

Thomas made an approach and Kelly was instantly interested. But what really swung his decision was that he would be riding with Ivan Mauger. The Kiwi was signed from Exeter in a shock move as Thomas aimed to bring success to the club.

After just one professional season in the States, many thought that making the trip to Britain was just too soon. Yes, he had had a sensational debut season, but he didn't have the experience. After all, more established riders than him had tried their luck in the BL and failed.

'We were always hearing about how good Ivan was,' said Kelly. 'It was always Ivan this and Ivan that. So when Ian Thomas offered me a chance to go and ride with Ivan at Hull, I couldn't wait. It was a chance to ride with Ivan Mauger! Bruce Penhall thought I should stay at home for another year. He was going to sponsor me with a van and such, but all I could think about was riding with Ivan.'

Penhall would be joining Kelly on his trip overseas. He had already resisted offers to join a British team, even though he qualified with Mike Bast for the Intercontinental Final of the World Championship at White City, London in 1977. However, Bruce would be joining another equally ambitious British team, Cradley Heath. With two of America's brightest talents heading for Britain and the world-renowned British Speedway League, it seemed that these two stateside stars heralded a new era for American speedway racing.

2
RAIN AND ROUNDABOUTS

The year 1978 was a season of double celebration in Britain. Not only was the World Final scheduled to return to Wembley for the first time since 1975, but it was also the Golden Jubilee year for speedway. It was widely believed that the sport officially arrived on British shores at the King's Oak Arena, High Beech, Essex, in February 1928.

Speedway in Britain was, by and large, in a healthy state when Kelly Moran made his first trip to race in the UK. The British speedway league was split into two divisions in those days. The British League was the top league, and the National League was a lower league. Only British and Commonwealth riders – Australians, New Zealanders and Canadians – could participate in the NL. This was because the NL was designed to develop their own youngsters – a stepping stone to move up to the BL – and riders like Kelly were excluded from racing in that league. A league match was run over thirteen races; after a short interval, an individual second-half event would follow to determine the rider of the night, which would sometimes carry a prize for the overall winner.

His team, the Hull Vikings, were entering their fifth season of British League competition, and had yet to finish in the top half of the table – although the club tasted cup success in 1976 when they defeated Wolverhampton in the Inter-League Knockout Cup. However, with the arrival of Mauger for a £12,000 fee, it seemed this unhappy record was about to change. Other team-mates were Tom and Joe Owen, Frank Auffret, Bobby Beaton, Graham Drury and Phil Kynman. During the season, other riders would 'double up' from the National League to replace riders who were injured or unable to ride for some reason.

For the teenaged Kelly, his arrival in England must have been a bit of a shock after spending his years in sunny California. There was a lot to get used to. Hull raced at the Boulevard, which was a stadium they shared with the local rugby team, and it was the fifth largest track in the top league at 380 metres (418 yards) – it would be the largest home track of their careers. In the US, most of the tracks were less than 200 yards in length, and only Ascot Park was close to a European-sized circuit.

'There was no sun! It was often grey and miserable,' Kelly recalled of his first year. 'It was so different. It was only the second time I had been outside California, and it was definitely good for character building.'

The expectations were high for the club to do well, and Kelly was fortunate that Ian Thomas was experienced when it came to dealing with Americans racing in Britain for the first time. Indeed, Kelly had replaced Mike Curoso who moved to Poole after two seasons with the Vikings, and Steve Gresham also had a brief spell with the club. Ivan Mauger was instrumental in helping to develop the potential of Scott Autrey at Exeter – who was then the top American racing in Europe – and it was hoped that the Kiwi would also be able to do the same with the latest Statesider.

'All the teams I rode for in England, I always had a say in who rode in the teams,' explained Mauger. 'I always had a say in who we got rid of and who rode with whom, who started on the inside and who started on the outside. I wasn't only a captain in name like a lot of people. A lot of those Americans came from schools we had out there. Kelly wasn't one of my students, but I knew about him coming up through the ranks.'

There were many critics who still doubted that the American riders possessed the necessary dedication to actually make it in Britain. DeWayne Keetar was the first American of the new era to try his luck in England, when he spent a promising season with Leicester in 1969. Keetar was a good rider, but he did not return and eventually left the sport to take up Short Track racing. There was much anticipation for the highly-rated Steve Bast and Rick Woods, but they only lasted a few weeks with Wembley and Newport. It seemed that the Californians were not willing to trade the sun, sea and surf for damp summers and tough, dedicated racing. Autrey was considered an exception to the rule, although with the continued participation of both Gresham and Curoso, it was clear that the new breed of American racers were eager to prove that they could compete among the world's best.

Among the first things that Kelly had problems with was England's road system. Following a Vikings' practice session, it took the little American an hour to make an eight-mile trip from the Boulevard back to his home in Beverley.

'It's the roundabouts that threw me,' he confessed. 'I had never seen one until I went to England. Ian would give me a map and point at an area on it and say, 'you're here and that's where the speedway track is'. And that was it. I used to get some funny reactions when I asked for directions, with me being a real Yank and everything.'

Kelly made his British League debut in a Frank Varey Northern Trophy match at home to Halifax, on 29 March. He started quietly by scoring 1 point and his team lost 42-36. It was clear that it was going to take him a little while to get used to things in England, and it had to be taken into account that this was only his second professional season. In many ways it was to his advantage that Bruce Penhall had made his debut the same year, as much was expected of the blonde-haired Penhall after his performance the previous summer at White City. All the attention was focused on him as the next 'big thing' from America, while little was known of Kelly outside of California.

In another Northern Trophy match at Belle Vue, Kelly was able to illustrate his track craft to good effect thanks to a cheeky manoeuvre from his team-mate, Mauger. In heat one, the Kiwi moved over the 1976 World Champion

A youthful Kelly Moran in Hull colours in 1978.

Peter Collins to create a space which Kelly seized upon and joined him at the front for a memorable 5-1. Little triumphs like this were a big confidence boost for him as he was determined to make it in Britain.

The opening weeks of the season were hard; he was in a strange country, with a different culture and terrible weather – although it was supposed to be spring! – and racing on tracks that were not only bigger than what he was used to, but were often wet and heavy from the rain. He was also in the main body of the team to begin with, which meant that he always faced the more experienced riders. Eventually, he would move down to the reserve spot, where he would meet riders who were less experienced and, on paper at least, he would get a few easier races.

His inexperience was illustrated to good effect in one match, when he put his team-mate Auffret under a lot of pressure because he wasn't aware of the bonus point system.

'Kelly didn't realise he got paid the same for finishing behind Frank as beating him,' recalled Thomas. 'When Frank told him, he apologised and promised to form a strong team-riding partnership.'

While he found points hard to come by during the opening months of the season, his cheerful and happy-go-lucky nature made him a popular rider with the public. He also fought hard for all of his points, and the public were left with no doubt that he was giving his racing all the effort he could. His mechanic, Bernard Harrison, was also instrumental in helping the youngster to concentrate on his racing by helping him adjust his bike to the different tracks he came up against.

'I didn't really know much at that time about the gearings and set ups I needed,' Kelly admitted. 'Bernard used to be Briggo's mechanic, and if I came in and said that the bike's rear tyre was spinning too much in the middle of the corner, I wouldn't really know if I needed to reduce the tyre pressure, change the sprockets or whatever. But Bernard knew, and I learned a lot from him. One day we were sitting around talking and he told me that when he used to work for Briggo, he used to have a complete bike in bits in the back of the car for spares. I always had good competitive bikes and they were always there.'

However, the turning point came in an Inter-League Cup match at National League Eastbourne at the end of May, when he top-scored with a morale-boosting 11-points, and only an engine failure prevented him from adding more points. He dropped just one point to Eagles' number one, Mike Sampson, and he certainly caught the eye of Eastbourne's boss, Bob Dugard, who made a mental note of this young man's talent as he revealed in a correspondence with the author.

'I saw him with Hull, and I thought he was the most naturally gifted rider I had ever seen,' he said.

Soon others were seeing that this young man from Lakewood was a rider with a big future ahead of him. His bravery when coming from the back was attracting admiration from all circles. In a league match at home to Reading, he brought the crowd to their feet when he split the experienced pairing of Dave Jessup and Doug Underwood. He passed Underwood with a wonderful second corner, and swept past Jessup to join Tom Owen for a memorable 5-1. He was starting to score well both at home and away and scored an impressive 15 points at Wimbledon. At home to Coventry, he was just 0.01 outside the track record set earlier in the evening by Mauger, and he would have achieved the record too, if he hadn't slowed up to avoid the fallen Frank Smith.

Unfortunately, he was forced to miss the match at Ipswich when his van broke down at Newmarket. But it was not through a lack of effort that he failed to line up for the Vikings as he hired a taxi to get to the stadium, but he arrived just as the match had finished.

By now Hull had begun to win some matches, but Phil Kynman quit the club at the end of May and then Joe Owen crashed heavily in a second-half race. For a time, his life seemed in the balance, but happily Owen recovered from his internal injuries, although he would not race anymore that year. Then Mauger, the club's talisman, sustained an injury which kept him out of the saddle for a time and the pressure began to mount on the little American. But he carried on his impressive performances, and even defeated an in-form Ole Olsen – who was crowned World Champion at Wembley later that year – in his first ever race at Coventry!

After observing the 'Wizard of Balance' at work, *Speedway Star* journalist Bob Radford was moved to write in his column: 'Kelly caught the eye, rarely have I seen a young rider with such balance. He straightens his bike so quickly coming out of the turns, and by doing so picks up the all-important drive that much earlier.'

In July, he underlined his talent and progress when he finished in sixth place with 10 points in the Yorkshire TV Trophy. Another engine failure denied him a place on the rostrum in a meeting won by Vaclav Verner with 13 points. Among the world-class riders in the field were Olsen, Michael Lee, Mauger, Penhall, Peter Collins and Terry Betts.

It was essential that he did well enough to achieve a 6-point average, as this was the minimum figure required for him to automatically qualify for a work permit for 1979. This was a necessity for all non-Commonwealth riders in those days. By the time the speedway press deliberated his and other riders' chances during the middle of the season, Kelly was below that average. But such was his form at that point that it seemed more than likely that he would reach that figure. His fellow countryman Penhall was doing all and more than was expected of him, and had an average exceeding the all-important 6-points. Frustratingly for Kelly, as he was still not yet 18, he was too young to qualify for an international licence so he was not able to join Penhall and the rest when they raced for their country. Perhaps this may have helped in his first year, as he could concentrate on getting used to the demands of British League racing without the extra pressure of international competition. However, by July it seemed that he could more than handle that type of situation.

His form had improved sufficiently by August to take him well above the 6-point limit required for a work permit for 1979. He made his first appearance in the Northern Riders' Championship at Sheffield and scored 8 points in a meeting won by Reg Wilson. His growing reputation as one of the finds of the season, led to an invitation to race at Exeter in the 'Westernapolis' individual. The track at the county ground was one of the fastest in the country with a fearsome reputation among the riders because of its hard safety fence. Kelly scored just 3 points in a meeting won by Phil Crump, with Scott Autrey coming second on his home track.

On 25 August, Hull travelled to Hackney for the quarter-final of the Inter-League Knockout Cup. Hackney were experiencing a poor season and were languishing near the foot of the table. Hull, by comparison, had climbed the table and were enjoying their best British League season to date. The Vikings travelled to the London venue without Mauger, and Hackney was also missing their top rider, the Danish star Finn Thomsen. Hackney chose to promote their number eight Ted Hubbard, while Hull booked Robbie Gardner – a guest from National League Newcastle.

It was hoped, and some experts even expected, that Hull would win this round and book their place in the semi-finals. Kelly won the opening heat and with Frank Aufrett taking second, the Vikings were off to a good start. However, Kelly crashed in his second outing, and by the time he lined up for heat 8, both teams were level pegging on 21 points each. But then disaster struck.

Kelly lifted on the pits bend and his rival, Bobby McNeil, rammed into the American. Gardner was unable to avoid the fallen pair and ploughed into them in a horrific crash. It was an accident of such impact that Gardner had to be retrieved from the flower bed on the centre green. McNeil was able to take his place in the re-run and he went on to win the race, but the crash meant a trip in the ambulance for the Vikings' duo.

Gardner was released with just bruising, but for Kelly it was the end of his season. He suffered multiple injuries – a fractured pelvis, two broken vertebrae, hip and shoulder injuries, a broken arm and a broken left leg. He faced five weeks in traction at Whipps Cross Hospital, but made an appearance at Hull's home fixture against Exeter on 27 September as a spectator. He received a rapturous reception from the crowd when he hauled himself out his wheelchair to address the fans over the radio microphone, and he promised that he would return in 1979.

However, as he would later reveal, that accident would have a lasting effect on his body. 'They drilled holes in my shinbone and I was put in traction with 28 lb weights. It was left in traction a little too long, and my left leg is a tad longer than my right one,' he said. 'They had to do it because the impact of the accident shoved the leg right up. But it never affected me when I raced.'

His crash brought his debut season to a premature end, and also ended Hull's outside hopes of making a serious challenge for the league title. Kelly finished his first season with a 7.01 average and so made sure of his work permit for 1979. Furthermore, he had done enough to prove that here was a young rider who had a bright future in the sport. In its end of season review of Hull's 1978 campaign, *Speedway Star* noted: 'As the season went on the Yank got better and better and better, helped no end by the help he got from Ivan and the rest of the lads. It was his smash, the second catastrophe to hit the club in the year, that really put them out of the title running. Hull not only lost his great scoring ability, they also lost a number one personality kid as well.'

Kelly could take great pride in his debut season performance, and would have received even more plaudits but for the wonderful season that Bruce Penhall had had. But at this point, Kelly was concentrating on recovering in time to race in the American Final of the 1979 World Championship – which, surprisingly, was planned for December 1978! This did not give him much time to recover from such serious injuries, but such was the debate of where and when the final would take place, that he was hopeful that he would get more time as the arguments dragged on.

Meanwhile, across the Atlantic in California, Shawn was turning his first wheel as a professional racer on board a 500cc machine. His fall at Briggs' training school was a distant memory as he began to make a name for himself at places like Costa Mesa and San Bernardino. However, it was on the bigger

Shawn Moran in early race action at Costa Mesa.

Ascot circuit that Shawn really displayed his ability.

'I kind of struggled a little bit on the small tracks,' he admitted. 'Don't get me wrong, it was still fun, but I didn't care for all the locking up and stuff. But I really liked the bigger Ascot track. I think it was Ascot that really got me excited about racing seriously. Racing on the small tracks was okay, but racing on the Ascot half-mile was real neat. You could go really fast there.'

As if to underline this, he startled the big crowd at Ascot in the American Long Track championship by finishing second to Bruce Penhall when he was still only seventeen. Watched by his brother, who was still recovering from his injuries, he saw off America's best riders and only missed out on the title itself by a few points.

This performance attracted the attention of Hull boss Ian Thomas, who had come over to America with Kelly to have a look at his younger brother, and to offer some support to Kelly as he battled to be fit for the American Final. Eager to sign another American rider, Shawn seemed the obvious candidate.

'Myself, KK and Ian discussed the possibility of going to England,' recalled Shawn. 'But, as I said, I hadn't really got to grips with some of the American tracks, and I felt that I still had a bit to learn. We sat round the table and discussed it, but it was decided that I should stay home for another year.'

Although disappointed, a gentleman's agreement was struck that he would try his luck in Britain in 1980. Thomas did not go home empty-handed though, as he agreed a deal to bring over Dennis Sigalos, one of Penhall's close friends. It might not have been the American he wanted, but it was another one of the fast-emerging US stars.

Amazingly, and against all the odds, Kelly took his place in the American Final and finished in third place behind Mike Bast and Bobby Schwartz. This meant that he would line up in the next round as reserve, which was not the result he had hoped for but a good one considering his lack of fitness. (See chapter three for the full story.)

Kelly though was eager to return to Britain and prepare for his second BL season. But Thomas advised him to avoid the winter months in England, and to take advantage of the warm Californian sunshine to help speed along his return to full fitness.

The Hull team for 1979 changed very little from the one that did so well during the previous season. The signing of Sigalos filled the vacant reserve berth which had been a problem since Phil Kynman quit during the late spring of 1978. So, with a largely unchanged side, the biggest news was that the club had secured a lucrative sponsorship deal with the car manufacturer Lada. They would be known as the Hull 'Lada Vikings.' This arrangement meant that Kelly and his new team-mate, Sigalos, would benefit by having the use of Lada vehicles for the new campaign.

On the eve of the new British season, experts predicted that Hull would do well if Kelly could recover from the injuries he had sustained at the end of the previous campaign and continue his progress. The same remarks were also levelled at Joe Owen.

However, Shawn once again showed his liking for the Ascot track when he raced in the USA team that lost 63-43 to the Rest of the World select at the third international of the series. Racing on a 2-valve Jawa prepared by George Wenn, he won his first three races to top-score with 15 points. His defeats came at the hands of ex-world champions, Peter Collins, Anders Michanek and Mauger. America won the series 3-1, with the last match, scheduled for Ascot, falling victim to the weather.

Shawn continued to thrill the crowds at Ascot, and it was his fantastic fence-scraping racing here that earned him the nickname of 'The Miracle Worker'. This performance proved that, in time, the younger Moran would cope well on the bigger tracks in England; however, he would continue to thrill the Californians for another year yet.

America was attracting a bit more interest than usual, as Barry Briggs' youngest son, Tony, had decided to follow in his father's tyre tracks and enter speedway racing. The British League tracks were instantly interested in acquiring his signature, but it was decided that he would be better off spending a season in the USA. Barry was quoted as saying that that the small American tracks would teach him a great deal, and would also give him time to develop without the pressure that comes with racing in Britain.

As the US season unfolded, it was Shawn, Tony and another teenage sensation, Lance King, who were catching all the headlines and interest. Shawn began to adapt to the smaller tracks and won a main event at San Bernardino in May, but it was at Ventura where he liked to go to race.

'It was a lot of fun, but I especially liked going to Ventura because it was close to the beach,' said Shawn. 'We used to go and surf in the afternoon, and then in the evening we would race speedway. It was neat being with all the guys, we had a good time.'

His brother recalled that their father was a little concerned about Shawn's feet. 'I remember my dad calling me when I was racing for Hull and he was worried because Shawn wouldn't wear any socks when he raced. Those boots are quite hard to wear without them, but it was because he was a surfer you know. In America, we used to change out in the open and I used to say to him, 'Aren't you going to wear any socks?' And he would say, 'No, I don't need them, I'm a surfer.' It was like, okay, whatever, you know. I said to Dad, if he's happy and he's winning races, then don't worry about it. Of course, when he came to England to race, because it was colder, he soon started wearing them then.'

Kelly moved house in England and his address attracted some local press interest. He took up residence at Spurn Head, Bridlington, Yorkshire, the site of the famous Spurn lighthouse which warns ships of the treacherous shallow water. He handled the interest with a typically humorous response: 'It's pretty bleak after California,' he said. 'But it does bring a regular spot of light into my life.'

The opening match of the new season saw the Vikings lose 42-36 at home to Halifax in the Northern Trophy. But this was just a case of blowing the cobwebs away, as they came away from Belle Vue with a narrow 40-38 victory. Kelly had proved in both matches that he was suffering no ill effects from the previous season's injuries, but he did reveal that he was experiencing pain from spinal arthritis. However, a 10-point return at home to Belle Vue showed that it was not going to hold him back.

Hull's problem during the opening weeks was the 50-point limit that had been imposed during the winter. Each team's combined average could not exceed 50 points when assembling their sides for the new season. Thomas, eager not to break up a promising team, decided to drop a rider from the side for the first few weeks until the new averages were issued after the first full month. This meant that Kelly missed the home Northern Trophy match against Sheffield and he was replaced by Rod Hunter, the star of the National League.

It was not an ideal situation, but with Sigalos on an assessed average and Joe Owen also likely to take a bit of time to get back into his free scoring mode, Thomas was sure that his intended team would by then fall under the limit. By doing this, he could then re-declare his side and track the seven riders he wanted to mount a serious challenge on the league championship.

It was a devious plan and it looked as though it would backfire when Hull were thumped 50-27 at BL newcomers Eastbourne in their first league match of the season. The man to make way this time was Mauger, and his replacement, Graham Clifton, failed to score. The bright spot, though, was Dennis Sigalos winning two races. However, the side made amends by thrashing title rivals Coventry 51-27 at the Boulevard, an encounter which saw Kelly drop just one point in his 11-point total.

Kelly's promising performances would prove to be no fluke as he began to fill the role of a second heat-leader to Mauger. He scored his first maximum in the Inter-League Fours at his home track and then he scored a paid maximum in a Knockout cup match against Sheffield. His bravery on the track was as much in evidence this year as it was the previous season – if there was a gap, he would go for it.

Unfortunately, this type of racing may be exciting to watch but it can, and often did, lead to a number of tumbles. He was chasing Reading guest Les Collins in one match when he caught the rider's back wheel and was sent cart-wheeling fifty yards into the Hull safety fence. He severely bruised his hip and was forced to rest for two weeks. This accident forced him to miss an important international for the USA, as his form was so good at this point that he was now becoming an automatic choice to ride for his country. Furthermore, he missed Hull's victory in the Fours Team Finals at Sheffield. However, he defied the doctor's instructions and raced a week later, when he scored a paid maximum in the Vikings' 56-22 victory over Hackney.

Racing alongside the legendary Ivan Mauger was of great benefit to him during his early years, as he explained: 'Ivan taught me a lot about speedway racing. Most of all though, he gave me an insight on how to read riders and the tracks. Ivan and people like KK were a great help because they would tell me

Kelly in Hull colours in 1979.

about certain riders to look out for. For example, Ivan said that you don't go around the outside of a certain pair of brothers who used to race for Exeter as they didn't like it, you know. Another rider wouldn't like you going down their inside, and it was stuff like that that prevented you from having problems out there. I think he used to think I was a bit crazy, because he used to tell me that I couldn't do such and such, and I'd ask him why, and he'd just say, "you just don't do it that way." In the Northern Trophy meetings against Halifax at the start of season, myself and Kenny (Carter) used to pull wheelies, drop the front wheel into the puddles and try and splash each other with water. Ivan used to shake his head and say something like, "Crazy American".'

By July, Hull were showing the rest of the league that they meant business. They were second behind Coventry in the league table and were still in the Knockout Cup. Their new recruit, Dennis Sigalos, like Kelly before him, was settling in and starting to score some valuable points. The Vikings then struck a psychological blow when they knocked Coventry out of the cup, and followed that with a victory at Belle Vue to close the gap at the top of the league. However, they suffered a set back when three of their riders failed to make the fixture at Wimbledon after a motorway breakdown. Bobby Beaton, Graham Drury and Frank Auffret all missed the match which was lost by just 5 points. This unlucky incident would come back to haunt the team later in the year.

On an individual level, Kelly showed just how much he had improved when he finished third in the Yorkshire TV Trophy. Mauger won with an immaculate maximum, Michael Lee was second with 13 points and the American third with 12. He was thrilled when he learned that he would replace Mike Bast in the World Championship, and took full advantage to reach his first World Final. At this point, he was obviously repaying the faith that Thomas had shown in him.

'In my view, he is probably the most exciting speedway rider the world has ever seen,' said Ian Thomas. 'He liked to drink, he liked to party and he took some handling. But I like to help all my riders if they're right for me. I try to help them whether they're a world champion, a potential world champion or an ordinary run of the mill speedway rider.'

'Run of the mill' is certainly not a phrase that one should use to describe Kelly Moran. His off-track antics were becoming the talk of the terraces, almost as much as his performances on the track. But this all added to the charisma of Kelly Moran, speedway rider. He was one rider in an exciting team which had transformed the club from an unfashionable Yorkshire side into a team that every track loved to have to visit. They had become box office material.

'We were where we were, simply because of enthusiasm,' said skipper Mauger. 'We won so many matches 40-38. It was the same when I was with Exeter in 1974.'

With matches in hand, Hull continued to close in on the Coventry Bees at the top. They travelled to Swindon in late August, and once again found themselves a rider short. Joe Owen broke down en route to Swindon and his absence cost the Vikings a victory. Sigalos rallied with a superb 15-point maximum, Kelly

Kelly outside his team-mate, Graham Drury, and King's Lynn's Michael Lee at the Boulevard, Hull in 1979.

dropped just one point to an opposing rider, and Mauger contributed another double-figure performance. But in the end they could only manage a 39-39 draw against a Robins team for whom Bob Kilby was in scintillating form.

Everything seemed to be clicking into place when Ivan Mauger returned from Poland with a record-breaking sixth World Championship, and Kelly took a brilliant fourth. Hull's biggest crowd for three years packed the Boulevard to welcome the club's first World Champion as they defeated Halifax 43-34. They then qualified for the Knockout Cup final after defeating Exeter in the semi-finals, when Kelly top-scored at the County Ground with 11 points. It seemed that everything was building up for a memorable climax – and so it would prove.

The Vikings' emphatic 52-26 victory at Wolverhampton meant that they only had to draw their last match of the season to clinch the championship. However, the celebrations of a job well done were tempered by a second-half crash to Kelly, who was taken to hospital where it was diagnosed that he had broken his collarbone. Thomas was 'sick', and his accident couldn't have come at a worse time for the club, as he was in flying form – as was demonstrated when he top-scored in the win at Wolves with 10 points.

Hull's last league match could not have been tougher as they had to travel to reigning champions Coventry. Both clubs were locked at the top with 50 points, with the Vikings in pole position because of their superior points difference. The Bees had to win to retain the title, but Hull just needed a draw. It was a tall order without Kelly, and it was a task made doubly difficult as they were unable to operate rider replacement as Coventry had been using this facility for Alan Molyneux for most of the year since he broke his arm. Consequently, both clubs had to promote their number eight riders. Ordinarily Thomas would have called up National League star Tom Owen, but he was sidelined with a broken leg. Eventually, they plumped for Kiwi Graeme Stapleton.

The showdown to decide the destiny of the 1979 British League Championship caught the public's imagination in a big way. The car park at Brandon Stadium was full two hours before the scheduled start time and the television cameras were there to lap up the occasion. A crowd estimated to be in excess of 20,000 people packed into the stadium to witness this showdown, and extra police were drafted in for overtime duty to cope with the occasion.

However, the already beleaguered Hull team suffered another devastating setback, as early as the second race, when Stapleton crashed heavily and was stretchered off – sadly, he never appeared again. They gamely battled on, mainly through the efforts of Mauger, Beaton and Joe Owen, but although they never let Coventry off the hook until the penultimate race, the Bees never looked as though they would relinquish their lead and they eventually ran out winners 42-36 – and retained the title.

'Stapleton broke a chain and that was it really,' recalled Mauger. 'I'm convinced that if Kelly had been fit to ride we would have been champions. We tried hard at Coventry, but it was too much of a handicap without him.'

At the time, Hull co-promoter Brian Larner criticised some of his riders for their previous indiscretions and a lack of professionalism. Years later, Thomas would echo those sentiments. 'We didn't lose the league at Coventry; we lost it by riders not going to Exeter and Wimbledon. We lacked professionalism when it mattered. It should have been sewn up before we went to Coventry.'

Their final chance of lifting a major trophy came with a Knockout Cup Final appearance against Cradley Heath. However, they lost 62-46 at Cradley in the first leg, which saw Graham Drury crash and sustain a broken wrist. But the second leg was abandoned after seven heats because of rain. Dan McCormick, the Cradley boss, was furious with the decision, as they were leading 23-19 when the referee called a halt to the proceedings, following a protest led by Mauger. Happily for the Vikings, Kelly made a return for the re-run of the second leg, but his eight points couldn't prevent an injury-ravaged side losing 58-50 on the night, and 120-96 on aggregate. In the final analysis, Hull finished the year as the league's bridesmaids and could only look back on what might have been.

Before the second leg was re-staged, Hull held a four-team tournament between Hull, a USA select, Sheffield and Exeter on October 24. The home team finished ahead of the USA team by a narrow two points, who would surely have won had Kelly been able to take his place. But the result was academic really, because making an appearance for the USA side was a rider by the name of David East. East scored 6 points, which included a heat 9 victory over Reg Wilson, Ales Drmyl and Wayne Brown. It later transpired that this promising Yank was in fact Kelly's younger brother Shawn!

'I came over to check things out,' recalled Shawn. 'Ian wanted to see me race, but I never had the necessary permit or something. So he had an idea to run me as David East, and I rode Kelly's bike. He said that no one would find out, but of course they did.'

'Obviously, knowing Kelly and the family, I knew Shawn, and brought him over a year before he could ride,' explained Thomas. 'He came across to have a look and for me to have a look at him. I rode him as David East in a second half first and the Speedway Control Board found out and I was fined for that.'

It was a controversial start for Shawn's career in Britain – he was also fined $50 by the AMA – but he liked what he saw and agreed to join the Vikings. As the season came to an end, it looked as though Hull would not have one, but two Morans in their team for 1980.

Shawn had enjoyed a much better year at home and had qualified for the US National Championship, which was won by Mike Bast. However, the younger Moran's place in the top meeting of the domestic calendar looked under threat

Shawn displays his spectacular all-action style of racing in the USA.

when it was discovered that the fuel he was using during one of the qualifying rounds contained an illegal additive. He was forced to miss the last qualifying round, but he had already scored enough points to make sure of his place in the final. However, as he had purchased the fuel over the counter, he was allowed to take his place in the meeting, where he finished well down the order with 7 points.

The last big meeting of the domestic calendar was the US Long Track Championship, which was held at Ascot. Shawn Moran had already established himself at the circuit with some sparkling performances, but he produced a spectacular display to see off the challenge from BL stars like Bruce Penhall, Bobby Schwartz and Scott Autrey, and won the meeting with an unbeaten 15 points. Shawn's only real challenge came from Tony Briggs, who was leading Moran when he crashed; Briggs lost his momentum after that, and Penhall ended up taking overall second to 'The Miracle Worker'.

'I remember Shawn at the Ascot half-mile,' said Bill Cody. 'He was especially good there, riding up against the wall and winning – he was great. But what I remember most was his happy-go-lucky attitude.'

Before 1979 came to a close, Kelly took part in the first indoor meeting to be held in Britain at the Wembley Arena, on 2 December. The promoters behind the event had a very distinctive Hull flavour about them as the men involved were Ivan Mauger, Ian Thomas, Brian Larner and Barry Briggs – who also raced for Hull in 1976. The event was staged as an individual contest and it was unique as the track was a 180-yard concrete surface. It required some getting used to and Kelly produced an incident-packed performance to finish on 6 points, demolishing the pit gate into the bargain. The winner was Mauger with 13 points.

'Oh, myself and Kenny Carter had a great time,' recalled Kelly. 'We were both teenagers and we thought it was great fun. I remember I got my bike locked together with Jimmy McMillan's and we couldn't prize them apart. But the concrete was hard when you came off. If you slip off like you were laying it down or something, it would really hurt and give you shocks and stuff, which you just wouldn't get on a normal track. Jan Andersson (Sweden) was the king of that kind of racing in the eighties. I was on borrowed machinery which I think Ian sorted out for me, and we just had to make sure we really pumped up the rear tyre.'

Just as it seemed that both the Morans would be riding at Hull, in early 1980 it was reported that they had both increased their demands and Thomas was 'disappointed'. He had made an agreement with Shawn and now it seemed that he was going back on this deal. He was quoted at the time as saying that he was looking forward to racing in England and wanted everything to be right: 'I would like to take a full-time mechanic with me, which accounts for the extra money I asked of Mr Thomas.'

Kelly, meanwhile, was placed on the transfer list for £12,000 and it seemed that he was keen to remain at home for the 1980 campaign. He would later deny this and say that it was Hull who wanted to offload him. Leicester and Wolverhampton were reported to have made enquiries, but it seemed incredible that a rider who was fourth in the world would be lost to British racing.

Fortunately, Shawn had a change of heart and contacted Thomas and travelled to Britain for his first season of British League racing. It was a team with a very distinctive American flavour about it as Dennis Sigalos was joined by new recruits Moran and John 'Cowboy' Cook, who was third in the US Long Track Championship. Mauger, Beaton, Joe Owen and Frank Aufrett were the familiar names in a Vikings team who hoped to go one better in 1980 and win the championship.

Shawn made his debut on 26 March with the traditional Northern Trophy opener against Halifax, and he made the best possible start by winning his first race. As was normal, Hull lost their first match 41-37 and Shawn finished his first night with 6 points.

'I arrived in England with three big suitcases, full of stuff like food which I thought I wouldn't be able to get to over there,' said Shawn. 'It was hard work carrying them around the train stations as I made my way to Hull, and my arms were really hurting. It was certainly an advantage that everyone spoke English. I couldn't believe that they expected us to race in the rain. In America, even if it looked like it was going to rain they called it off, because they knew that they wouldn't get the crowds. But winning my first race, well, that was just bitchin'.'

Happily, Shawn settled into a scoring groove quite quickly at Hull, with a paid 11 points in a 12-point victory over Belle Vue. He followed this with 7 points at Halifax. Just like his brother, his cheerful, happy-go-lucky nature was a hit with the fans, and it seemed that they had another success story on their hands.

He shared digs in Hull with John Cook, but the garage wasn't big enough so they did all their machine maintenance indoors. This did not go down well with the landlady, but it was an incident of a more serious nature that meant that they had to look for alternative accommodation.

'Our bedroom was damp and we always had a bar heater on,' explained Shawn. 'One night, a pillow fell on the heater and burst into flames. Cookie jumped out of bed and tossed the pillow out into the street. Unknown to us, the pillow fell on the boyfriend's car and it just happened to have a soft top.'

Unfortunately, the Vikings were not to have a particularly successful campaign. An early indication that it was not going to be such a memorable year was when Hackney won at the Boulevard in late April – even though Shawn top-scored with 13 points. By rotating their side, they were still trying to beat the 50-point rule. It was a tactic which may have worked in 1979, as all the riders were used to each other, but with new faces and a side low on confidence, it was not working out this time. Ivan Mauger spent the year battling against injury, illness, and just plain bad luck. And his scoring was restricted as a result.

Kelly made a late start to his season in the US as he had to wait for the AMA to issue him with a licence. But he soon lit up San Bernardino with some char-

Shawn smiles for the camera as he prepares for another night's racing.

acteristic racing in a marvellous tussle with Lance King. Journalist Gary Briggs reported that only an engine failure prevented Kelly from taking the ultimate prize, and he enthused: 'Lance King was overshadowed in one of the greatest races ever seen at San Bernardino. Kelly used every inch of the track with some amazing balancing tricks.'

But moves were afoot to bring the elder Moran back to Britain. Birmingham, who had made a disappointing start to their new campaign, stumped up Hull's asking price and signed the diminutive American.

However, Kelly got off to a troubled start when a mix-up occurred over his debut for the 'Brummies'. He eventually made his first appearance in a Knockout Cup match against Coventry, and he scored 10 points in their 56-51 victory.

'I'd just failed to qualify from the American Final, and I was really choked,' said Kelly. 'It was such a big disappointment, especially after finishing fourth the year before. I was so disillusioned at the time, the last thing I wanted was to return to British speedway. But then Birmingham was interested in me and the prospect of a new challenge began to appeal.'

It didn't take him too long to adjust to the Perry Barr track, but he didn't enjoy the same level of support from his team-mates here as he had at Hull. Andy Grahame, Steve Bastable and Zdenek Kudrna were the only riders to offer regular support, but even their contributions were inconsistent. It wasn't difficult to see why the team were struggling near the foot of the table. However, Kelly's scoring did make the side a more formidable proposition, especially in the Inter League Four-Team Championship qualifying round at Belle Vue, when he dropped just one point to top score for the team and sneak a two-point win – and guarantee the Midland's club an appearance in the Finals.

But bad luck ruined their day in a feast of speedway racing during the tournament held at Wolverhampton. Birmingham finished joint top with Halifax in their semi-final with 28 points and joined the Yorkshire club in the final, where they also met Cradley Heath and King's Lynn. Kelly rose to the occasion to top score with 9 points, but he scored half the team's total as they finished third with 18 points. The tournament was won by Cradley, but it was such a disappointment after a battling display in the semi-finals. Their cause was not helped when Phil Herne was called away to be with his sick daughter, but more was expected.

However, behind the scenes, Birmingham boss Joe Thurley handed over the reins to the charismatic Dan McCormick. McCormick had transformed Cradley from a Cinderella club into Cup winners and championship contenders. He was also the man responsible for bringing Bruce Penhall and Bobby Schwartz to Britain. He saw that Birmingham, a one-time giant in the National League, had the potential to become the giants of the British League too.

In a Midland Cup match against McCormick's old club Cradley, the biggest crowd for some time assembled to watch this meeting. Unfortunately, Kelly was an innocent victim of a spectacular three-man pile up which left him with a chipped bone in his right elbow. Cradley's Dave Perks had reared up and took Moran's team-mate Finn Jensen with him, and they completely demolished a section of the safety fence. But poor Kelly was left with no time to avoid them and ploughed into them both. Perks broke some vertebrae in his back, but Jensen was able to continue.

The accident threatened Kelly's hopes of qualifying for the US Nationals and his American commitments began to cause a few problems for both himself and the club. Understandably, a struggling Birmingham needed his point-scoring, but he also had to honour his commitments in the USA – commitments he had made when it seemed that no British club was going to offer him a team place. Consequently, he missed a large chunk of August to race in America.

Murmurs and grumbling came from the Brummies' camp. But there were no complaints when he scored a paid maximum in a narrow victory over Poole, and then followed that two days later with another in a Knockout Cup fixture against Sheffield.

The Moran brothers were both willing participants when it came to promoting their sport. As a result, Kelly appeared before a massive crowd in the Birmingham City Centre to publicise the motor show at the NEC. Predictably, he was a big hit and thrilled the crowds with a display of wheelies around the famous 'Bull Ring'.

'Oh, that was great fun,' Kelly recalled. 'There were a lot of famous people there from car racing like James Hunt, Keke Rosberg, Dan Gurney, and Barry Sheene and others. We were in a parade and the announcer said, 'And here comes the Brummies,' or something like that. And it was like, well, what do we do now? So I just started pulling wheelies and they loved it. The rest of the team were there too. But how we got our bikes to do that distance, I just couldn't tell you. But it was a real fun day.'

It was about this time that Shawn's form had begun to slip at Hull. Something appeared to be amiss. 'I wasn't happy,' he said. 'I don't really know what it was. I got along fine with Ian and the rest, and the track was okay. Although, being around a rugby pitch, the wall was exposed on the back straight and you didn't want to hit that. So I sat down with Brian Larner and Ian and told them how I felt. They agreed to let me go, and then this opportunity came along with Sheffield.'

Ironically, in his last match for the Vikings, he scored his first paid maximum of his British career as Hull won with a massive 60-18 thrashing against … Sheffield!

Shawn was signed for the remainder of the season as a replacement for Reg Wilson, who had broken his leg. Sheffield Tigers boss Ray Glover was delighted with his new signing, whom he purchased from his rivals for a fee believed to between £6,000 and £8,000 – depending on which publication

Kelly Moran in Birmingham colours in 1980.

Kelly after winning the Studs Champion of the Evening at Birmingham in 1980.

one was reading. 'I am sure I've got the bargain of the year and a future champion,' he said.

It was the end of an era for Thomas, as neither of the Moran brothers would race for Hull again. And in 1981 there was not one American in the team! However, they remained friends and he followed their careers with interest.

'They were both very flamboyant, on and off the track,' recalled Thomas. 'But Shawn was a little quieter than Kelly, but still a very spectacular rider.'

Shawn made his debut for the Tigers on 11 September 1980 in a league match against title-chasing Hackney. The Sheffield faithful must have wondered just what Glover thought he was doing when Moran failed to score and Hackney won 40-38. He was disappointed with his own performance, and just couldn't put it together on the night. There was very little in his first three matches to suggest just what a star he would be for the Tigers in years to come. He managed just 3 points in three matches – hardly the performance of a 'future champion'.

'In his first meetings he didn't get many points at all,' Reg Wilson remembered. 'But he did get going after that and there was no stopping him. Most people could see at the time that he was keen and he had loads of ability on a bike. You could see that he had something special. That was the start of Shawn Moran at Sheffield.'

Steps were taken to assist him with his bikes and a much-improved display against Halifax saw him collect 6 points. Then he received a massive confidence boost the night before his home match against King's Lynn, when he teamed up with fellow American Ron Preston and won the Sheba Travel Best Pairs at Poole. Just to make sure that the Tigers' fans realised that was no fluke, he top-scored with 13 points as they saw off King's Lynn 43-35. He followed that up with his first paid maximum for the club with a hero's display in the 43-34 defeat at the hands of Poole. This was the talent and ability that Glover was so excited about.

On 9 October, the Sheffield public were afforded a genuine glimpse into the future if they did but know it. They staged a challenge match between two sides, the Stars and the Starlets. The latter featured some of the brightest young talent currently racing in Britain, against a Stars side which featured more established riders. The Starlets ran out comfortable winners with a 67-41 victory. It was significant as far as the Tigers fans were concerned, as the joint top scorers for the victors were Shawn and Kelly with 13 points each. It was the first time they had raced together in the same team in Britain and, of course, they preceded their famous double act at the Owlerton track by six years. This may have been a fixture put together to fill in a blank date caused by the club's lack of on-track success, but with Neil Collins also present in the side, it was closest that the club would ever get to a crystal ball reading of what was to come.

Sheffield finished 1980 at the foot of the league table, but with Shawn already set to return in 1981, they had good reason to feel optimistic. Birmingham and Hull finished marginally better in a year when the championship was won by Reading.

Kelly's late start to the season, plus his American commitments, contributed to a year when his scoring slipped a little. Birmingham had signed him to fill the role of a number one, but his circumstances meant that he didn't quite fulfil that requirement. But his best individual performance was a third place in the prestigious Golden Hammer at Cradley Heath, which was won by Chris Morton ahead of runner-up, Scott Autrey.

Shawn returned to America and proved that he hadn't forgotten the quickest way around Ascot when he retained the US Long Track title ahead of his ex-Hull team-mate, John Cook. With his future settled, he travelled to Australia with fellow countrymen Cook, Bobby Schwartz, and Denny Pyeatt.

Although he never made it public knowledge, it was widely believed that McCormick was not a big fan of Kelly Moran. The *1981 Daily Mirror Speedway Yearbook* indicated that the Birmingham boss was not happy with his 'unprofessional attitude.' McCormick had bought Wolverhampton, and planned to run them in the National League. Therefore he inherited their senior riders, which included World Finalist, Hans Nielsen. Despite the fact that Kelly had stated that he didn't want to leave the Brummies, it seemed that the spectacular American was not in McCormick's plans for 1981.

In a long and complicated transfer saga, Eastbourne had expressed an interest in signing him. Eventually, it came down to a rider swap deal after they had agreed personal terms. Kai Niemi was offered to Birmingham and Kelly would join the Eastbourne Eagles. However, Bob Dugard, the Eagles' boss, was perhaps mindful of the American's unpredictable reputation, as he insisted that Niemi could not leave until the American had arrived in Britain and signed his contract. Therefore, Niemi actually raced in Eastbourne's first match of the 1981 campaign.

However, the American eventually made his debut for the South Coast club on April 5 in a League Cup match at home to King's Lynn. He missed his first two programmed rides though, when his flight was delayed from LA; he was detained further at Heathrow because of a problem with his work permit. He was whisked to his new track and was on a bike within five minutes of arriving at the Arlington Stadium. He signed his contract on the centre green, but only contributed 3 points as they lost 57-38. Nevertheless, he promised the Eastbourne faithful that he would do better – and he did. Two weeks later, he scored his first maximum for the club – 15 points at home to Wimbledon – and this had followed 9 points at Ipswich and 10 points in Eastbourne's first victory of the season over Swindon. And so began two memorable seasons for the club.

'Of all the British teams I raced for, I enjoyed it at Eastbourne the most,' he revealed. 'Sheffield, Belle Vue and the others were great too, but Eastbourne was different. Bob Dugard was an ex-rider and he was a great promoter. It was a family-run track. It was like being part of the family, there was Bob, his father Charlie, the two boys, Martin and Paul, and there was so much experience there. Charlie used to ride as well, and then there was Eric Dugard, and of course Martin and Paul went into it too. Bob knew what you were going through as a rider – he understood. It wasn't just a business to him. There was a better climate down there too. I heard a lot of stories about Bob in his riding days. One, in particular, was that he would drill holes in his helmet so that he could hear the riders coming up behind him! I don't think I would have liked to race against him,' he laughed.

Eastbourne had only joined the British League in 1979, after enjoying many successful seasons in the National League. Bob and his promoting partner Danny Dunton, a former rider with Harringay, used to run a BL team at White City – they lifted the championship in 1977 – as well as Eastbourne during the mid 1970s. But White City was closed to regular league racing at the end of 1978 – although it would continue to run international and World Championship events until it was closed for good in 1984. So the promoting duo transferred their BL licence to Eastbourne and brought some of the White City team with them too.

Both seasons had been a hard slog for the Eagles' fans and management. After tasting so much success in the NL, two seasons spent languishing near the foot of the table were hard to stomach. For most of the time, it was left

Shawn Moran, Sheffield Tigers, 1982.

to the reliable scoring of Gordon Kennett and Kai Niemi to spare the Eagles' blushes. The arrival of Kelly Moran marked a new era for the Sussex club. He formed a powerful spearhead with former World number two Kennett, while the rest of the side included local discoveries Paul Woods and Trevor Geer, Robert Slabon from Poland, Dave Kennett and another promising rider from Finland, Olli Tyravanien. On paper, the side had potential, but it was emphasised that this was a first step to more successful times, and Kelly was looked upon as a major part of that plan.

The American invasion of British Speedway peaked in numbers in 1981. When the tapes lifted on the new campaign, there were a record 14 US riders trying their luck in England. Among the newcomers that year was Brad Oxley – Harry's son – who turned out for Wimbledon and made a favourable impression.

If there were any doubts about Shawn Moran's capabilities, then they were quickly dispelled by some spectacular and brave riding. Ray Glover was particularly proud of this exciting young American. After he had produced 50 points in four matches during a 10-day period in April, Glover said before setting off for a match at Shawn's old team, Hull: 'Hull couldn't buy Shawn back for any amount of money – and that goes for any other track. The lad was just what we needed and he's already licked Mauger and Olsen this season.'

Glover was building his team around the 'Miracle Worker' and when they travelled to Edinburgh for a Cup match, Shawn passed Dave Trownson and Chris Turner. Glover gleefully turned to the Edinburgh boss, Alan Bridgett, and said, 'I bet you wish you had a rider like that.' But the Scotsman had the last laugh, as they pulled off a shock 49-47 victory.

The American's sense of humour also proved to be a massive hit with the Yorkshire folk. In one race, he was lining up to make a pass when he lost control and hit the deck. His reaction when he returned to the pits typified his fun-loving outlook on racing: 'I was only testing the track in readiness for my next race,' he said.

And in that next race he proved what a talent he was. Coming out of the first bend on the second lap, the Tigers fans roared with approval as he burst between the Hull duo of Mauger and Billy Sanders, and they just couldn't catch him. He quickly established himself as the club's number one rider and although the Sheffield team improved on their previous season's performance, they still lacked the strength to seriously challenge for honours.

Wilson made a return to captain the team, and his team-mates included Dave Morton, who was signed from Wolves, the experienced Alan Molyneux and Eric Broadbelt, Phil White and promising young Australian, Mark Fiora.

While Shawn was still proving himself, Kelly was finally performing at a level of consistency that everyone knew he was capable of, but seldom did so with the Brummies. His ability from the back and his entertaining showmanship made him a legend at Arlington.

In a feature called 'The Entertainers' which was published in *Speedway Mail* in 1986, the author described him as the 'darling of the Arlington crowd'. He was amazing around the tight Eastbourne track and produced some wonderful racing from the back, and he would pass riders anywhere on the circuit. On many occasions, he would clinch the match for the Eagles with a match-winning performance during the last race. He set a new track record of 58.26 seconds on his way to another full house in a 48-30 victory over Hull.

In July, Eastbourne did a short tour of Poland. It was an agreement made with the Polish Federation that enabled Slabon to race for the Eagles. For the first two matches, Kennett and Moran were not able to ride due to World Team Cup commitments, and they were replaced by Wimbledon's Malcolm Simmons and Edward Jancarz. They lost 49-29 at Wroclaw, but did a lot better at Gdansk, losing by a narrow scoreline of 47-43.

Kennett and Moran returned to participate in a pairs meeting at Gdansk which the pair eventually won with a combined total of 23 points. But during the third race, Kelly took a heavy tumble and injured his knee. For a moment it looked as though their challenge was at an end, but he bravely carried on. He was helped to his machine for the remaining races and won his final heat. As winners, they picked up pair of attractive crystal vases. The Polish pair of Bobby Nowak and Marek Towalski took the runners-up position.

Disappointingly, this was the only success the Eagles enjoyed, as the British team was defeated heavily in the last two meetings. They lost 55-35 to Gniezno, despite Kelly top-scoring with 13 points and Kennett offering good support with 10. However, at Leszno, Eastbourne was forced to race on worn out tyres and they were struggling with the lack of spares afforded to them by their hosts. Predictably, they lost 70-18 as they could hardly compete at this stage.

When Bob Dugard enquired about the tyres and spares that had not arrived, he was offered new rubber at such a high price that it was more than a rider would be paid if he was to score a maximum! As a result, by the last few races only Robert Slabon's Jawa was still operational. Kelly burnt out the clutch on his Weslake and he tried Roman Jankowski's machine, but he still finished on just 1 point.

'It was a lot different racing in Poland in those days,' recalled Kelly. 'It was the time of the Iron Curtain and all that. I remember at the start line, we would dig in to try and get good traction out of the start, and the dirt was so deep it was like lining up in trenches. Sometimes, I would try to pull away and my progress would be restricted because my exhaust pipe, or foot rest, would get caught up in the dirt.'

Both Eastbourne and Sheffield did well on their home tracks, but lacked the strength in depth to seriously trouble the opposition on their travels.

Nonetheless, the interest in the Morans in opposition was immense when Sheffield came to visit Eastbourne in a league encounter. The Eagles defeated the Tigers 46-32 and Kelly defeated his brother twice during the two occasions they met. Shawn top-scored with 10 points and pushed his brother all the way in their opening exchange, but couldn't do anything about him later as Kelly swept to 9 points.

The sequel to this duel of the brothers took place at Sheffield, where the Tigers ran out easy winners with a comprehensive score line of 56-22. Shawn met his brother three times during the match, and set the fastest time of the season in the first of his three wins. Among the crowd that evening were their grandparents, Mr and Mrs Garth Ganes. Their grandfather had recently retired and part of his golden handshake was two airline tickets to anywhere in the world. They decided to travel to the UK to see their grandsons in action and to take in the World Final at Wembley.

Unfortunately, both of them were eliminated from the World Championship before the final at Wembley. Kelly missed the cut at the last stage, while Shawn concentrated instead on the European U-21 Championship and successfully won the title.

It was indeed a shame that Kelly did fail to make the final as he hit a purple patch of form around that time, and would surely have been a contender for a rostrum placing. In eight matches, he was averaging around 10.50 and scored four full maximums. He scored maximums in both the

A rare photograph of the Moran brothers in opposition at Eastbourne in 1982. Shawn is on the inside for Sheffield, with Kelly challenging on the outside.

home and away clashes against King's Lynn. Although he missed his first programmed ride at Belle Vue – through being held up on the motorway because of an accident – he hopped on his machine and was never beaten as he fought a lone battle for the Eagles. Such a run of excellent form could have been put down to a change of accommodation, as Bob Dugard revealed.

'Kelly was always a difficult house guest because he was a real party animal. I will always recall he had exhausted staying with all of his friends, and his only option was to come and live with my family under strict rules: one pint of lager per day, and not allowed out 48 hours before a meeting. He settled in and was the perfect guest. He was great with my children and lived with us for six weeks and dropped just a handful of points in 13 meetings – which showed the talent he had. But the strain of being on such a tight rein proved too much and he asked to move back with friends, and his form dipped.'

There was much interest a few years ago in the pre-race routine that Grand Prix rider Chris Louis used to go through before settling down to start a race. One of the curious quirks that Kelly displayed in his early years was knocking his front wheel against the safety fence before continuing his journey toward the tapes.

'I did that to straighten my front wheel. It used to get bent because of the way I used to try and scrub off speed in the corners. It always used to happen in the early days for some reason, and it became a bit of a habit.'

However, there were other things that he never stopped doing right up until he retired. He would be the last to emerge from the dressing room when the engines were warming up in readiness for the competition ahead. He would also invariably be the last rider to emerge from the pits – quite often with only seconds to spare while under a two-minute time allowance.

'He had a routine,' said Craig Cummings. 'On his way to the tapes, he would kick the clutch arm three or four times which he did until the day he retired. He'd leave everything for the last minute. He would always clean his leathers, his boots and helmet about 10 minutes before he would leave for the track. It was almost as if he wasn't bothered, but he was. He liked to portray that devil-may-care attitude.'

On the face of it, Shawn did not have any of these little routines, but he did later reveal that he always walked the track and would always take the same position in the dressing room. However, he believed that other riders must have done that too, otherwise he would have lost his place.

As Shawn was the undisputed number one rider at Sheffield, he found himself lining up at Belle Vue in the British League Riders' Championship – an annual meeting which was regarded as being a tougher event than the World Final itself. Despite displaying his best BL form to date, Kelly missed out to Gordon Kennett and took little comfort from the fact that he would have been the number one rider at most of the other teams in the league.

In spite of lifting the Under-21 title, smashing the track record at Poole, and carrying a Green Sheet average of a shade over 9 points, *Speedway Mail* journalist John Hyam put Shawn in the 'no-hopers' bracket in his preview. But Shawn, riding a Godden machine, produced a magnificent display to finish in third place with 13 points. He lost a run-off to Chris Morton for second in a tremendous shoulder-to-shoulder tussle, which was a repeat of their heat 12 encounter – but Shawn came out on top in that one. The meeting was won by the England and Halifax star Kenny Carter with a perfect 15 points.

This meeting, along with the Under-21 championship, was the highlight of his individual season. He also took third in the Yorkshire TV Trophy and, at the expense of his brother's misfortune; he won the Trevor Geer Testimonial at Eastbourne. Kelly was on an unbeaten score and leading his brother when his fuel lead came adrift and relegated him to fourth place. Shawn won with 15 points, while Kelly had to settle for third behind John Cook. His response was typically philosophical: 'That's racing, but at the least the trophy stayed in the family.'

At the end of the season, both of them were settled at their respective clubs and went into the close season with high hopes for the following year. Sheffield had improved on their previous year's position to tenth place, while Eastbourne climbed three places to thirteenth – their poor form away from home prevented them from climbing further up the table.

Clearly both sides needed to find support for their star riders if they were to challenge for honours. For Eastbourne, it was Kelly who alerted Dugard that Ron Preston was looking for a transfer from Poole and he eventually signed for the Sussex club. Two Swedes, Borje Ring and Lars Hammerberg, were also added to the tail-end alongside Dave Kennett. Paul Woods was expected to continue his improvement and for the first time in a few years, it looked as though the Eagles were going to be a real force in the BL. On the eve of the new season, Dugard praised Kelly's first season at Arlington on the front page of *Speedway Mail*, while he acknowledged his off-track reputation.

'Kelly is the best thing to have happened at Eastbourne for a long time,' he said. 'There are aggravations with him as everyone knows and perhaps at times he is his own worst enemy. Basically, there is no harm at all in Kelly and the public love him. A lot of riders don't appreciate the public and then they wonder why the American riders are so popular.'

Meanwhile, at the Tigers' den little had changed. While experts agreed that Moran needed solid reliable backing, Glover continued with his youth policy. At one stage, it looked as though American Keith Chrisco would be joining the Tigers, but the deal folded because a work permit was not granted. Instead, Glover signed promising Kiwis David Bargh and Wayne Brown. Bargh had a good season with Newcastle in the National League, while Brown had won the 1980 National League Riders' title. These were the only two changes made to the team, and they proved to be wise ones too.

Eastbourne had a mixed start to the new season, and Preston did not arrive until Easter. But it was soon apparent that the team was top-heavy. The two Swedes and Dave Kennett were not supplying the back up for the top four, and this was a problem when they faced solid teams away from home.

Kelly was paired with Ron Preston for the opening weeks of the season, as the latter had missed the bulk of the 1981 season due to a serious knee injury. Many thought that the signing of 'Rapid' Ron was a gamble because of the injury, but he soon settled in. While racing with Moran he could have the choice of gate positions, and this didn't seem to thwart Kelly's own form. He scored maximums in the home and away clash with King's Lynn – just as he did in '81 – and generally carried on where he had left off.

However, it seemed at one point that Kelly would not make the trip to King's Lynn, when the vehicle that he, Borje Ring and Hammerberg were travelling in broke down at the Dartford Tunnel. Minutes after a desperate telephone call to Hove, Sussex, Dugard was racing to their rescue to transport his riders to Saddlebow Road, where they won 40-38. Another home and away maximum followed at Swindon, which included a sweet

Eastbourne Eagles, 1982. From left to right, Kelly, Dave Kennett, Ron Preston, Gordon Kennett (on bike), Bob Dugard (team manager), Lars Hammerberg, Paul Woods, Borje Ring.

inside pass on Phil Crump at Blunsdon, after the Aussie had brought the Swindon crowd to their feet by blasting by the unbeaten American.

Controversy shrouded Sheffield's match at Coventry, which ended in a 41-35 defeat for the Yorkshire team. In the final heat decider, Bees' guest, Scott Autrey, leapt into the lead, but before the end of the opening lap, the other three riders had hit the deck. Shawn was adjudged to be the cause of the accident and was excluded. Protests from the Tigers camp followed which held up the meeting for twenty minutes. Then Reg Wilson was excluded under the two-minute rule, and the Tigers management declined to put out a replacement and withdrew their riders from the second half.

Wilson had been struggling with his form and the captaincy was handed over to Shawn, whose form was even better than last year. It was hoped that by removing the responsibility from the shoulders of the experienced Wilson, it would kick start his season and mark a return to the form which was expected of him. For Shawn, it was a role he would continue with.

'Although I was their number one, I didn't mind stepping down if it was for the good of the team,' said Shawn. 'When they had the nominated riders' heat, I used to tell the team manager to pick the riders who were going well. They didn't always have to pick me because I was the captain or their number one. If someone was going well, or I was having a poor night, then I'd always put the team first.'

In May, Kelly's reputation went before him in a fixture at home to Wimbledon. He had just flown back from racing in the States, and rushed to the stadium to take his part in the match. However, in heat three, he crashed and then fell again in heat five. The referee decided that all four riders were eligible for the re-run, but in a hectic first turn he took another tumble – only this time they excluded Wimbledon's Brad Oxley. The Wimbledon Dons' management retaliated by demanding that the track doctor carry out a fitness test on Moran. The doctor ruled him fit and he won his next race in a match that finished as a 39-39 draw. But it was an incident that left a foul taste and Dugard sought legal advice over the matter.

The Eagles had just registered nine matches without a defeat when Dugard put Kelly forward for a crack at the Golden Helmet Match Race Championship. This competition was run over two legs between two riders only, and Kenny Carter was the holder.

'Although he would be a popular nomination among speedway supporters, for some reason he doesn't seem to be so highly rated by some promoters,' wrote Dugard in his programme notes. 'Some of the points he has dropped this year are as a result of trying to team-ride. I suppose he could go all out for personal victory all the time, but he is very team conscious. And I wouldn't want him any other way.'

He was overlooked; but his brother wasn't. Shawn was announced as the challenger for Carter and he relieved the Halifax number one of the title. He successfully defended it against Swindon's Phil Crump – although the Aussie was unfit to participate in the decider after they had both won their home legs. He went into the close season as the holder as he saw off the challenge of World Final runner-up, Les Collins.

Although Eastbourne was enjoying their best British League season to date, it was turning out to be a mixed one for Kelly. He was fined £1,000 and had his equipment impounded by the management when he failed to arrive for a home meeting against Ipswich on 20 June. He telephoned to say that he couldn't get a flight back to London after he had been riding in the American Final of the World Championship. He had postponed his original departure date for which he was originally booked and, as was confirmed by the Eagles' bosses, the flights back to London on the date in question were indeed full. They maintained that he should have flown on the original date and his absence undoubtedly cost them the match as they were held to a 39-39 draw. His replacement, Keith Pritchard, failed to score.

Kelly went onto the centre green and publicly apologised to the fans. Dugard refused to remove the punishment and he had to race in the Intercontinental Final of the World Team Cup on borrowed equipment. But they put the incident behind them, and Dugard said that it was all in the past.

After qualifying for his second World Final, Kelly returned to Britain and travelled to Belle Vue for the Eagles match. However, the Belle Vue management insisted that he take a fitness test before racing and the doctor ruled him unfit to race. He was fined £10 by the meeting referee and was reported to the Speedway Control Board. The Eastbourne management, who lost the match 48-30, warned him of his future conduct and issued this short statement. 'The rider had been celebrating reaching the World Final the previous night in Sweden, and had not slept in 24 hours and was obviously in no fit condition to ride. We agree with the action taken by the Belle Vue management.'

In his defence Kelly Moran responded: 'You can't expect someone to go home and have a night's rest after they have qualified for a World Final. But basically the whole thing was a big mix up in Sweden. There was some confusion about the homecoming arrangements, and we seemed to be driving round Sweden for half the night. I was tired, burned out and a little hung over. But I was only half as tired as I was when Wimbledon made their protest.'

Despite these indiscretions, he was still scoring well and Eagles' fans continued to support him.

'He was worshipped,' said Dugard. 'They always forgave him for all of his off-track slip-ups, which were well recorded at the time. But they realised he really could help himself, and he did try hard to reform. For Kelly to have ever realised his true potential would have robbed him of his natural thirst to party and his happy-go-lucky personality. And I don't believe he could do that.'

For some reason, speedway racing in Ireland has never caught on, but on 13 July stock-car promoter, Robert Mather and the then Cradley team manager, Peter Adams, staged a meeting at Ballymena Showground, County Antrim, Northern Ireland. They took the reigning British League champions Cradley across the Irish Sea, and assembled seven star riders to race in an Ivan Mauger World Select team. The 440-yard tarmac track, which was normally used for hot rod and stock cars, was covered with shale and a temporary wooden safety fence was installed. A crowd of 5,000 witnessed the last speedway meeting to take place in Ireland, which was won by Cradley.

Shawn Moran made the trip over to ride in the World Select and scored six points, which included a win over Erik Gundersen. 'I was still a bit green then and I was pretty concerned by all the soldiers and guns about,' he said. 'I had never seen those kinds of checkpoints at home and it scared me a little. I was always hearing about the IRA and Sinn Fein and all the troubles while I was in England, but I didn't get involved in all the debates. But it was scary. I remember the track was really big and slick, but I guess the costs of ferrying riders and their equipment across to Ireland has made it too expensive to run a team over there.'

The close-knit American riders who raced in Britain were shocked when their fellow countryman, Denny Pyeatt, was killed in a track crash at Hackney on July 16. The likeable man from Woodland, California, was in his second season at Reading, and beginning to show some true form when the accident occurred. Bobby Schwartz, Pyeatt's team-mate at Reading, was particularly upset, but it affected all of the riders. It was a bleak year for British speedway as Zdenek Kudrna, Brett Alderton and Martin Hewlett (who collapsed after a race at Swindon and died of a haemorrhage) all lost their lives.

'Zdenek was my team-mate at Birmingham,' Kelly recalled. 'It was hard as Denny was a great guy. I remember calling Kenny Carter and Mike Lee and asking just what was going on? You know, we all think we're Superman when we put that crash helmet on, and we're wearing all the protective clothing, but something like that makes you realise how vulnerable you are – it makes you think. The only good thing to come out of it was that it pulled all the riders together – which is kind of sad to think that it can sometimes take something like that to do it.'

'Denny was a sweet guy,' agreed Shawn. 'Bobby used to call him the 'Koala Kid', because we spent time together in Australia. It was very sad, because he just loved racing.'

Reading hastily arranged an emotional memorial meeting, which Shawn won. Kelly was unable to take his place due to shoulder and rib injuries sustained in a crash at home to Wimbledon. Other tributes followed and an inquest was called. It was the beginning of America's loathing for the Waterden Road circuit, where Kelly had sustained multiple injuries in 1978.

Kelly in the pits before another match with Eastbourne.

Despite Shawn's disappointment at his elimination from the World Championship, he was in fantastic form as he added a point to his average. In addition to winning the Pyeatt memorial, he also lifted the Northern Riders' Championship – the first American to do so – and set a new track record at Sheffield of 63.2. And to top it all, the Tigers' gamble on assembling a young side paid off, as they eventually finished in fifth place – a big improvement on the previous year.

If anything Kelly's form was better than his first year with the club, and he increased his average slightly in 1982. He made his second World Final appearance and finished in fourth place. Shortly after the staging of the sport's premier event, Britain staged a British Open Championship at White City and the field for the World Final was largely reassembled. Bruce Penhall had retained the World title and promptly made his retirement speech on the rostrum. The meeting at White City was consequently billed as a second World Final. On a slick track, which produced very little passing, Kelly finished third behind Hans Nielsen and winner Dennis Sigalos.

'I know I could have done better, but the track was dreadfully slick. But to think that you could produce a World Final at White City a week later, was absolute nonsense,' he said.

In a stormy 54-24 victory over Poole, Vaclav Verner speared Kelly and the American was taken to hospital with a broken collarbone and a cracked shoulder blade. Verner was later fined £50 and suspended when he became embroiled with an irate Eagles fan. This injury put paid to his chances of heading Kennett and making his first appearance in the British League Riders' Championship. Although he returned to bolster Eastbourne's assault on the Southern Cup during the final month of the season, he was too late to prevent the club's exit from the Knockout Cup at the hands of Cradley in the semi-finals.

Once again, Shawn represented Sheffield in the British League Riders' Championship. The Sheffield star avoided all the controversy that occurred between defending champion Carter and Dennis Sigalos, and coped well with the wet track, producing another magnificent display to finish runner-up to Carter.

But his season wasn't over yet. He returned to America to ride in the US National Championship and swept all before him to win the championship with 14 points, and looked a certainty to take over the mantle left by Penhall as the new US number one.

It became a close season of discontent as far as American riders were concerned. Brad Oxley went on record to describe his living conditions as a 'slum'. Scott Autrey retired after a long and difficult year with Poole, and John Cook announced that he would not be returning to Ipswich.

Then came the news in early December that rocked the very foundations of Eastbourne Speedway – Kelly Moran was quitting the British League. Dugard dismissed the news as a rumour. So sure was he that the news was

Shawn is doused in champagne by Karen Meister following his victory in the 1982 US National Championship.

untrue, that he finally let the unsettled Gordon Kennett move to King's Lynn as he planned to make Kelly his number one and build his team around him. The ever faithful and loyal fans refused to believe it too; surely the darling of the Eagles' fans would be back?

However, as Kelly proved elusive to track down, team planning was put on hold while the new season crept ever closer. Then the horrible truth was confirmed – Kelly was staying in sunny California. Dugard was very upset by his decision as he had stood by the little Californian throughout his troubled season and, understandably, he felt let down. But when the news came through that fellow American Ron Preston was also planning to remain in the USA, the future of the club did start to look very bleak indeed. With very little time to assemble a competitive team, *Speedway Star* even went so far as to sensationally indicate that the very future of the club was in jeopardy.

'I had been racing in the BL since 1978 and I needed a break,' said Kelly. 'I only had one professional season at home before I went to England. Shawn had just won the Nationals, and he said that he wouldn't get the chance to enjoy it because of his BL commitments. It's more relaxed at home; if you have a bad night it's not affecting anyone except yourself, where as in the BL it affects the whole team. Besides, Costa Mesa was my favourite track.'

However, it was reported that a rift had surfaced between the rider and the promoter, but the scale of this was exaggerated in the sport's press. But one thing was certain; and that was that Eastbourne faced a difficult year in 1983. 'Yes I was upset, but it never stopped us from being friends,' said Dugard. 'Kelly was promised a massive deal to stay in the USA, but it never worked out for him.'

There were no such worries for Sheffield as Shawn returned for his fourth British season. But he was one of only six Americans that travelled across the Atlantic to race in England. After the USA had won a clean sweep of all the major competitions during 1982, suddenly the American influence in Britain was drastically reduced. They could barely field a test team with the resources they had in Britain, and the planned test series against England seemed to have lost some of its appeal. The retirement of Golden Boy Penhall marked the end of an era, but America and, the Morans, were not finished yet …

3

CHASING GOLD

We ride for the big occasion. The bigger the pressure, the better we go,' wrote Kelly Moran in his column in *Speedway Magazine,* when asked about what motivates the Morans. And they don't come much bigger than the World Individual Championship.

Until 1995, the World Individual Speedway Championship was decided in one glorious night of action. Throughout the year, qualifiers were held to determine the sixteen riders to contest the one-off night of tense racing. It was usually held in September, and such nights like this, at world famous venues like the legendary Wembley, had a unique atmosphere of expectation that was all their own. The road to get to the last sixteen was a hard and torturous one, which grew progressively more difficult as it went along.

It was in 1978 that Kelly first turned a wheel in the World Championship, in the controversial American Final. There was much debate and argument in the States about where and when this World Championship qualifying round was going to take place. The FIM, the sport's world governing body, had regulations for the track size that these rounds had to conform to. Therefore, Costa Mesa was ruled out because it was too small. The American Motorcycle Association, meanwhile, did not seem to know what they were doing when it came to organising a speedway World Championship event.

The first American Final was staged in 1977, when only two qualifying places were available – which went to Mike Bast and Bruce Penhall. The following year, the British-based riders earned their places based on their British League averages at a certain cut-off date. Therefore, Scott Autrey and Steve Gresham took the two American places for the Intercontinental Final. But this method was wholly unpopular and unfair, as the riders racing at home were not even given an opportunity to qualify.

However, such was the talent emerging in the USA, that it was vital that they had their own qualifying round like most of the other nations. Eventually, it was decided to stage the meeting at Santa Ana – a venue twenty-five miles south of Los Angeles. Immediately, the AMA came in for criticism when they announced that this round would take place in December 1978. A World Championship qualifying round for the 1979 World Championship being held in 1978 seemed, well, Mickey Mouse! It certainly didn't do much for the credibility of the competition.

The date especially concerned Kelly Moran as he was still recovering from multiple injuries sustained in a track crash at Hackney in September. He was in a race against time to be fit enough to ride.

But there were more problems on the day of meeting. Scott Autrey had finished in a brilliant third in the 1978 World Final at Wembley, and had become the first American since 1938 to stand on the rostrum. He was not at all happy with the organisation of the event when he arrived, and became so upset and disillusioned that he withdrew from the meeting and threatened to retire from the sport altogether. Happily, he did not carry out his threat to retire, but the AMA took a dim view of his stand and overlooked him when selecting riders for the international events in 1979. Eventually Harry Oxley stepped in to resolve the World Championship situation. Although Scott said that he had 'no regrets' about making his protest, he must have wondered just what might have been when he experienced his best season of his career and was arguably the best rider in the world during 1979.

Kelly had little time to think about all the arguments and the discontent among his rivals, as he had enough problems of his own. The fact was that he was far from fit to race. Since the accident, he had not even ridden on a bike until the practice the night before the final. And yet here he was, aiming to finish in the top two places to qualify for the next round.

He could hardly walk on the night, and his father and Ian Thomas had to lift the brave little Californian onto his machine so that he could take his place in the races. It was a top-class field and, after he had completed his five rides, he tied for first place on 12 points with Mike Bast, Steve Gresham and Bobby Schwartz. This meant a run-off was needed to determine the two qualifiers and the reserve for the Intercontinental Final at White City, London in August. Schwartz led with Kelly second, but Bast passed Moran on the third lap. Then, possibly due to fatigue, he slid off. Luckily, Gresham had already fallen and so Kelly was awarded third place overall.

At this point, he was all set for the reserve spot and, understandably, was disappointed after all the hard work. But the story wasn't over yet. As the year progressed, noises came from California that Bast would not be making the trip across to England. And eventually Kelly's brave efforts were rewarded as he stepped up to take his place in the Intercontinental Final.

'When you get a break like that, you don't throw it away,' said Kelly. 'The dice rolled in my favour and in many ways I still can't believe it. When Bast withdrew, the AMA weren't going to put me in, they wanted to put Scott Autrey in. But Ian Thomas got on the phone and made sure that I was.'

Kelly was just five races away from making his first World Final. The 1979 Intercontinental Final was described as 'the day of the battler.' It was a dry, warm Sunday afternoon, and some of the world's best riders from the West were all hoping to make the top nine. Kelly had been in fine form all year, but his inexperience at this level was viewed by most people as being too much of a handicap.

At the interval stage, he had three points to his name. There were a number of riders all hovering around the edge of qualification or failure – including Mauger, Olsen, and Billy Sanders. Kelly gave his chances a tremendous boost when he won heat fifteen ahead of John Titman, Gordon Kennett and Hans Nielsen. He had to wait until the penultimate race to make sure of his place in the final, where a second place should have been enough to qualify. By this time Schwartz had blown his chances, so it was down to Moran to ensure that America was represented in the World Final.

He was off the inside gate, and faced John Davis, Dave Jessup, and Larry Ross. Davis was out of contention, but Jessup needed a win to force a run-off for overall victory. The Kiwi, Ross, would be a danger man as he needed to win to stand a chance of getting through. Kelly hit the front and was pursued by Ross, while the English duo didn't really figure. In an exciting race, Ross just clinched the win on the finish line, but second was enough for the American, while New Zealander Ross had to wait for the outcome of the final race to determine his fate.

Kelly was elated and would line up at his first World Final in Katowice, Poland as the youngest rider in the field. 'Now I've got to stay in one piece,' he joked. 'I felt I had the worst gates for my weight early on, but after the fourth outing, with the inside gate to come, I felt confident.'

As if to tempt fate, just ten days before his debut appearance in the sport's biggest showpiece, he suffered concussion when he crashed trying to pass fellow World Finalist, Edward Jancarz. Happily, he recovered in time to take his place in the line-up.

He was not among the favourites and was expected to be making up the numbers. But speaking before his big day he said: 'I'm going there to win. If you don't go with that attitude, then there's little point in setting off. Having never ridden the track, I do not know what to expect, except what people have told me. I think we've planned everything – as far as you can – and if I do succeed much of the credit will go to my mechanic, Bernard Harrison. My only real fear is that the track is too slick. This would really kill off what chances I have.'

It was a strong line-up. Among the favourites were that year's Intercontinental and Commonwealth champion, Michael Lee, reigning champion Ole Olsen, former World Champions Peter Collins and Ivan Mauger and, for once, you couldn't discount the Poles in front of their own fans, especially the claims of Zenon Plech. Add to that the undoubted talents of Billy Sanders, Dave Jessup and Finn Thomsen, and it wasn't difficult to dismiss the chances of the inexperienced Moran.

There was a massive crowd at Katowice, reported to be over 100,000 fans. He may have been the lone American, but he had plenty of support and advice on hand. He flew to Poland with his trusty mechanic, Bernard Harrison and was joined in the pits by Harry Oxley and his Hull boss, Ian Thomas – although the latter also had an interest in Ivan Mauger's performance too. On such a big occasion, and for a young man who was still not yet nineteen years old, one wouldn't have been surprised if the occasion got to him – but it didn't.

He had no time to get nervous after the presentation of the riders as he was in the first race. He lined up in gate three against Peter Collins, the Soviet rider Mikhail Starostin and Billy Sanders on the outside. Australian Sanders led from the front and held on for a win despite the close attention of Collins. Kelly finished in third and scored one point. Heat seven saw Kelly take the outside gate against Zdenek Kudrna, Mauger and Plech. No one at the time realised how significant the outcome of this race would become to the overall result. Moran's Vikings' team-mate, Mauger, hit the front and Kelly tucked in behind him, with the local favourite Plech in third. While Mauger held station, Plech set about putting the American under pressure. Roared on by the partisan Polish crowd, Plech tried everything to find a way past Moran, but it was to no avail as Moran held off his every move. It was the best race of the afternoon, and demonstrated that the Californian was not out of his depth at this level.

There are no easy races in a World Final, but Kelly's third race was as close as he would get to one – but only on paper. This time he was off gate three with Robert Slabon, German Alois Weisboch and Australian John Titman off the outside. Titman hit the front with Kelly in hot pursuit. All of the American's spectacular efforts were rewarded when he took his first win by inches on the finishing line. This put him on six points and with a real chance of a top three finish.

He finished second behind Jessup in heat fifteen, and ended the chances of Olsen and Lee who were behind him. Two races later, Mauger made history when he won the race and clinched his record-breaking sixth world title. A victory in his last race over Denmark's Finn Thomsen and Edward Jancarz meant that Kelly finished on 11 points, and would face a four-man run-off for third place against Sanders, Olsen and Lee.

Once again, Kelly was off gate three with Lee outside him. It was Sanders who made the start, but Lee pulled clear out of the second turn. Kelly was enjoying a tremendous tussle with Olsen when the Dane's engine stopped and the American took off after Sanders and snatched second in the race to claim a marvellous fourth place overall.

It was such a sensational performance that Kelly joined the top three of Mauger, Plech, and Lee on the podium. Deservedly, he celebrated his achievement as he had set himself a target of a top four finish, and everyone who saw that final in Katowice agreed that the American was a potential World Champion.

'Kelly wasn't a bit nervous because he didn't think he had a chance,' said Mauger. 'He wasn't the type of person to get nervous – I don't think he ever was. He was so laid back, life was a bit of fun to him and I expect it still is.'

'Kelly wasn't nervous at all,' agreed Thomas. 'He stopped Zenon Plech from winning even though he was up his leg for the whole race. It was fantastic speedway. We had to shell out a small fortune to the management of the Novotel in Katowice, because young Kelly autographed all the white leather

Kelly leads Zenon Plech and Zdenek Kudrna at the 1979 World Final in Poland.

chairs in the lounge. What a talent he had, but he caused us a few headaches I can tell you.'

'The 1979 World Final was my best,' said Kelly. 'There was a big crowd, over 100,000 I think, and no one really expected me to do as well as I did. It was especially satisfying for me because the year before I was in hospital with a broken back.'

The week before the World Final, Harry Oxley called a meeting with all the UK-based Americans to try and resolve the qualifying round issue which saw Autrey withdraw under protest. He was now the AMA representative with the FIM for all speedway matters, and he tried to get the Americans' allocation of places in the Intercontinental Final increased from two to three.

The venue for the American Final was changed to Anaheim, but took place in November 1979 and there were still only two qualifying places up for grabs. Shawn joined his elder brother in the final, but it wasn't to be an occasion of celebration this time.

The meeting was a disaster for Kelly, as he suffered a mechanical breakdown in his first race; then he finished third in his second race, before a crash in his third outing left him with a knee injury and he was forced to withdraw from the rest of the meeting with just 1 point. Shawn made a bright start with two victories, but could only add a further 4 points from his last three rides to finish

Harry Oxley (left) with Kelly and Ian Thomas at the 1979 World Final.

on 10. This time, the qualifier ran to the form book, with Bruce Penhall emerging the winner, while Scott Autrey took second after a run-off. A crowd of 5,000 was a little disappointing, but at least the event was relatively trouble-free this time. Penhall went on to qualify for his first World Final, which was won that year by England's Michael Lee.

Although he was not European, Shawn was eligible to enter the European Under-21 Championship as he was now racing in the British League. This competition was the forerunner to the World Under-21 Championship, which was officially launched in 1988, as it was looked upon as a World Championship in all but name. The Morans' fellow countryman, Ron Preston, was the first American to win it when he was crowned champion in 1979.

Shawn was not the only American taking part, as his Hull team-mate Dennis Sigalos also lined up with him at the first qualifying round in Bado Polesine, Italy, on 1 June. Siggy won the meeting with a maximum, while Shawn came second with 12 points and progressed to the semi-finals in Hungary, where their performances were repeated – except that on this occasion, Shawn scored 13 points. The final itself, held at Pocking, Germany, was a disappointment for Moran as he finished with just 2 points, and was plagued by mechanical gremlins. The meeting was won by Denmark's Tommy Knudsen ahead of runner-up Tony Briggs, with Sigalos finishing third.

There was much celebration in American Speedway racing when it was announced that they would stage the 1982 World Final at the plush Los Angeles Memorial Coliseum – the venue for the 1984 Olympics. The men whose job it was to insure that the event was a success was a group of individuals called *World Class Inc.,* and they were Harry Oxley, Jack Milne, Barry Briggs and Ivan Mauger. Furthermore, their progress in international racing had seen their World Championship allocation increased from two to four places for the newly installed qualifying round called the Overseas Final.

However, the Moran brothers' pursuit of individual glory for 1981 had to be put on hold until 30 May, when the American Final was staged at the LA Coliseum as a practice run for the World Final the following year. It was Penhall who again won with an immaculate 15 points; Dennis Sigalos came second after he defeated Kelly Moran in a run-off, having both tied with 13 points. Scott Autrey grabbed the fourth and final qualifying place after a four-man run-off with Shawn, Alan Christian and Denny Pyeatt. This staging of the American Final saw experienced international Billy Sanders fly over to race in a series of match races to test the suitability of the 400-yard track, and a FIM delegate, Charles Ringblom, was also in attendance to report on the success of the venue as a speedway track.

'The LA Coliseum does not have a race track,' Oxley explained in an interview he gave to *5-One* magazine. 'So we had to lay down a track and run a meeting on it, and then tear the whole track up again. It was a useless exercise just to show the FIM we knew how to lay a race track. Now the American Final's a good event, and it used to draw 10,000 to 12,000 people in those days, but it's not an LA Coliseum event. We ended up losing $100,000 because of the expense of putting it in, and the status of the event.'

Shawn's fifth place meant that he would qualify as reserve, but instead he withdrew to concentrate on the European U-21 Championship – and he didn't regret it. He proved what potential he had when he won the qualifying round in Pocking and the semi-final at Abensberg, Germany, both with unbeaten scores. He travelled to Slany, in Czechoslovakia and, despite the wet conditions, he was crowned the Under-21 Champion. The seeded Czech Antonin Kasper took second – losing only to Moran – and another Czech, Jiri Hnidak, was third.

'It was a title,' said Shawn of that victory. 'That was pretty good, so early in my career over there (in Europe). Everything went well; and the bike was hooking up real good. In the semi-final at Abensberg, I was going for the maximum and in one race I couldn't see the start light because someone was in the way. I signalled to the referee, but he let the race go. I wasn't too happy and I left my bike on the start line and walked back to the pits to make my protest. They saw my point – for once – and I was allowed back in the re-run which I won. After I won the meeting, I got a telling off from the authorities. It was nothing too bad, but I was warned not to do it again. Normally I wouldn't do anything like that, but I was hungry for the maximum.'

He had remained unbeaten throughout the whole tournament, including qualifiers, and that was an achievement which would not be repeated too often. His Sheffield boss, Ray Glover, accompanied his rider to the final: 'He was in a class of his own,' he said. 'It was a wonderful performance in the face of fierce opposition on a track made almost unrideable by heavy rain. The Czechs had been practising on the circuit for a fortnight, whereas Shawn only got a couple of laps in the night before.'

The first staging of the Overseas Final was won by Dave Jessup – who was destined to be speedway's nearly man – but it was notorious for the first world-wide public dust up between Bruce Penhall and Kenny Carter. Kelly qualified comfortably for the next round with 10 points and fourth place. Now nicely settled at Eastbourne, he was in top form when he travelled to Vojens, Denmark, for the Intercontinental Final at the end of July.

If there is one thing that you can be sure of in speedway racing, then it is that it will rain in Vojens – and the 1981 Intercontinental Final was no exception. It was a meeting that got off to a poor start for Kelly as he crashed in his first race and failed to score. The rains came and fourteen of the sixteen riders thought that the surface was so bad that it should have been postponed for twenty-four hours. The meeting was held up for ninety minutes while the officials and the riders discussed the conditions. Eventually, the meeting resumed and was won by Penhall, who went on television to say that it should have been stopped.

Kelly struggled in the wet conditions and failed to score and, along with his fellow countryman, Sigalos, was eliminated from the title chase. However, it seemed that he was a victim of some clever gamesmanship from his rivals. Bob Dugard was present in the pits with Kelly at both the Overseas and Intercontinental Finals, alongside his mechanic, Eric Richardson – father of former Eagle Colin. 'The worst memory was at that last qualifying hurdle in Denmark,' he recalled. 'He was at the top of his game, when rival competitors and mechanics smuggled him out of the hotel the night before the meeting and got him hopelessly drunk, and he failed to qualify.'

'I was suckered,' said Kelly. 'A bunch of them got together and said, "Hey, let's go out and have a few drinks and get a few girls." They were egging me on and the temptation of these beautiful blonde Scandinavian women was too much. So I went along and had a few drinks and thought to myself, "I hope I get on the podium tomorrow". But they sure messed me up for the meeting the next day. The rain and all the trouble didn't help, but I was definitely suckered by my rivals.'

In arguably the greatest World Final ever staged, the Morans could only watch as Bruce Penhall thrilled the 90,000 crowd at Wembley as he became America's first World Champion since 1937. The stage was set like a Hollywood film script for the final at Los Angeles the following year – and Kelly and Shawn intended to be there.

Shortly before the American Final, Kelly revealed his thoughts on his assault of the World Championship in an interview he gave to *Speedway Star.* 'I've got two special motors and I can almost taste the atmosphere – but if I make it, I

Shawn on parade at the 1982 Overseas Final at White City.

want to get into the top three this time.'

To make matters more difficult, Penhall had been seeded directly to the Overseas Final, which meant that there were only three places available at the American Final. This time it was held at another new venue, the Veterans Stadium, Long Beach, California – famous for the location of the British cruise liner *Queen Mary,* where it is shored as a museum/hotel-convention centre.

Dennis Sigalos won the meeting on the 400-metre track, with Kelly in second and Shawn taking the vital third. However, the Morans faced Scott Autrey in a run-off to determine the qualifiers after they had all tied on 13-points. It appeared that Scott was a victim of their team-riding tactics as so many would be.

The new track received the thumbs up from all who raced there, although the surface did cut up a little at the end. Shawn said after clinching his place: 'The points don't come easy. I found my steering stiff in my first two rides, so I switched bikes and felt a lot happier. Everything was well presented and we got good TV coverage the next day. I'm pleased with my Godden engines and my two mechanics did a terrific job, and Don Godden helps a little bit too – though I am not anything like a works rider.'

It was American Independence Day when the Overseas Final took place at White City. It was a highly competitive meeting, and as the Yanks entered their final races, only Penhall had made sure of his place in the next round. All four of them met in their final race and something had to give. What followed is still talked about with mixed reactions to this day.

Penhall could have clinched overall victory, but instead he languished at the back and let his three countryman battle it out amongst themselves. Sigalos was the winner, Kelly took second and Shawn third. It was an unselfish action, but one which incensed the large White City crowd, who felt that he had cheated. A chorus of jeers greeted them on their return to the pits, and missiles were thrown at the four Americans on their slowdown lap. Penhall had not helped matters by attempting to 'entertain' the crowd with wheelies during the race, and Kelly's two-fingered gesture to the crowd couldn't have helped matters much either! The outcome was that both Siggy and Kelly were through while Shawn faced a run-off against Peter and Les Collins to determine his fate. This time the British duo kept the younger Moran at bay and he finished as reserve for the next round at Vetlanda, Sweden.

'It was such a hard afternoon and to end like that, well, I was close to crying,' revealed Kelly, 'it was like that, emotionally. I was disappointed for my brother. We are very close and he deserved to go through with the way he was riding.'

The events at White City did serious damage to the popularity of not only Penhall, but the Americans in general. Penhall cut a lonely and sad figure in third place on the rostrum behind the winner, Dave Jessup and his arch-rival Kenny Carter.

It was another tough meeting at Vetlanda, but all three of the Americans made it to their World Final in LA. Kelly finished in fifth with 9 points and

On parade at the 1982 World Final in the LA Coliseum, Kelly (left) and Peter Collins.

seemed happy to sit back once he had made sure of his place in the last sixteen. However, a fall in a match at King's Lynn meant that he was making regular trips to Brighton Football Club for intensive physiotherapy on damaged shoulder muscles.

'It won't affect me at the final,' he said before leaving. 'It's going to be a real special time. To race in a World Final in front of your own countrymen, your friends and your family will certainly be the pinnacle of my career. Nerves won't eat me, in fact I go better in that type of situation. My motors have been to Trevor Hedge so I have no worries on that score.'

Drawn at number one, Kelly Moran was scheduled to appear in the first race against Peter Collins, Mikhail Starostin and Sigalos. It was Siggy who leapt from the start; while Kelly produced a spectacular sweep inside Collins on the fourth bend of lap one to finish second. In his second race, he faced the favourite, Penhall. He couldn't do anything about his fellow countryman, who was fired up after a surprise defeat at the hands of Les Collins, but he had to do something about the German Georg Hack and Sweden's Jan Andersson. As he emerged from the first bend in last place, he used all his finesse and speed to pass Hack and was unlucky not to wrestle second from Andersson. He won his next race with an inside pass on Denmark's Hans Nielsen and wheelied his way to the finish line to put himself on 6 points.

The meeting was delayed by the controversial events of heat twelve. Penhall and Carter clashed, with the Briton crashing out of the race. Carter was livid when the referee excluded him, and delayed the re-run with his on-track protests, which were eventually ended when security staff led him away. Penhall won the re-run and was on course to retain the world title.

Kelly made light work of winning his delayed heat thirteen, defeating Edward Jancarz, Jiri Stancl and Kai Niemi. Despite leading coming out the first bend of his last race, he was overhauled by Les Collins and he had to settle for second ahead of the unlucky British duo of Carter and Dave Jessup. When Dennis Sigalos won his last race of the evening, Kelly was fourth again on eleven points.

'I remember I was cheering Siggy on,' recalled Kelly, 'and my mechanic said, "What are you cheering him on for?" And I said, "Well, look it's Siggy, and he's in front." Then he told me that if he finished second, then I would have a run-off for third place with him. I didn't realise. But the final was a big success and it did a lot of good for American Speedway. But it would have been nice to have got on the podium.'

'We didn't make a lot of money on the event, but we didn't lose any money and we paid back what we lost the year before,' revealed Harry Oxley. 'The FIM made it as tough on us as they could. We just went up against them and did our job, and I think we had a wonderful World Championship. We had beautiful pageantry, as good as anyone, a wonderful race and an American winner.'

But the drama wasn't over yet. Penhall, who was the first American to win two World titles, announced on the podium that he was retiring to pursue a career in Hollywood. Whatever happened in 1983, the world would have a new champion.

With still only four riders qualifying from the American Final, it had to be one of, if not *the*, toughest domestic rounds in the world. One poor race and you were staring elimination in the face, two poor races and it was all over for another year. And that is exactly what happened to Kelly in the 1983 final.

Possibly the meeting came a little early, as he was spending 1983 racing at home and, after years riding Weslake engines, he had switched to Godden and was taking time to adjust to them on the small tracks, never mind the bigger Long Beach circuit. Nevertheless, a third place in his opening race put him under pressure, and when he fell and was excluded from his fourth, well that was it for that year. In his column in *Speedway Magazine* he said: 'I want to be world champion and at twenty-three, I know time is on my side. It will require a little more time and dedication, and even if it's not my year for the world championship, I am still making progress.'

Once again, it was Sigalos who won with a maximum, but taking second was Mike Faria, who had never raced regularly outside of the USA at that point. Lance King took third, while Shawn once more had to win a run-off to qualify, with Rick Miller and John Cook having to give in to the 'Miracle Worker'.

The Overseas Final was held at Belle Vue, and it was so wet that one publication described it as 'The Belle Vue Bog'. Once more, it was disappointment for Shawn. Until his last race he was looking good to qualify with 7 points, but he finished at the back in his last race behind Phil Collins – who won the title – Andy Graheme and Michael Lee. Amazingly, despite being in good form, he would take no further part in the championship, which was won that year by Germany's Egon Muller.

Muller was best known for his performances in Long Track racing, where he was World Champion several times. As its name suggests, Long Track takes place on much bigger tracks of up to 1,000 metres in length – it was sometimes known as the 1,000 metres championship. It is slightly different to conventional speedway, as the bikes are purpose-built 500cc machines with a longer wheelbase, rear suspension and two gears. These bikes can reach speeds of over 100mph on the long straights. It is a discipline of motorcycle racing that is particularly popular on the European continent; in many ways, it can be considered a big track version of conventional speedway, creating an overlap between the two fields.

Shawn had excelled on the Long Track scene in America, and he had his first taste of the European version in 1982. So he entered the 1983 World Long Track Championship and qualified for the final with a second place to Muller in the semi-final. Sadly, on 5 August he suffered a broken leg in a track crash at Hackney, and with the final scheduled for 18 September, it seemed that his last shot at individual glory had gone.

However, Bobby Schwartz, Reg Wilson and Norrie Allen rescued Shawn from the hospital in London and took him to Dr Carlo Biagi – the wonder doctor in Galashiels, Scotland – to weave his magic and get him fit enough to race in the final. Shawn had already visited Biagi earlier in the year when he broke his arm in the USA. This time, the doctor inserted two pins as big as carriage bolts into his left leg, and it immediately began to feel better. Moran's thoughts thus turned to racing in Marianske Lazne, Czechoslovakia. But healing time was at a premium …

Kevin Godden, a physiotherapist in the Sheffield hospital, put Shawn through the pain barrier to get him walking again. With a week to go, Shooey – as Schwartz had now christened him – threw away his crutches and began practising at Belle Vue. After studying the x-rays, Biagi and his team agreed that he could put his leg foot down, and Shawn informed his sponsor, Maurice Ducker, and the Tigers' boss, Ray Glover, that he intended to ride in Czechoslovakia. He put in around forty practice laps at Scunthorpe, and then followed this with another long stint at Sheffield's Owlerton stadium on the Wednesday and Thursday, before the big event. Shooey's practice sessions were intended to get him race fit, because if he was going to ride he needed to be a sharp as possible to compensate for the leg injury.

'He didn't like the idea of me racing in the final,' said Shawn of Biagi. 'He thought it was too soon after he began working on my leg. He thought we were taking a bit of a risk, but it was the only World Championship meeting of the season left for me. In the end he let me go with a letter to the track doctor in Czechoslovakia saying it was okay for me to race.'

In *Speedway Magazine,* Biagi told journalist John Chaplin: 'When we watched Shawn set off to ride in the Long Track Final, one of my colleagues turned to me and said, 'He shouldn't even be out of bed!'

Shawn left for Marianske Lazne on the Friday and arrived at the track the following day for the practice. However, the track doctor was not happy about the American's wish to ride, and at one point he wasn't going to let him participate. But perhaps that letter did the trick, because he was allowed to take his place in the meeting. He bumped his leg during the practice, but his Godden engines were going really well and, despite the injury, he felt reasonably confident.

'I didn't take any tablets or have any injections. When I was racing, I didn't think about the pain and the track was in good shape. Tiredness was the big problem,' he said.

Fortunately, Long Track doesn't require quite so much pressure applied to the left foot as conventional speedway, and this helped Shooey in his quest for glory. Thankfully, he started making the gates when he needed them, and his confidence increased with each race. He was beaten only once in the qualifying races – by Germany's Alois Weisbock. And against all the odds, he entered the final knowing that the World title was his.

'After I had dropped just one point, I knew I had a chance of winning,' recalled Shooey. 'Karl Maier passed me in the last race, and I was just hanging on. I was tired and my arms were hurting and I was sure pleased to see that chequered flag. But it was worth it. I was a dark horse and no one expected me to win.'

Shawn with the World Longtrack championship trophy.

It was a courageous effort in front of over 25,000 fans, and he won the title with 22 points, with Jiri Stancl second on 20 and Maier in third place with 18. My enduring memory of that day is of Shawn hobbling toward the rostrum to step up as a World Champion. It was a brave performance and one which is worthy of any Hollywood script.

'It really meant more to me than perhaps winning the World Speedway title, because although the immediate prize money was not as high as the one for winning the US Nationals, the benefits will come from riding in Europe next year,' Shawn told *Speedway Magazine*. 'Don Godden himself and his two mechanics prepared my Long Track bikes. I switched to Weslake for speedway, but the Goddens do a better job on the Long Track.'

A celebration was arranged at Sheffield's Pinegrove Country Club, as Shawn recalled: 'I bought some champagne in Czecho, mainly to use up their currency because it's no use to you when you get back. So I bought three bottles of good quality champagne at a cheap price. The trophy was a crystal vase, a very nice thing, and I put the three bottles inside. They weren't wedged in there or anything like that, but when I got them out, the last bottle knocked the bottom out of the trophy. It was like, "Oh God," you know. I got some scotch tape and taped it up.'

Shawn Moran was the first, and so far, the only American to win the World Long Track title. But the speedway crown still eluded him and his main aim for 1984 was to qualify for the World Final.

Originally, the venue for the 1984 World Final was to be Britain. But Wembley closed its doors to speedway racing, and then it was discovered that White City was closing too. Therefore, the final was switched to Sweden's magnificent Ullevi Stadium in Gothenburg, with Britain allocated the 1985 World Final instead.

Kelly had aimed to show that you didn't have to race in the British League to qualify for the World Final. As the reigning US National Champion, he seemed to be better prepared, both mechanically and mentally. There was never any doubt that he had the talent, but with a good sponsorship package behind him and a more relaxed outlook, he was racing better than ever.

Consequently, he made light work this time of qualifying from the American Final in second place, and was only beaten by eventual winner, Bobby Schwartz. Shawn took third with 13 points and Lance King completed the quartet with 11. The event saw Dennis Sigalos crash out with a nasty broken ankle which would lead to his eventual retirement.

Don Godden, who supplied the engines that Shooey rode to World Long Track glory, then ruined the relationship by sending the reigning champion a bizarre letter. This highly personal attack made its way on to the back page of the tabloid paper the *Daily Star*, as well the sport's usual weekly publications. With headlines like: 'No Sex for Shawn Moran?' and 'US Speedway Star's Sex Ban', it did little for the credibility of Godden or the image of the sport.

In the letter, which he admitted that he sent, he said that he was disappointed with Shawn's early season form and said that he had 'no future.' He went on to outline the following requirements: 'If you want to continue using my equipment you will have to observe the following:

    1. You must be race fit – that means train hard.

    2. You do not drink the night before the race.

    3. You do not have sex the night before the race.

  Only if you observe these rules, which I know are necessary, will the bikes be unloaded at the tracks.'

  'Looking back on it it's quite funny, but it wasn't so funny at the time,' admitted Shawn. 'What happened was we were going to a Long Track meeting in Herxhiem, and I was talking about having some fun that evening and scoring a few points with the girls. I had a few beers and had some fun, but it wasn't a particularly late night or anything. Well, at the meeting the next day, I wasn't going very well and the Goddens were not getting me out of the starts. So I tried somebody else's bike and it just flew. Don didn't like it; it was like "Oh you gotta ride my bikes" and all that. As a racer, you want to win and sometimes you just cannot get the set-up right, and you jump on someone else's and its just right for you. It's one of those things. For example, when I was at Belle Vue, I rode one of Shawn Venables' bikes and it was just hooked up right for the track

Shawn powers out of a turn at San Bernardino in 1983.

and it flew. He couldn't understand that and moaned that I had to use his stuff, that's how petty they are sometimes.'

'I used to do Grass Track for him and I absolutely hated that. Simon Wigg was brilliant doing that kind of racing, but I couldn't see the point. The tracks were full of ruts and stuff, and it was a lot different to speedway or long track. It wasn't for me. I was never a works-sponsored rider and I paid for everything, so he had no reason to send me that letter. And yes I'd go out and party the night before, that's how I relaxed myself for the meeting. I can't remember who I gave the letter to, it was ridiculous really.'

It was an amazing outburst, and one that may have been inspired by jealousy. The Moran brothers' main sponsor was STP International. Nigel Tubb was the European co-ordinator for STP, and he said that a lot of the people involved with the Morans did not like the amount of exposure that STP would get from their association with the brothers.

'Shawn called me one evening and said that he was having a problem with Don Godden and the STP sponsorship. Apparently, Godden wasn't happy that STP stickers were appearing on his machines. Now, both the Morans were contracted to display the company's logo on their leathers and use our products. So I wrote a letter to Don Godden explaining that situation, and that if Shawn was a fully sponsored works rider who received bikes in exchange for advertising, then I would therefore make sure that STP's logos did not appear upon his bikes. It was a very firm but polite letter. I received a reply stating, in the frankest of terms, that Shawn Moran had nothing for nothing. There was a lot jealousy that STP was getting all this exposure through Shawn and Kelly.'

Lance King won the Overseas Final at Belle Vue, with Shooey taking third. He seized his engine in an exciting dual with King, but was only beaten by Phil Crump, who took second overall. It was harder for Kelly, who was earning his points from the back, which included an on-the-line effort to overhaul England's Jeremy Doncaster for third – a point which proved crucial in the end. He faced Les Collins in a run-off for the tenth and final qualifying place. For the first time that afternoon, he got the drop on his rival and led on the opening lap. Riding his brother's bike, as he came round the pit turn he nodded his head in the direction of his watching brother and crew, to acknowledge that he had done it – even though there were just over three laps to go!

The Intercontinental Final at Vojens, Denmark followed less than a week later. Kelly was involved in a controversial clash with Hans Nielsen in his second race, which saw the American excluded from the re-run. He protested to the referee, but it was all to no avail.

'I was in gate 3 and before I could do anything I was hit,' he said in an interview in *Speedway Magazine*. 'I was taken straight out in the first corner. This was really obvious though and I talked to the referee but he didn't want to hear my side of the story. Everybody in the pits was saying they couldn't believe the referee's call.'

However, Kelly comfortably qualified for his third World Final with 8 points, and but for that exclusion he could have been in the top three. His brother, however, was in the top three – first in fact. He won the Intercontinental Final with 13 points and only lost to his brother and Nielsen, but he was a little disappointed with the trophy.

'Before the start, we all walked the track, and we saw all these nice big trophies on the centre green for the presentation,' said Shawn. 'So when I won the meeting and stepped up to take the top spot, I expected something like that. But I get this puny little trophy which was about eight inches tall! I never understood that.'

The Morans and King were America's representatives in the 1984 final, and the sports press was so excited about the prospect of both the Morans in Gothenburg that they debated whether it was the time for the Moran brothers to dominate the sport.

Four times World Champion Barry Briggs, stepped in to assist Kelly in his preparation for the final: 'I knew Kelly as a young bloke back in America,' recalled Briggs. 'He was a brilliant rider, but he wasn't very organised, and I knew Hans Zierk [the celebrated engine tuner] in Germany and borrowed him an engine. That's how I got to help him. I know people, and I thought he was going to be a talent that was never going to be recognised of how good he was.'

The boys' father came over to see them race in Sweden and there was much press interest in the two Moran brothers. When Kelly was asked who his biggest rival was, he instantly answered that it was his brother.

Kelly practises at Gothenburg for the 1984 World Final.

'If we're both in the run-off for first place, we'll cross the line shaking hands,' he said. 'We really will do that. It may cause a bit of a problem for the officials but we are ready to make it a photo finish. I'm not bothered about it (the final). I ride for the occasion and never worry about the pressure. I look at it as any other meeting, except the payback is a little better.'

For Shawn, he was among the favourites and he said of that expectation: 'Everybody wants that number one. I'm going to give it my best shot and hope that lady luck rides with me. I think I have as much chance of winning as anybody else and my confidence is really high. It doesn't bother me being one of the favourites. I'll treat it like any other meeting.'

It wasn't a great debut for Shawn, who was pretty much out of the running after he had scored just 1 point from his first two rides. He switched from his Godden to his Weslake, which proved more effective and he added six points to finish on 7 points – winning his third ride. However, his preparation had not gone according to plan, as *Speedway Mail* reported that he was spotted testing an engine on the local harbour just twenty-four hours before the big night.

Did the occasion get to Shawn? Craig Cummings was in his first season as a mechanic for him, and would also later turn the spanners for Kelly too. He offered this opinion on how they would handle the big occasions: 'Shawn got a little nervous at the World Finals, but he was not overly nervous. He was that kind of guy, a typical Californian, real laid back and took everything in his stride. Kelly never got nervous at all, no matter what.'

Kelly performed a lot better, but soon found that the slick Gothenburg track would not suit his style when he was unable to make an impression on Simon Wigg in his first race. And this was how it continued, but he had a big say in the destiny of the title when he lined up alongside Denmark's Erik Gundersen and Hans Nielsen in heat fifteen. At that stage Nielsen was unbeaten, while Gundersen had dropped just one point. The Czech Petr Ondrasik was not really a factor, but Kelly still had a good chance of a rostrum finish.

Kelly was sandwiched between the rival Danes in gate three, with Gundersen on his outside and Nielsen inside him in gate two. Ondrasik pulled back as the green light went on, and both the Danes nervously nudged the tapes. As the tapes flew up, the two Danish riders sped away and were so worried about each other they forgot all about little Kelly Moran. Nielsen gave his fellow countryman an almighty shove as they hit the first turn, but Erik cut back inside. But Kelly was the spoiler as he produced a wonderful first corner, and for a brief moment he was alongside Gundersen, but crucially ahead of Nielsen. Gundersen pulled ahead on the back straight, but Kelly had all but finished Nielsen's chances of winning his first world crown.

In his autobiography, *The Main Dane*, Nielsen acknowledged Kelly's vital part in that heat fifteen showdown, which led to Gundersen winning the championship ahead of runner-up Nielsen – who defeated Lance King in a run-off to decide second and third. 'I did not make a good start, while Erik was just ahead of me on the first bend and Kelly Moran turned on a sixpence to come under me in incredible style on the second bend. That incident lost me the world title.'

Kelly won his last race and was fourth again. But he admitted in his column in *Speedway Magazine* that a spell in the British League would have enhanced his performance.

'I was pretty happy with my performance in the World Final. I would have liked to have taken it, obviously, but fourth wasn't bad. I think it would have helped if I'd ridden in the BL for a month or so before the final to sharpen up a bit, because the gating was so important over there. Heat fifteen with Gundersen and Nielsen was a good race. They were so concerned with taking each other out that they forgot about me. Again, it was the gating. In my last race I had a good gate and won it by half a lap, so you can see how important the gating was.'

It is my opinion that if he had raced in the BL that year, he would have won the championship. Never again would he have such an opportunity when he looked in such a comfortable position, both with experience and machinery. Briggs agreed that the track wasn't suited to his style of riding, and he went on record to complain about the slick nature of the surface.

'He had the drop on most of the boys,' said Briggs. 'Nielsen lost the title

Kelly (left) receives advice from the great Barry Briggs, who assisted the American at the 1984 World Final in Sweden.

because of Kelly. He was trying to bang into Gundersen and while he was doing that, Kelly passed him. He was virtually impossible to help, because he always wanted to shake hands with everybody and be friendly, when he needed to be focused. He had so much talent, but you couldn't get him to focus. I think I could have helped him more if I spent more time with him. His lifestyle was very different and foreign to mine. I mean he never looked after his body he just had this brilliant natural talent.'

Briggs once described Kelly as the 'best passer in speedway' but said that it took more than that to win a World Championship.

'You can't rely on passing in every race. When you go to the start, you've got to go there and concentrate. Otherwise you're last from the start. Really he was too talented; he was a very good motorcyclist and it came natural to him, but it takes more than that to win a World Championship. Shawn was the same. He was also very naturally talented, but they were too loose.'

Shawn qualified for the World Long Track championship at Herxhiem, Germany and, as the reigning champion, he was expected to do well. But it wasn't to be his year, as the Godden engines were not getting him out of the start and he finished in eighteenth position with 3 points in an event won by Erik Gundersen.

'I just couldn't get out of the gate fast enough,' he recalled. 'So Bo Petersen, who was the reserve, he offered me his bike for my last race, and I thought what the hell, and jumped on it. And it just flew; it was hooked up real good. I finished third in that race and PC (Peter Collins) passed me. It was the first time that I had ridden a bike with one side of the handlebars slightly higher than the other and, I don't know if that made a lot of difference, but Bo's bike was pulling stronger than mine. Of course, Don didn't like me changing over.'

For 1985, the number of qualifiers from the American Final was increased from four to five. John Cook was in flying form at Long Beach and won the meeting with a 15-point maximum. Sam Ermolenko took second with 13, and Shawn was third with 12. But there was a real scramble for the final two qualifying spots. Kelly, Lance King, Rick Miller and Bobby Schwartz all finished the evening with 11 points. A run-off was required to determine the lucky duo.

Kelly had won his last two rides to get in the run-off and he was odds-on to make it through. It was King who took the lead, while Kelly was involved in a hectic scrap with Miller. They passed and re-passed each other, until Kelly overcooked it trying to get down the inside of Miller and bit the dust. Schwartz was a distant third and Kelly's Championship hopes were over for another year.

The Overseas Final was held at Bradford's Odsal Stadium, which would be the scene for the World Final itself later in the year. Shooey had displayed his liking of the newest track in England, with 15 points in the USA's victory in the World Pairs semi-final with Schwartz.

He got off to the best possible start when he won the opening heat over local hero Kenny Carter, and in the process set a new track record of 59.4. Shawn dropped just one point to Kelvin Tatum, which meant that he faced Carter in a

Shawn (left) with Craig Cummings celebrates their success at the 1985 Overseas Final at Bradford.

run-off for the Overseas title, after they had both finished with 14 points.

It was a classic showdown between the recently-crowned British Champion, Carter, and Yorkshire's adopted son, Moran. Carter made the start and took the lead, but as he moved out to block the expected attack from the American on the outside, he quickly changed direction and cut underneath to take up first place. Carter shadowed Shooey for the remainder of the race, but he just couldn't find a way past. Shawn was a deserved winner as he had produced some wonderful racing that included another from-the-back victory over Cook.

Shawn travelled to Vetlanda for the Intercontinental Final, where one of the favourites for the World crown, Kenny Carter, crashed out with a broken leg in another rain-affected qualifier. But Shooey retained the title he had won the previous year with 14 points, and booked his place in the final at Bradford. Lance King took second, with Hans Nielsen – who was the only rider to defeat Moran – taking third. Four Americans qualified from Vetlanda – Moran, King, Sam Ermolenko and John Cook – which made it the country's biggest representation yet in the sport's top event.

As in 1984, Shawn was installed as one of the favourites for the title. In a regular column in *Speedway Mail* called 'The Thinker', this journalist spelled out the reasons:

'Moran's record at Bradford is impressive to say the least. Apart from his Overseas Final success, he took 15 points in the World Pairs semi-final and was the highest individual scorer in that meeting. Truly he is at home on the new

Yorkshire circuit. That, plus the lack of experience there for Nielsen and Gundersen, plus the fact that they have both received injuries of late, is the reason why Moran starts as the number one favourite.'

He had also been in excellent form throughout the season – the best of his career – and was in fact top of the BL averages during the week prior to the final. In his column in *Speedway Mail*, Shooey gave his views on his chances.

'I'm in a confident mood to win the title and I don't think I could be better prepared. Last year was my first World Final and I wasn't prepared for it either physically or mentally. Now I'm 100 per cent and I'm going all out to make that title mine! I've got a lot of testing to do, and when that is over I will know what bike I'm going to use for the final. Whichever it is, it will be a GM, because they have been going really well for me and I'm very happy with them. I really think I can do it this time. All I need is to go out on the day and make five good starts.'

Watched from the pits by his brother, Shawn got off to a good start with a victory in his first race over Kai Niemi and Karl Maier – while Cook took a tumble. Denmark's Tommy Knudsen crashed in heat five as he diced with Shawn. The race was stopped just as Shawn had edged ahead of Ermolenko and Kelvin Tatum. Knudsen was allowed back in the re-run and went under Shooey to follow Ermolenko home. It seemed that this race was a turning point for the American's title hopes, as he followed this with another third in heat ten, which was won in spectacular fashion by Nielsen from Sweden's Jan Andersson.

However, he stormed to a race win in heat fifteen that put him on 8 points, and in contention for a podium finish. No one could have predicted heat twenty, which saw reigning champion Gundersen swoop round the outside of Moran and King to put himself in a run-off with Nielsen and Ermolenko for the title. The little Dane won the run-off to retain the championship, with Sam Ermolenko taking third behind Nielsen in his debut World Final.

Shawn Moran eventually finished in fifth place with 10 points and it was a big disappointment for the Moran camp, as his mechanic, Craig Cummings, explained:

'It was a huge disappointment for him, for us and everyone who was associated with him,' he said. 'I think there were circumstances that were out of his control. He had a guy who was sponsoring him at the time (Maurice Ducker) who was also the promoter of Sheffield Speedway. I'm sure that he decided at the time that he was going to do Shawn's engines, and the engines were absolutely flying until two weeks before the World Final. He stripped them down and rebuilt them, and they never went properly at all after that. Pressure wasn't a big factor to him, that wasn't his problem, his problem was his engines.

'Shawn was the kind of guy who took everything in his stride. If it didn't happen, it didn't happen – that's the way it goes.'

'I was disappointed,' said Shawn. 'I kind of pumped myself up for it. But it wasn't to be. I don't know why, it's all about what happens on the day. Erik did well and it was his day, but for some reason it didn't happen for me. I felt good

The face says it all ... Disappointment for Shawn at the 1985 World Final.

and the track was okay, although it rained a bit. I was having a good year, but who can say?'

After winning the World Long Track semi-final in Scheesel, Germany, Shawn was through to his third final. Although he improved considerably on his eighteenth place of the previous year, he finished in fourth with 17 points, and just missed out on a rostrum finish. England's Simon Wigg was the winner – the first of many Long Track successes.

'He almost won the Long Track,' said Cummings. 'But when he got to the final, he got filled in and had to pull out. The dirt actually knocked out a lens in his goggles and he had to pull over in the first corner, because he couldn't see where he was going, which was a real disappointment.'

Kelly made his first appearance in the British Final working for BBC Radio 2. He was sat alongside Tony Millard to offer his expert opinion and analysis. He proved such a hit that he was asked back to perform the same thing the following year. 'That was Tony who set that up because he used to be the announcer at Eastbourne,' recalled Kelly. 'That was fun, I think it was for a programme called *Sport on Sunday* or something like that. Tony was great. He was responsible for getting me the sponsorship with Travellers which was great. It was free air travel with British Caledonian and the flight attendants on that airline are the best. They really look after you even if you're travelling with the cattle!'

As attention turned to the 1986 World title chase, it was expected that Shawn would build on his the 1985 season to mount a serious challenge for glory. His brother had made a return to British racing after a three-year absence, and it was thought that the extra sharpness which BL competition brings would be the last part of his World Championship jigsaw.

Both of them were now mounted on the Italian GM engine – which was the engine of choice among the front runners. This engine had powered both Gundersen and Muller to glory, and Shawn enjoyed his best season in 1985 on this machine.

However, it seemed that Shawn's World title hopes would be over before they had begun when he crashed at his bogey track, Oxford, and broke his right ankle while riding for his BL team, Sheffield. The accident occurred just ten days before he was scheduled to appear in the American Final.

For any other rider, this may have spelt the end of their World Championship dreams, but this was Shawn Moran – who wasn't known as the 'Miracle Worker' for nothing. He arrived at Long Beach and, with the aid of crutches, he hobbled around the pits, determined to make it through to the next round.

Shawn was able to take part in the meeting with the aid of a special fibreglass cast which encased his ankle. This was then squeezed into his boot and taped up, and then it was unwrapped between races to allow the blood to circulate. Once again, he was producing a courageous performance against all the odds

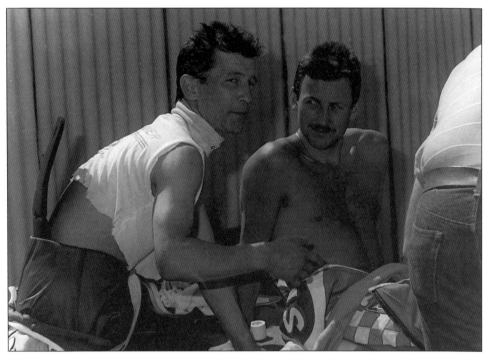

Kelly and Shawn in the pits at the 1986 American Final at Long Beach, USA.

and he finished the night as the American Champion with 14 points – dropping his only point to Bobby Schwartz in his final outing. Once again, he had lived up to his nickname; indeed, his performance begged the question: if he can do this when he is less than 100 per cent, what will he do to the opposition when he is fully fit?

'I remember Shawn came out on the riders' parade on crutches,' recalled Billy Hamill, who was a junior racer at that time. 'He just smoked everybody and that was pretty cool to watch.'

Kelly also made it through with 11 points to finish in a comfortable fifth place, and joined second-placed Lance King, Sam Ermolenko and Schwartz in the next round.

Shawn arrived at Coventry as the defending Overseas Champion and, along with his brother, he was expected to get through. They met in their first outing in heat four on a dry and hot afternoon. It was just eight days since his Long Beach triumph and his ankle was still not properly healed.

Kelly was off the inside gate, with the newly-crowned British Champion Neil Evitts alongside him in two, Shawn was off gate three with Paul Thorp from England on the outside. As the four riders roared into the first bend, Shawn was marginally behind and he kept the throttle wound on until, suddenly, he was flying over the top of his machine and into the dirt. Catching sight of his brother, Kelly quickly laid down his own bike and ran over to check on his little brother's condition. Unhappily, Shooey had damaged his ankle and another hospital visit was required.

'I had a look over and saw Neil Evitts going wide,' said Kelly later. 'I thought he was kind of silly 'cos there was no dirt out there – especially in the first five or six races. I caught sight of Shawn and thought, 'What the heck,' and ran over to him.'

'I've got a picture which showed that Neil Evitts moved out,' said Shawn in his column, 'but I'm not complaining about anyone's riding. I was just behind Paul Thorp off gate three – which wasn't the best gate, so I was quite happy with the start I made – but I came off worst in a first-bend bunching situation. I don't blame anyone for the accident.

'Despite my broken ankle, I went to Coventry confident that I would get through and win.'

Kelly made it to the next round with 8 points, in a meeting which was won by Sam Ermolenko. But he had problems with the slick surface at Coventry.

'I had some awful trouble trying to get by riders. You would think these promoters would kick in a couple of extra tons of dirt, but they don't. It makes it very boring for the spectators, and riders certainly don't like to see dust flying off the track after the third race. But I'm happy to get through.'

With the World Final scheduled for Katowice, Poland – the scene of Kelly's impressive World Final debut – plus the fact that Kelly's BL form was nearing the level he was at before he decided to forgo British racing, it seemed that he was set to safely negotiate the final round and make his fourth World Final appearance.

But just as a track accident had ended Shawn's chances; it was an accident of a different kind that ended not only Kelly's World title hopes, but his season too. Whilst competing in Poland as part of the *JMS All Stars* troop, he was seriously hurt in a hotel accident.

'I stepped forward to push open a door, but it was locked and I slipped, pushing my arm through the glass window instead,' he recalled.

His left wrist was badly slashed and it was only the quick thinking of Chris Morton which prevented him from possibly bleeding to death. Morton applied a tourniquet to stem the flow of blood – an action which saved his life.

Typically, Kelly made light of the accident at the time, but admitted that he was 'glad to be alive'. He received two skin graft operations and had micro-surgery. 'It was pretty scary,' Kelly says now of that terrible accident. 'I just about severed everything in my wrist, artery and tendons. I was really grateful for what Chris did. I remember up waking in a Polish hospital and I wanted a cigarette. I got one from another patient, but boy they were strong! I wouldn't try any of them again!'

Hans Nielsen finally defeated his great rival Gundersen to win in Katowice, but the latter lifted the World Long Track title at Pfarrkirchen, Germany. Shawn also qualified for that final and finished in tenth place with 8 points.

The 1987 World Final was scheduled to be an experimental two-day event. One meeting would take place on the Saturday evening and the next the following afternoon. The riders' scores from both days would be combined together to determine the overall winner. It was the first and last of its kind.

Even with the benefit of hindsight, it's difficult to understand the wisdom of the FIM. They were tinkering with the product with no clear idea of what they were trying to achieve. The final itself would take place at the Olympic Stadium, Amsterdam, Holland – a nice plush venue – but to stage the sport's premier event in a country whose speedway's pedigree was questionable to say the least made a mockery of cries of disbelief in the corridors of power when it was announced that the USA would stage the 1982 final. But it does make some semblance of sense when you realise that the man behind this venture was Dutchman Jos Vaessen.

It was as well that the Dutch Federation could seed a rider, as it was doubtful that they had a rider who was good enough to qualify. They chose Henny Kroeze, a former British League star with Halifax, Bristol and Sheffield, who had never previously qualified for a final of any description. Needless to say, he failed to make much impression when the day(s) arrived.

Nevertheless, an unofficial 'dress rehearsal' took place in May for the Dutch Golden Helmet, which was won by Sam Ermolenko – after a little help from Kelly Moran. In the final race, Sam slid off in the wet conditions and the referee excluded him. However, Kelly intervened and persuaded Vaessen to reinstate his World Pairs partner. 'The public came to see a six-man final not a five-man one,' he said.

Kelly (left) with his injured left arm is pictured at Bradford in 1986 for the Intercontinental Final, with Chris Morton (centre) and another injured rider, Andy Smith.

Sam was involved in a tenacious battle with Kelly for the all-important second place that would clinch the helmet. It was Ermolenko who got the verdict by a narrow victory at the finish line. Kelly's unselfish act had cost him overall victory, and his sporting gesture of fair play was a far cry from the win at all costs outlook that is associated with sport – it was remarkable in 1987, never mind now. His brother was also present and finished in fifth place overall.

Harry Oxley was not happy about the inclusion of Canadian riders in the American Final. He was anxious to give as many American riders the opportunity to progress in the World Championship as he could. Therefore, he introduced five rider races and so increased the number of competitors from 16 to 20. 'The Canadians belong in the Commonwealth Final with the English, Australians and the New Zealanders,' he said.

Sam Ermolenko finished the night as American Champion – dropping his only point to the runner-up, Kelly. However, Shawn failed to make it after a second race fall after 'Sudden Sam' had locked up in front of him – leaving him with no alternative but to lay down his machine. Mike Faria, John Cook and Robert Pfetzing took the remaining qualifying spots.

'Sammy locked up in front of me going into turn one, and I don't know if I touched him or not, but I ended up having to lay my bike down,' said Shawn in his column in *Speedway Mail*. 'I'm not blaming Sammy for what happened out there. He came up to me afterwards and felt so bad about it – but I told him it's just one of those things. I reckon I was a bit unlucky, but I went home, had a few drinks and thought a lot about what happened. But the following day I was fine. I just want to forget about it as quickly as possible.'

It was a hot sunny afternoon in Bradford for the next round – the Overseas Final. Kelly won his first race by equally the track record of 59.1 seconds. He was never in danger of not qualifying and defeated Ermolenko in a run-off for third place, in a meeting won by Mitch Shirra. But during a compulsory return to America he clipped a rival's back wheel at Ascot's South Bay Stadium and dislocated his shoulder. Well, that was the original diagnosis. It later transpired that he had indeed broken it. With just over two weeks until the Intercontinental Final, it was looking unlikely that he would be able to take his place at Vojens. And, despite physiotherapy and being optimistic of being able to race, he had to withdraw. There was some justice, however, as his replacement was England's Chris Morton.

It was a bitter disappointment for Kelly as he had already shown a liking for the Amsterdam track, and was enjoying one of his best seasons. He travelled to Holland as a member of fellow American, John Cook's pit crew, as Hans Nielsen retained the title ahead of Erik Gundersen and another third place for Sam Ermolenko.

Shawn Moran defeated England's Martin Hagon in a run-off to finish third in the World Long Track Final at Muhldorf, Germany. It was his best performance in the competition since his triumph in 1983; the race was won this time by Karl Maier with Simon Wigg in second.

If 1987 proved to be a disappointment for the Moran brothers, then 1988 was an absolute disaster. In successive races in the American Final at Long Beach, their hopes for glory were dashed. In heat fourteen, it was Shooey who fell while chasing Ermolenko and he could only manage reserve for the Overseas round. Then in heat fifteen, while holding a huge lead over Canadian Shawn Venables, Kelly's primary chain came adrift and he ground to a halt. It was a meeting which was won by the in-form Ermolenko, with Robert Pfetzing, Rick Miller, Mike Faria and Schwartz all making it through to the next round. It was the first time since 1980 that neither of the Morans had qualified from the American round. Even the Long Track championship proved a disappointment when Shawn failed to negotiate the semi-final at Korskro, Denmark, which was the first time he had failed to make the final since his triumphant debut in 1983.

In 1989, things didn't get much better when Kelly withdrew from the Long Beach qualifier after he had broken his finger in his brother's testimonial meeting. And Shawn took his place in the qualifier while racing under an appeal following a ban imposed by the AMA for failing an alcohol test. He had been contesting a World Long Track qualifying round at Korskro, Denmark on Sunday 14 May, and was expected to qualify as he had been in blistering form for his new club, Belle Vue. When he arrived at the venue by taxi and just managed to get into his leathers and onto his machine in time to win his opening race, he attracted the attention of the officials. Following a fourth place in his next outing, he was asked to take an alcohol test which proved positive. A gap of ten minutes was left before a second test was carried out, which also proved positive and he was excluded from the meeting.

Shawn had crashed at Belle Vue on the Friday before and injured his arm. 'The night before the meeting a group of us went out for a meal,' explained Shawn. 'When I went to bed, my arm was aching and I couldn't get comfortable. I decided to have a few more beers and I eventually got to sleep. When I woke up, well, I was feeling terrible.

'I knew the meeting started at two and it was about 1.30, so I got a taxi to the track. When I walked into the pits, everyone was sitting on their bikes and getting rolled out to the track. I got changed as quickly as I could, got out there and beat Hans Nielsen. Once you're racing you feel okay, but when I got back I felt terrible again. They tested me and that was it. I was out! It wasn't for dangerous riding or anything and there have been loads of riders who have raced while they were hungover.'

He took his place in the American Final and finished in second place to Sam Ermolenko to qualify for the next round. As the USA had not provided more than two World Finalists since 1985, the number of qualifiers was reduced to four. Lance King and Ronnie Correy took the other places while Rick Miller awaited the outcome of Moran's appeal.

The original ban meant that he couldn't contest any world championship events for the remainder of that season – individual, team or pairs. His appeal against the ban was not successful and he lost his place in the next round, which went to his good friend, Miller. Furthermore, he was ordered to repay all the monies for travelling expenses to the association. The AMA issued this short statement. 'Shawn Moran's appeal was denied. Thus he remains suspended from all speedway World Championship competition for the year 1989.'

Just as Kelly was having a good year in 1987 when injury prevented his progress, so Shawn was experiencing one of his best seasons when the ban was imposed.

Nonetheless, they all started with a clean sheet for 1990. It was Shawn who led the qualifiers from the American round when he won a run-off for the title. However, the run-off was between four riders, Moran, Billy Hamill, Rick Miller and Greg Hancock, and all four had made sure of their places in the next round – this was simply to decide the winner. Unfortunately, the run-off was tinged with sadness as Hancock slid off while in third place, and Miller was unable to avoid him and ploughed into the young American. Hancock sustained a broken arm and, although he had qualified, it was pretty certain that he would not be able to take his place.

This meant that Ronnie Correy stepped up after he had beaten Kelly Moran in a run-off for what he originally thought was for the reserve place. And Kelly would now move up to take the reserve spot.

Shortly before the Overseas Final at Coventry, Shawn had crashed in a meeting in Sweden and there were some doubts as to whether he would be fit enough to take his place. Happily, he was able to and after three rides he was struggling with 4 points. Kelly loaned his brother his machine and Shawn won his last two rides, thereby qualifying for the Intercontinental Final and also finishing on the podium in third place behind Jeremy Doncaster and Australian Todd Wiltshire. However, this meeting would come back to haunt Shooey.

This was the first time since 1985 that Shawn had progressed beyond the Overseas Final and he produced a vintage display to win his third Intercontinental Championship at Fjelsted, Denmark – to date, he is the only rider to win three Intercontinental titles. He scored 14 points and only lost to Ronnie Correy. There was some talk that his rivals, Hans Nielsen and Jan O. Pedersen, had deliberately dropped points to get a better draw for the World Final, which was being held at Bradford, England.

'I'm not bothered about the draw,' he told *Speedway Mail*. 'It's all about what happens on the day. Winning has boosted my morale for Bradford.'

The engine that powered Shooey to victory in Denmark was prepared by 1980 World Champion, Michael Lee. 'I was able to set it up exactly as Shawn wanted it on the day,' Lee said in his column in *Speedway Mail*. 'He used it in practice and decided to stick with it for the final itself. With 14 points from five rides, he looked very happy with the decision.'

Shawn seemed to be coming into his best form as the final approached, which was one of the most open finals for years. Hans Nielsen was the favourite to retain the title he won the previous year, but Denmark's other finalist, Jan O. Pedersen, was ruled out through injury. Once again, Shawn was riding an engine prepared by Lee and his mechanic, Gordon Hemmingway. Also alongside Shawn in the pits

1990 Intercontinental Champion, Shawn Moran. This was the third time he had won the title; no other rider has won it more times.

were his brother, and Craig Cummings.

'I was working for Kelly full-time, but I had helped Shawn in the world championship rounds. He rode Kelly's bike, which I prepared for him at the Overseas Final, so that's how I came to help Shawn at Bradford,' said Craig.

The final itself produced some fantastic racing and was on a par with the classic Wembley 1981 event – it was certainly the best for many years. There was a lot of support for Shawn among the 26,000 crowd.

His first ride came in heat four and he was off the inside gate. He came in third behind the sensational Swede, Henka Gustafsson and Britain's best hope, Kelvin Tatum. It wasn't the start he had hoped for.

'It rained before the meeting a little and because it was a banked track, all the water runs to the inside,' said Cummings. 'So if you're off gate one, it's so wet and slimy that it's hard to get to the first corner in front. That was all that was wrong with his first race. Once he got away from that slimy gate one he was fine after that. We didn't really make any changes to the bike at all.'

And things didn't seem to be getting any better for his next race in heat seven. The starting gate malfunctioned and Richard Knight was left at the start in gate one and it also delayed Shawn's getaway in gate two. The American expected a re-start and shut off, but amazingly the referee let the race continue, with Ronnie Correy leading Hungary's Zoltan Adorjan, and Shawn a distant and unhappy third. The crowd made their feelings known in the direction of the ref's box and it was decided to stage a re-run. In the re-run, Shawn passed Knight on the second bend to collect his first win of the evening – but those extra four laps may have been more significant than it first appeared.

'I did seven rides,' Shawn told *Speedway Mail*, 'and it threw me off. I looked at Richard and as we got out of the start, I slowed. The referee let the race go, but why four laps? You look at stuff like that and you think, "why are they there?" He had the brains of my shoe!'

He followed this with another victory in heat ten, and then faced Per Jonsson and Todd Wiltshire in heat sixteen. As they lined up at the starting gate, it was this trio of riders who were looking the most likely contenders for the crown – and so it would prove. Jonsson was on the inside, with Wiltshire alongside and Shooey was digging in on the outside gate. England's Martin Dugard was off gate three.

On the first bend, Shawn went outside Wiltshire and up the inside of Jonsson to take the lead. The Swede hounded the Californian and at one stage he took the lead on the inside on lap two, but he couldn't hold the line and Shooey pulled off another majestic inside dash to exploit the gap and regain the lead on the third bend. Desperately, Jonsson made a final surge around the outside on the last two bends but failed to make it. Wiltshire finished in third. *Speedway Mail* said of the race: 'It was a race every bit as thrilling as it was crucial.'

He hardly had time savour the victory in the most exciting race of the evening, before he was out in the next race to face Hans Nielsen. The Dane could not win the title, but was still eager to get on to the podium. He occupied the productive outside gate with Shawn alongside him in gate three. Shawn dived into the lead

Shawn leads Per Jonsson during the classic heat sixteen of the 1990 World Final at Bradford.

and never looked back. It was his last ride of the evening and he had finished with 13 points. Had he done enough?

The Moran camp didn't have to wait too long to find out. Per Jonsson had to win the next race to force a run-off with Shawn for the 1990 World Championship. The only rider who looked like he could defeat the Swede was England's Kelvin Tatum. But Jonsson was in no mood to let this opportunity pass him by, and streaked away from the start and won the race.

And so it all came down to one race: Shawn Moran, the colourful and flamboyant American, versus Per Jonsson, the quiet but effective rider from Sweden. Shawn chose the outside gate and Jonsson the inside. The Swede rode away when Moran appeared at the start line and then the start marshal added to the tension when he made Per move over. Jonsson made the start and Shawn attempted to dive through on his inside, but his way was blocked. From that moment on, there was no stopping the Swedish rider.

'We had a bike problem in the run-off,' revealed Cummings. 'The engine lost compression and it was one of those engines that was built for just one night only – a special engine if you like. We had re-starts, and one race went a complete four laps for some reason and then it had to be run again. So I think the engine may have run its course by the time the run-off came around. We almost went out on the spare bike because we knew it was losing power in his last race, but he said: 'No, no, it'll be okay' – but it wasn't.'

The World Final was a great success and the highlights were repeated on television by popular demand. Michael Lee described it as 'speedway at its very best.' *Speedway Mail* said: 'It was the most memorable World Final for five years – it had it all' and its editor, Tony Barnard, said: 'it was a marvellous advertisement for speedway.'

For Shawn, it was a case of so close and yet so far. He would have dearly loved to add the speedway gold to the one he won at Long Track, but it wasn't to be. He was the closest any American had come to winning the world crown since Bruce Penhall's triumph in 1982, and would remain so, in most fans' eyes anyway, until Sam Ermolenko was crowned champion in 1993.

Sean Wilson, who was a team-mate of the Morans at Sheffield, was also watching the final. 'The way he rode that night was just out of this world,' he said. 'He deserved to win it. He let Per Jonsson move over a bit further on gate one and he lost it. That was one of the saddest days really.'

While British Speedway continued to bask in the applause of a job well done, dark clouds began to gather on the sport's horizon. Just over a week had passed since the dust settled on the Odsal track, when news came through that one of the finalists had produced a positive drugs sample during a routine test. It later emerged that the sample was produced at the Overseas Final. The sport braced itself as a second test was ordered.

On 26 October 1990, Shawn Moran was found guilty of a breach of the rule 09.09.92 of the FIM medical code. An FIM Track Racing Commission Tribunal, which comprised of president, Gunter Sorber, Renzo Giannini and Janos Nadasdi, had stripped the popular American of his second place in the World Final, and imposed a ban of twelve months, with six months suspended, for failing a drugs test at the Overseas Final. It went on to say that after the six months had expired, he could then obtain a licence on probation. But there was more to it than that.

As we know, Shawn was carrying an injury sustained in a track crash in Sweden which had prevented him from riding for Belle Vue in the British League.

'What happened was I borrowed a bike from, I think, Mikael Teurnberg, because mine wouldn't start. I got out the gate and this bike was flying, but I couldn't stop the bike from drifting out to the fence. Einar Kyllingstad was on the inside and he collided with someone and crashed into me. I got centre punched and all three of us hit the fence.

'I felt like I'd broken everything on my side, but it turned out that nothing was broken. But I was in a lot of pain at night, and I was having trouble sleeping. The doctor gave me these painkillers (Distal Gesic) which I took to ease the pain. I called Maurice Ducker, who was the BSPA (British Speedway Promoters' Association) chairman and told him that I'd taken these pills. I'm not blaming Maurice at all, but he thought it would be okay. Anyway, on the Saturday he calls me and says that I shouldn't have taken them. It was like, "Oh, it's too late now Maurice".

'When I got to Coventry, I told the Clerk of the Course and the track doctor, because the referee hadn't arrived or something. I had a doctor's note and I wasn't hiding anything. I told them that if there was going to be a problem then

Shawn Moran with the runners-up medal for the 1990 World Championship – or should that be the World Team Cup medal?

I'd rather not ride and my brother could take my place. Well, I guess it was difficult for them, to try and advise me because it would have been a big thing if I withdrew. Then in the interval, after I had ridden three races, I was tested.

'But I never heard anything about it, so I thought that it was okay. Then after the World Final I got a call from the FIM saying that I had to fly to Budapest and explain myself. It was Monday and I had to get there for Wednesday or something like that, no please or thank you – just make sure you're there. When I got there I was in a court, and I had Bill Boyce with me from the AMA and I had to go through it all again. We had to leave the room for about five minutes and then they told me that I had been banned from FIM meetings. They never said anything about losing the second place. It cost me a packet, and to cap it all the taxis were on strike in Budapest when the price of petrol was doubled,' said Shawn. 'I missed my flight and Belle Vue's last meeting.

'Of course it was on my mind for the Intercontinental Final, but why did they let me do all that? That made it tougher to take. You know when I received my medal at Bradford, when I turned it over it said World Team Cup. So they knew. They knew all along. I don't know what else I could have done. They were only painkillers, they wouldn't have given me an advantage when I raced.'

Shawn explained to the tribunal that he had informed the physician that he couldn't take any medicine that contained any of the banned substances according to Speedway Control Board (SCB) rules. In all innocence, the doctor prescribed the drug not knowing that it contained a banned substance. It was known as Co-Proxamol, which he couldn't find on the list in the rule book. Shooey said that he could not have raced without taking the painkiller, but it was *not* a performance-enhancing drug.

From the moment he arrived at Coventry, he was up front and honest about the situation, and was willing to give up his place to avoid exactly the sort of problems he now found himself with. On the face of it, perhaps Shawn should have withdrawn. But he had earned the right to be there and every rider wants to be World Champion, and you take the opportunities that come your way. Besides, he was under the impression that he could participate.

The meeting at Coventry took place on 24 July, and Shooey was permitted to follow the competition to its conclusion at Bradford on 1 September, and still he had not heard anything about it. The publications of the time revealed that the President of the Track Racing Commission was in possession of the facts before the day of the sport's biggest night of the year. The fact is, if you see any roll of honour in a World Championship programme, the FIM have not upgraded the rest of the field. That speaks volumes.

This unfortunate episode was handled badly by the officials, and yet the only person to suffer was Shawn when all he needed was some guidance at the appropriate time. What was he really guilty of? He was found guilty of providing a test result of medication that he told them he had taken! The situation became quite ludicrous when it was announced that American road racing star Kevin Schwantz had raced with the aid of painkillers to keep his championship hopes alive. It was difficult to explain to non-speedway followers what Shawn had supposedly done wrong, when other forms of motorcycle racing seemed to have an altogether more professional and understanding outlook.

Shawn was once quoted as saying that he wished that he had handed his place to his brother, and withdrawn from the meeting. He earned his runner-up place to Per Jonsson and as such I believe it's time that the FIM reinstated his second place as it wasn't that meeting where the incident occurred. There were more people at fault at Coventry than just Shooey, and it's time that the FIM acknowledged that fact.

At the AMA awards dinner, Kelly Moran made his feelings plain to the assembled officials and was fined $1,000 – although suspended – for expressing his disgust. Shawn, disillusioned by the episode and no doubt fed up with the whole scenario, chose not to appeal.

'I am not appealing against the test result; it is a fact that I was allowed to continue in the competition after telling the authorities what I had done,' he told *Speedway Mail*. 'If I shouldn't have been in the competition, that was time to have stopped me. It's such a let down for all my sponsors, the speedway public and the people who have helped me and I am sorry about it.'

The 1990 World Final was one of the best in the history of the championship, but it has largely been forgotten by the powers that be because of this incident. Within two months of that run-off, the FIM and the SCB, through their incompetence, managed to tarnish a product which was

Shawn helps Kelly, Bradford, 1991.

attracting praise from all the right quarters.

Shawn Moran would never ride in the World Championship again, and it seemed that he had lost his enthusiasm for the sport and was disillusioned with it.

'For them (the FIM) to take his name out of the World Final, I think that finished him. I think he should be re-instated because he told them that he was on painkillers for the Overseas Final,' agreed Sean Wilson.

'He was a fantastic speedway rider,' said Cummings. 'He wasn't as natural as Kelly and had to work a little bit harder, but he had a hell of a lot of natural talent and ability as well. I think, when he wanted to do it, there wasn't anyone in the world that could beat him.'

In spite of all this, Shooey retained his sense of humour about the situation. In the short-lived magazine, *Speedway Now*, he was asked to reveal his loves and hates. In a dig at the officials, he revealed one of his loves: 'I would love to represent the planet Uranus in next year's World Championship. Could someone tell me where my first round is?'

Kelly successfully qualified in fourth place from the 1991 American Final with 11 points, which was won by Rick Miller with a 15-point maximum. As America had three riders in the 1990 final, their allocation was put back up to five, and the other riders to make it were Sam Ermolenko, Ronnie Correy and Billy Hamill.

At the Overseas Final at Bradford, riding his brother's bikes, Kelly qualified with 7 points. As he entered his last race, it seemed he had done enough to get through when he came in last in his final race and caused 'a bit of sweat'. But it proved to be enough. He impressed the crowd when he passed home rider Gary Havelock from the back, in an event which was won by England's Kelvin Tatum.

The Intercontinental Final was temporarily dropped from the qualifying calendar and was replaced by a semi-final. Until now, the Intercontinental Final had just included the Western riders, while the Continental Final was run for the riders from the continent. Now there were two semi-finals and Western and Eastern riders were all mixed up together. To make it harder, only eight riders would qualify from each round for the Final, which would be held at Gothenburg, Sweden.

Kelly was scheduled to race at Abensberg, Germany. However, accompanied by his brother and Simon Wolstenholme, he missed the ferry from Dover and arrived an hour after official practice. Then his machines arrived late for the machine examiner to run his checks and, for a brief time, it seemed that he could be thrown out of the event. Happily, he was able to take his place, but was fined 250 Swiss francs because his bikes were not available on time for the inspection.

Kelly commenced his bid for his fourth World Final appearance with a fourth place behind Tommy Knudsen, Ronnie Correy and Kelvin Tatum. He followed that with two second places, and at the interval stage he still had a lot of work to do, with just 4 points to his name. While lying in second place to Ermolenko in heat sixteen, his engine seized and he stopped in mid-track

The end of the road for Kelly's 1991 World Championship hopes – his engine seizes in front of Denmark's Gert Handberg.

– leaving the chasing young Dane, Gert Handberg, with nowhere to go and they crashed. Kelly was immediately on his feet and he rushed over to check on the health of Handberg. The Dane would continue but Kelly was excluded from the re-run and his championship hopes were all but over. He finished second in his last race, but it wasn't enough. It was a disappointment, and but for the engine failure he would have qualified.

Nevertheless, this didn't prevent *Speedway Star* journalist Philip Rising from launching a scathing, critical attack on the charismatic Kelly. He described his performance as a 'sick joke,' and went on to criticise him for the next two paragraphs in his report of the Abensberg semi-final. Quite why he felt he had to do this is not clear, but the American went on video to describe the publication as *'News of the World Speedway Star,'* and said that he would have qualified but for the engine failure – which was true.

Kelly did not enter the 1992 World Championship. The expense of taking part was one of the factors, as he said that the travelling expenses hardly covered his costs.

There is no doubt that both brothers could and should have lifted the World Speedway title, but it wasn't to be. Many reasons have been put forward, but the overriding one is always that they were just not dedicated enough, and were happy just to enjoy their racing.

'Kelly and Shawn Moran: there was more talent in those two guys than any other two people I have ever seen,' said Ivan Mauger. 'They had the talent to ride the bike and they were fantastic. Shawn could have been World Champion that night at Bradford. But there were a few things he did that night that wasted the opportunity. It was just Shawn being Shawn. Everybody has their different way; they all have their own way of getting themselves up for the sport. The Morans' way was up all night, partying and all that stuff. Without that they couldn't perform, and you couldn't get them to be serious. If you got them to be serious, you ruined what the Morans were all about, you ruined what made them.'

4

FLYING THE FLAG

Although America was a strong world force during the pre-war years, they never assembled a team for Test match duty. This did not happen until the post-war years of 1951, when the USA sent out a team of young internationals, who based themselves at Shelbourne Park, Dublin, Ireland. It was here that they made their base and proved a popular attraction for the locals.

It was the then Wimbledon promoter, Ronnie W. Greene MBE, who arranged for this team of stateside speedsters to travel across the Atlantic and base themselves in Ireland – a country which has strong links with the USA, and with the two men who are the subject of this book. Greene had already been impressed by the signing of Ernie Roccio for his team in 1950 and it was through this signing that he returned from a trip to the USA with the signatures of Americans and one rider from Mexico – Manuel Trujillo – to ride under the banner of the Shelbourne Tigers.

On their own circuit this team were no pushover, as was demonstrated when they beat First Division clubs, Wimbledon, Belle Vue, Bristol and West Ham. As a nation they also saw off teams from England, Scotland and Norway. But then they took part in a proper five match international test series against an England 'C' team in Britain. They lost the series 3-2, but there was plenty of potential among the US side who were Ernie Roccio, his brother, Johnny, Nick Nicolaides, Royal Carroll, Don Hawley, Jimmy Gibb, Lloyd Campbell and Johnny Gibson.

Nicolaides attracted interest from Poole, but it was Ernie Roccio who went on to prove his ability. But then the sport suffered a drop in fortunes until the Jack Milne/Harry Oxley-inspired revival of late 1960s.

Soon they began staging internationals at their own tracks, usually a USA versus a Rest of the World select – often brought over as part of the Barry Briggs/Ivan Mauger-inspired Champions Troupe touring series. These events were not usually sanctioned by the FIM, but in 1976 a world-class touring side assembled to take on the Americans in their own backyard, and the sport's governing body agreed to give the series their official seal of approval. However, at the last minute, the FIM withdrew the official status of the event and Oxley was furious. To the astonishment of everyone, he took the FIM to court. His actions warned the speedway world that he was not a man to be messed around.

Finally, in 1978, the USA was able to enter a team in the World Team

Championship. But with only a handful of Americans racing in Britain, they could barely put together the five riders necessary to make a team. Then they were refused permission to use Kelly Moran because he was too young to hold an international licence. Therefore, with Scott Autrey, Bruce Penhall, Steve Gresham and Mike Curoso, they were still a rider short. They decided to call up Gresham's older brother, Jim, who hadn't ridden in Britain and was largely known for his skills as a mechanic. The surprise move was passed, and the USA took to the track to make their debut in the World Team Cup, UK qualifying round at Reading. Incidentally, the promoting of ex-riders/mechanics to make up the numbers instead of having the extra expense of flying in a rider from their homeland, was to become commonplace as the years went on. Mick Rooney was John Cook's mechanic when he was persuaded into action in the 1985 series, while Sean Diiullio was on holiday when he was suddenly drafted into the 1986 team – neither had ever raced in Britain before. At times, some critics felt that the Yanks were not taking it very seriously.

The formula for the World Team Championship in those days was a four-team tournament, with one rider from each team representing their country in each race. Each team would comprise of four riders and one reserve, who could be used to replace an injured rider or someone who was not doing well. This format bore little resemblance to the regular league competition, or test series racing – where pairs would represent their teams and team racing as a pair was encouraged. But this format remained in place until 1994.

The Americans faced England, Australia and New Zealand in the UK qualifying round and did well, finishing third behind winners England and just one point adrift of second-placed Australia. This meant that two more points and they would have qualified for the next round. Scott Autrey led the scoring with 9 points.

The following year, Kelly was eligible to ride and he took his place in the side which now included Bobby Schwartz and Dennis Sigalos, to add to Autrey, Gresham and Penhall. They also had their own manager, a stately English gentleman called John Scott, whose only apparent link with America was that he closely resembled the actor David Niven. In truth, he had been managing the affairs of Gresham and he agreed to step into the breach.

This round of the World Team Cup is best remembered for the wet weather and England's dismal display which led to their elimination. America finished in second with 26 points, behind winners New Zealand on 30. England were four adrift of the Yanks on 22. It was Kelly's victory in heat fifteen over the persistent Gordon Kennett of England which secured their qualification. He scored 7 points, which included a fall when he shed a chain in his second outing. It was particularly pleasing for the side because they were without their top man Autrey, who was overlooked for selection for all international events because of his withdrawal, under protest, from the American Final.

Therefore, Kelly teamed up with Bruce Penhall to represent the USA in the World Pairs championship for the first time. They travelled to Yugoslavia and

Kelly and Shawn, USA, 1982.

finished in third place on 23 points behind Poland (26), and New Zealand (25), and put America through to their first World Final. Penhall scored 14 and Kelly collected 9 points. Ivan Mauger was paired with Larry Ross for the Kiwis and recalls Kelly's laid-back approach to racing at the qualifying round: 'Kelly was with Bruce and I can't remember what happened to Kelly's engine in the practice. But he came back in the pits and it was making a rough noise. Anyway, he's really laid-back, couldn't care less, but as long as it was still running and the piston was going up and down, he didn't seem to think anything of it.

'The others around said that the engine was bad and it had to be changed. So they changed the engine the next day. It was a Weslake engine, and the engine they put in, the "W" and Weslake, was all written in red paint. Kelly rode in the meeting, and afterwards, in the night-time, we were all sitting around having a meal. The whole lot of us, Bruce, myself, Barry (Briggs), and a few other guys, when somebody happened to say, "Wasn't it a good job we changed Kelly's engine." And Kelly said: "You know, I can't remember having any red paint on it, like the Weslake being written in red." He was so laid-back, he didn't even know they had changed the engine. As long as it was a Weslake he hadn't noticed.'

Craig Cummings revealed that Kelly and Shawn only really knew the basics about bikes. 'Neither Kelly nor Shawn were particularly mechanically minded at all. I think you get really talented people like that, and all they can do is get on a bike and ride it,' he said. 'There are other guys who have a lot of racing talent but they think about things too much. They're riding around thinking, "well, if I had a bit more compression it would do this, or it would do that." They're never happy with what they've got. Shawn and Kelly got on with what they had and rode it to the best of their ability. If it was fast or if it was slow, it didn't matter. They got on it and gave it everything they could. Sometimes they would win races on terrible bikes.'

A bruised hip prevented Kelly from appearing in the final, which was won by Denmark's Ole Olsen and Hans Nielsen. But Penhall faced a lone battle when his replacement, Steve Gresham, failed to arrive due to an air traffic controllers' strike at Heathrow. Nevertheless, Penhall scored 14 points to put the USA in fifth place, ahead of New Zealand and Finland.

Kelly top-scored with 8 points in the Intercontinental Final of the World Team Cup in Sweden, but he couldn't prevent his country from being eliminated from the competition. They finished in third with 22 points, behind the winners New Zealand – who went on to be crowned World Champions – and Denmark. A World Team Cup Final place would have to wait for another year.

In 1980, Britain staged the first England versus USA senior test series. It was run over five matches and produced some of the most exciting racing of the year. The first test at Wimbledon ended in a 54-54 draw, and anyone who was present on that night witnessed some of the best test match action for years. Some of it was filmed for a documentary called *Test Rider* about Scott Autrey, who was back in favour and was installed as the captain. As Kelly was riding in the USA, he was not included in the teams. However, his brother Shawn was in his debut season in England, and was sure to make an appearance in the series. John Scott was given the position as the manager of the team, and Harry Oxley also flew in to add his considerable help and gamesmanship to the cause.

Despite the dash and glamour of the Americans, they were not really expected to win the series as only Autrey and Penhall were considered to be true world class performers. This belief was underlined when England won the second test at Cradley, 62-46. However, the third test at Hull saw America fight back with a 61-47 victory, helped no end by Harry Oxley winning a game of psychology before the test. In a 1981 book written by Richard Bott and England's co-manager, Ian Thomas, called *Speedway Grand Slam*, Thomas wrote of his disapproval: 'It was a real kick in the teeth to lose at my own track. The Yanks pulled a stroke before the start by arriving early, taking over the directors' car park and the home section of the pits. If they intended to niggle us, they succeeded.'

This test, which took place on 7 May, was the debut appearance in the series for Shooey. He was named at reserve on his home track, but took a surprise outing in heat two. The often temperamental Steve Gresham told Oxley and Scott that he didn't feel up to the task. Shawn was put out in his place while Oxley talked Gresham round. Shooey took third in his debut ride, but by the time he had returned to the pits, Harry had persuaded Gresham to race and he contributed a valuable 7 points. Shawn would appear again as a replacement for the out of touch Ron Preston, but in this race he actually failed to score.

America won the fourth test at Poole 63-44 – despite losing Preston with a knee injury in heat nine. Shawn had a busy night and scored 4 points. With the final test at Swindon, the unfancied Americans led the series 2-1 – with one drawn match. It was vital that England won the last test to draw the competition.

There was plenty of controversy in the pits before the deciding match, when England's skipper, John Louis, was told by Swindon's promoter, Wally Mawdsley, to move his equipment to the visitors' side of the pits! 'We were also installed in the visitors' dressing room. Now wouldn't you have thought that racing in England we would have been regarded as the home team? The Americans had actually been given a psychological boost by a British promoter,' said Thomas.

The USA took the lead with a 5-1 in the opening race from Bruce Penhall and Bobby Schwartz, and they never looked back. Shawn, starting in the team for the first time, gained his first paid win in heat three when he followed Dennis Sigalos home. He went on to score 6 points as America clinched the series.

England's John Davis registered his disgust at the treatment his side had received at Swindon, from both the promotion and the fans. To his great annoyance, the Californians were receiving more vocal support from the crowd than the home nation! This was the first real indication of how much these Yanks had been taken to the hearts of the British public.

When Kelly returned to Britain with Birmingham, he raced for his country in the Intercontinental Final of the World Team Cup at Vojens, Denmark. Selected at reserve, he finished third in his race during his only appearance that year for his country. America lost to England by just one point, with the in-form Dave Jessup clinching victory with a last heat win over Penhall as he scorched to an unbeaten maximum.

The USA made the World Team Final, but lost to an England side who won the Grand Slam of World Championship events that year – individual (Michael Lee) pairs (Peter Collins and Dave Jessup) and team. They were the first country to do so. But that defeat in the test series clearly rattled the England management partnership of Ian Thomas and Eric Boocock.

But, despite their success, they lost their roles to Len Silver, who took over the reins of the toughest job in English speedway. It seemed that he concentrated on gaining revenge in the test series against the Americans, as the wounds inflicted by America's test series win were still smarting as the 1981 season came along.

By the time the third test arrived at Swindon, England held a 2-0 lead. Bruce Penhall had taken over as captain and he said before the match that his team were deadly serious and had no time to entertain the crowd with wheelies. And so it appeared, as Penhall and Bobby Schwartz opened up proceedings with a 5-1 encounter. Kelly Moran won his first race and then pulled a huge power wheelie in his second outing while exiting the final bend on the last lap, but the pursuing Jessup was not able to find a way past to deny the American his second win. But England was in no mood to let their grasp on the series slip, and they clawed their way back and eventually won the match, 64-43, and clinched the series. England went on to win the series 4-1, with the USA's solitary success coming at Ipswich.

Kelly and Shawn had made occasional appearances in the competition, with Kelly scoring 9 points at Swindon – but mechanical breakdowns restricted his scoring. Shawn's best was a 7-point return at Cradley Heath in the final test. However, they were both selected for the three-match series in Sweden.

The Swedes were not the world power they had been, or would be in the 1990s, but they still managed a 2-1 series victory. America won the first test with a narrow 54-53 scoreline at Norrkopping, but the last two tests at Stockholm and Kumla saw the Swedes win by comfortable margins. The Moran brothers rode in all three matches, which were run over a three-day period. Kelly scored 11 points on two occasions, but Shawn's best performance came in the last test with 7 points.

Kelly's performances saw him selected as reserve for the first qualifying round of the World Team Cup at Reading. Heavy rain before the start made the track heavy, but England won with 36 points and the USA grabbed the second qualifying place with 32 points. Kelly made one appearance in heat fourteen, and finished in second place behind England's Chris Morton.

By the time the next round came along, at King's Lynn, one of Kelly's favourite tracks, his impressive form for his club, Eastbourne, meant that he was promoted to the main body of the team. This was a close fought contest between the England, USA and Denmark – the world's top three speedway nations – and with only the top two teams progressing to the final, it was the USA who missed out with the following scoreline: Denmark 31, England 30, USA 26 and Sweden 9. Kelly scored 5 points and won his first race, and he was involved in a classic race with Ole Olsen and Dave Jessup, when you could have thrown a blanket over all three for the entire race.

However, gold was finally struck for the US when Penhall and Schwartz won the World Pairs Championship at Katowice, Poland with 23 points, and then Penhall was crowned World Champion at Wembley. But, considering that America had more British based racers to choose from than ever before, or after, they were disappointed to lose as many competitions as they did.

In 1982, all the talent and potential that the Americans had displayed since their first entry into World Championship competition in 1978 would finally come to bear gold medals in abundance during this exciting year.

First up was the England *v.* USA test series. A big rivalry had developed between these two nations and the Americans looked upon their success in this series as the key to their season. After losing the first test at Wimbledon 63-45 – a meeting at which Shawn stole the show with some fantastic racing to top-score with 13 points – the series was poised at 2-2 when the last test took place at Poole.

There were concerns about whether their inspirational captain, Penhall, would make the trip back in time from a racing engagement in Germany.

'The next day, in Germany, was Christihimmelfahrt – or Ascension Day – a public holiday and a qualifying round for the World Long Track Championship,' explained

The victorious USA team at Ipswich in 1982. From left to right: Shawn Moran, Bobby Schwartz, John Cook, Ron Preston, Dennis Sigalos, Scott Autrey, Bruce Penhall, John Smith (USA co-team manager), Kelly Moran.

team manager, John Scott. 'Practice for the Long Track was the day before – that is the day of the Poole test. Bruce practised between 2 and 3 p.m. at Herxhiem; he was flown by helicopter to Frankfurt airport. He then flew to Heathrow and again was taken by helicopter to Poole Stadium.'

To the relief of the team, Penhall arrived with less than an hour to go before the scheduled start time and, inspired by their captain's efforts to make the fixture, America ripped England apart 69-39, to win the match and the series.

Shawn Moran had emerged as America's top performer in the series with a 14.19 average and raced with his brother in all the test matches. They proved to be the most productive pair as they averaged 21 points a match. They scored nine 5-1s, six 4-2s, drew nine races, conceded one 5-1, and five 4-2s, for a total of 107 points. Their race average was 3.56 as a pair. Kelly scored more bonus points for the team than anyone else with 12 and finished the series with a 10.20 average.

'Kelly and Shawn would go where angels feared to tread with great effect,' said Scott.

Next up was Sweden, who were beaten 2-1 by the USA in a series in which Kelly Moran averaged 12.33. America achieved this success by using some of their lesser lights.

The USA lost the UK qualifying round of the World Team Cup at King's Lynn by the narrowest of margins. England and the USA had finished with 39 points each and a run-off was required to decide the day's victor. Kelly had finished with a

Kelly leads Australian Billy Sanders during the 1982 UK qualifying round of the World Team Cup, in which Kelly scored a maximum.

maximum and he was nominated to face England's Peter Collins. It was Collins who won despite Kelly's best efforts to find a way past the former World Champion.

'I remember when I beat PC during the match I pulled a big power wheelie as I came out of last bend and I held it to the chequered flag,' said Kelly. 'PC came up to me afterward and said, "How did you control that wheelie? That was brilliant." I just said, "I don't know." I could never explain those kinds of things. It doesn't do to question it, I don't think.'

The Morans were now an integral part of America's team, and Shawn scored 9 points in that round. Kelly found himself having to borrow Bruce Penhall's bikes and equipment for the last qualifying round at Vojens because his own equipment was impounded by his club as punishment for failing to arrive at a meeting. It didn't make any difference however, as he joint top-scored with Penhall on 10 points as they won the meeting with 34 points ahead of Denmark on 28. England were eliminated which was a big blow to the competition, as they were the hosts for the final at White City. Shawn scored 9 points in another solid display, while Dennis Sigalos scored five. The reserve, Schwartz, was not called upon to ride as the team qualified for their second team final.

Greg Hancock, the 1997 World Champion, was a protégé of Penhall's and he recalled: 'I remember Kelly rode Bruce's bikes a number of times; and wrecked a few of them too, but someone was always there to lend him another one. He was a gentleman and never meant any harm. He was just there because he loved speedway and he loved to help people too.'

The team spirit in the American team was second to none. To the amazement of their opponents, riders who were not racing particularly well for their club would often produce match-winning performances for their country. They would share bikes and equipment; and would always be there to encourage and gee up each other for each race.

Shortly before the final at White City, the US team suffered three setbacks. The first was the death of Denny Pyeatt at Hackney and the second was the ankle injury to Dennis Sigalos. Bobby Schwartz, who was particularly close to Denny, was promoted into the team to replace Siggy, and Scott Autrey was brought in as reserve. Their popularity with the public also took a nosedive when their captain, Penhall, deliberately finished last in a race in the Overseas Final of the World Individual Championship, to allow his team-mates, Kelly, Shawn and Sigalos, to progress to the next stage. It might have been viewed as an unselfish act of a national captain by some, but for many, it was little short of cheating. Many fans were outraged and boycotted the World Team Final in protest.

Once again, the rain threatened to spoil the day as America faced reigning champions, Denmark, Czechoslovakia and West Germany. From the beginning, one could see that it would be between the Yanks and the Danes. The Americans took the lead in heat two and never really looked back. Shawn Moran made sure of the gold by winning heat thirteen, while Schwartz – who was unbeaten after three rides – unselfishly gave up his last ride so that Scott Autrey – the man who

World Team champions 1982 – USA. From left to right, back row: Scott Autrey, John Scott (team manager), John Smith (team manager), Kelly Moran. Front row: Bobby Schwatz, Bruce Penhall, Shawn Moran.

started it all in the early 1970s -could participate and feel a part of this historic success. Kelly and Bruce again top-scored with 10 points each, Schwartz scored 9, Shawn 8, and Scott 0, as America won with 37 points, Denmark 24, West Germany 18 and Czechoslovakia 17. As the team posed for pictures, Schwartz carried a picture of their fallen team-mate, Pyeatt, and the victory was dedicated to his memory.

However, in the press conference, captain Penhall announced that he was quitting British Speedway to concentrate on a career in Hollywood. Later at the World Final in Los Angles, he would quit the sport altogether as he retained the World Championship. With two competitions left, their number one rider would be missing.

However, the strength in the USA side was such that, even without Penhall and Kelly – who had broken his collarbone – they still won the International Fours. It was another four-team tournament against England, Denmark and Australasia. America only lost at Sheffield – which Denmark won, with England coming second and the USA third – and hit 46 points at both Reading and Eastbourne. They scored 150 points and were 28 points ahead of second-placed Denmark.

Shawn scored a maximum at Eastbourne and totalled 37-points and appeared in all four meetings He was again his country's top scorer and finished with an impressive 9.25 average.

'I enjoyed riding for my country, it's a great honour,' said Shawn. 'All the meetings were important, but as a team we had a lot of fun as well.'

When Schwartz and Sigalos won the World Pairs in Australia, they had completed a Grand Slam of competition victories. It was a tremendous feat for a country that was still young in terms of international speedway racing experience.

The team manager, John Scott, who also had assistance from John Smith during 1982, was particularly proud of that team, whose celebrated team spirit was worth a few extra points alone. In an interview he gave to the author shortly before he passed away in 1997, he said: 'A team of all the talents. Every one of them was capable of winning races on their own or helping team-ride their partners. Personal glory took second place to the victory of the team. We had a good choice in 1982, strong heatleaders, and plenty of enthusiastic back-up, all willing to ride with anybody else in the team. It was a tremendous year, and marked the end of an era.'

'It was a good team,' agreed Kelly. 'It was one of those years when everything clicked together; no matter what happened we always pulled through as a team. I don't know what it was, but it was the same with the Danes when they were winning everything, you just get on a roll and the confidence carries you through.

'John Scott was a good team manager. For example, if one of the other boys was going well, or we thought he deserved a chance, we would say so to John and he

Plenty of encouragement for Kelly as he prepares for a race during the 1982 World Team Cup at White City. From left to right: John Smith, Kelly Moran, Scott Autrey, Bruce Penhall.

used to listen to us. I think all that helped with the team spirit, as everyone was involved.'

After such a year of domination, the retirement of Penhall and the decisions of Kelly, John Cook, Ron Preston and Scott Autrey not to return to the UK seemed to suggest that the USA would not be able to continue that good run of form. Some critics even predicted a walk-over for the English team in the test series. But the Americans did not walk away with all the medals in 1982 for nothing ...

They flew in Kelly for the series and also Mike Faria – although he would return after the first two matches to be replaced by John Cook. There were also some doubts about the fitness of Shawn, as he broke his arm in the US Spring Classics just before the start of the British season.

However, America proved that they were still a match for England, who just won the series 3-2, with the outcome in doubt until the very final race of the last test at Sheffield. The Morans raced together in each test and, although they weren't quite as dominant as the previous year, they still scored 13 heat advantages and five 5-1s in 29 races together. In the third test at Poole, Dave Jessup must have felt as if he was seeing double as, in one movement on the third and fourth bends, Shawn slipped through on the inside and Kelly around the outside, to link up for another 5-1. Shawn scored an 18-point maximum in the fourth test at Ipswich – his first in the series.

Despite these important internationals, both of them continued to enjoy themselves off the track. Reg Wilson, who was Shawn's team-mate at Sheffield, recalled an occasion the night before a World Team Cup round.

'They were at Halifax and the next day they were due at Reading in a Four-Team Tournament. They went to a party after the meeting and they were totally out of it at two o'clock in the morning when they set off. The next day we all thought they were going to get nothing, but they didn't. They both did well and cleaned up. I remember thinking that was incredible after they had been out of their heads on booze the night before and still did well. Someone like Hans Nielsen would probably have been in bed at ten o'clock, and there's these two partying 'til two o'clock and they go to Reading and clean up – fantastic really.'

The US had to concede the World Team Cup to the host nation Denmark, as they were weakened by the absence of Shawn, who had broken his leg. In fact, America slipped to third behind the Danes and England. It was the start of the Danish domination. However, in his column in *Speedway Magazine*, Kelly was not happy with some of the tactics employed by the host nation. 'Ole Olsen led the Danes to a so-called victory by being the promoter and grading the track whenever it suited his team, instead of every four heats.'

However in 1984, after the USA had won the test series against England 4-1 – and Shawn was once again in fantastic form with another 18-point maximum at Ipswich – they made it to the World Team Final at Leszno, Poland, and were hot favourites to win. But it was not a good day as Denmark exploited the tape rule and ran away with the gold. America were pipped to second by England and they struggled on the big slick Polish track. Unlike today, riders were allowed to touch

The Moran brothers head for a 5-1 victory for the USA. Shawn, inside Kelly, leads England's Chris Morton.

the tapes and would only be excluded if they broke them. It was a rule which the Danes especially took advantage of. There were rumours of discontent and even arguments among the American team.

'Some of us were overconfident,' wrote Kelly in his column in *Speedway Magazine*. 'It's good to be confident, of course, but there is a limit. It wasn't like Carl Glover (England team manager) said about us fighting in the pits. There were little quarrels, but nothing out of the ordinary. Tempers were short because this was such an important race. And the Danes were playing games at the tapes – really cheating. The referee didn't help out at all either. There was no warning whatsoever, so that was really unfair, I think.

'At the World Final we were told in the riders' briefing that the referee knew who the rollers were, and he said that whoever pushed the tapes, the tapes would go up and he'd put on the red light and he'd warn them once. That never happened.'

Shawn rode in the World Pairs for the first time in 1984 with Bobby Schwartz. They made it to the final and finished in fourth place with 19 points (Schwartz 11 and Shawn 8). The event was won by the English pairing of Peter Collins and Chris Morton – who raced together at Belle Vue.

The USA was the hosts for the 1985 World Team Cup, and they staged the event at Long Beach. Therefore, they did not have to qualify for the final. They faced the holders, Denmark, England and Sweden.

117

Kelly Moran was unable to ride as he was injured with a broken foot, but the team of Shawn, Bobby Schwartz, Lance King, John Cook and Sam Ermolenko at reserve, combined with their home-track advantage, seemed destined to win their second World Team title. Their team manager for this event was Bruce Penhall.

The meeting was once again promoted by *World Class Inc.* and they felt that the FIM were losing the plot, as Harry Oxley explained: 'The FIM track inspector said that the track was sub-standard, and then the World Champion, Erik Gundersen, said it was the finest track he'd ever ridden on in his life.'

Indeed, the surface produced some of the best racing ever seen in a World Team Cup Final. The razzamatazz and the presentation were second to none, even if it was biased to an American victory.

It was a straight fight between the USA and Denmark, as the English and the Swedes never managed to provide a race winner. In a close fought contest, the Danes won by just two points, thanks to a match-winning performance by reserve Preben Eriksen and a full house from Tommy Knudsen. For the USA, Shooey and Schwartz led the scores with 11 points each, both only losing to Knudsen. Shawn produced a classy inside pass on Gundersen in heat ten, but John Cook's below-par display probably cost them the overall victory.

Denmark's team manager, Ole Olsen – who quit as manager after the meeting to spend more time with his son, Jacob – was a little annoyed about the way that everything was geared to a USA success, as he revealed in an interview he gave to *Speedway Mail:* 'We've had a rough time here, especially early on. The Americans were really pumped up and the atmosphere was too much.'

Shooey was messing around on a mini-motorcycle during practice when he crashed and tore some skin off his arm. The leathers made the wound sore, but he still put in a sterling display in the meeting.

'The atmosphere in the pits for us was great,' wrote Shawn in his column in *Speedway Mail.* 'We were motivated to win right up 'til the last heat, when we knew we couldn't pull it off. That's what it's all about after all, and it's great when you have that kind of feeling in the pits. But you can't win a meeting in the pits alone, and it's just one of those things.

'None of us can feel bad about the way we rode. We were pushing all the way and you can't ask any more from the riders. You just can't give more than 100 per cent and that's all there is to it.'

Shawn and Bobby 'Boogaloo' Schwartz scored 22 points (Shawn 11 and Schwartz 11) and went one better in the World Pairs to take the bronze medal in the final at Rybnik, Poland. Denmark's Tommy Knudsen and Erik Gundersen took the gold this time. It was a little disappointing as they had won their semi-final at Bradford, with Shawn in brilliant form, scoring 15 points.

America ended the season on a high, however, when they completed a whitewash over England in the test series with a 3-0 victory. Shawn was in good form throughout the series, and his brother also put in an appearance at the Ipswich test for two rides. But he failed to score on either occasion while using his brother's equipment and leathers.

The parade, Californian style – Shawn acknowledges the applause of the crowd and his surroundings at the World Team Cup Final at Long Beach, USA in 1985.

Shawn prepares for another race during the 1985 World Team Cup Final.

In 1986, the format for the World Pairs was changed to include six rider races. It was a controversial move as many riders complained that there weren't enough tracks wide enough to safely accommodate six riders racing into the first bend. Shawn was undecided and explained in his column:

'You've got to now try and hold off two pairs and I'm not sure I like this new format,' he said. 'We have six riders in a long track meeting, but even that gets scary.'

Nevertheless, through Shawn and his partner Schwartz, the USA qualified for the final in Pocking. However, neither would appear in the final. Schwartz was dropped in favour of Kelly, who was running into the form at the right time, but it was felt that the Moran brothers' unique on-track understanding would be an advantage in the new format. They were immediately installed as favourites to win America's first pairs title since 1982.

'When I'm on the track with Shawn, I know exactly where he is all the time,' said Kelly. 'I think we would be good partners in the best pairs for that reason.'

However, just four days before the final, Shooey crashed at Oxford and sustained a broken angle. He was out of the final. Sam Ermolenko was drafted in at the last minute to replace Shawn for the final in Germany.

Riding Shawn's equipment, which had already been shipped out for the meeting, Sam and Kelly produced a brilliant display to pick off their opponents in the German sunshine. It was the first time that Kelly had ever raced at Pocking and he teamed up with Sam to finish first with Denmark on 46 points (Kelly and Sam both scoring 23). A run-off was required to determine the destiny of the gold and silver medals.

'It was a last minute deal and I had no time to get anything together,' recalled Sam. 'So I just jumped on a plane to get over there and rode Shawn's bikes.

'We didn't realise how close we were to winning it until it came down to the run-off between America and Denmark. I bowed out of it because I thought, it was Shawn's bike and it didn't really suit me that well, and I was just doing my best. Kelly knew his own bike and it was a majority rule that Kelly should go in it.'

Unfortunately, starting has never been Kelly's strong point, and as the Pocking track was by now very slick, it was very important to get a good start. He faced Hans Nielsen, and the Dane made the start and led all the way. Although obviously disappointed not to have taken the gold, both of the Americans were pleased with their performance considering that they hadn't raced together before until the practice the day before the final.

The World Team Cup was also revamped, to be run over a series of three finals. The matches were extended to twenty heats and the placings were decided on a league basis, 3 points for the winners, and 2 points for second and so on. Kelly was unable to take part due to a wrist injury sustained in a Polish hotel, but Shawn produced three good performances; however, America could only finish in

The 1986 World Pairs Final. Kelly is outside his partner, Sam Ermolenko, as they lead the traffic at Pocking, Germany.

second overall, as Denmark won again. The formula was not popular and it was changed again for 1987 by aggregate race points. And although the USA won the round at Coventry, they could not improve on their third place overall.

The Moran brothers finally teamed up together in the 1987 World Pairs semi-final at Norden, Germany, and won the meeting with 49 points (Kelly 26 and Shawn 23).

'They were difficult to race against as a pair because they had a telepathy between them,' explained Billy Hamill. 'Because they knew each other so well they could anticipate each other's moves. Usually it was Shawn on the inside and Kelly on the outside. They would slow their opponents down to allow one or the other to catch up and come through. They were so good that they had it all covered.

But Shawn was uncomfortable with his own form and his machinery by the time the final came round at Pardubice, Czechoslovakia. Once again, Sam stepped in – only this time he had plenty of time to prepare. Unfortunately, the pair struggled a little bit on the big track, but still finished in third place on 36 points (Sam 18 and Kelly 18) behind runners-up England and the winners, Denmark. At one point, Kelly was threatened with exclusion from the meeting because he wasn't at the track four hours before the scheduled start time. Team manager, John Smith and Kelly, carried out a lengthy protest

Shawn leads England's Steve Bastable, while Kelly prepares to make his move during the 1983 England v. USA test at Sheffield.

and he was allowed to take his place but was fined for not being on time.

America lost the test series to England 3-0 in 1986 in a series which was marred by riders being fined and excluded for pulling celebratory wheelies. At Oxford, Simon Wigg was denied a maximum as he celebrated his last race win by entertaining the crowd with a wheelie and was excluded! Luckily, England had already clinched their win.

The following season, the second test was scheduled to take place at Hackney. The Americans' hatred of this track was well known. Kelly once described it in his column as 'the armpit of world speedway.' Both the brothers had sustained serious injuries here, and their fellow countryman, Denny Pyeatt was killed at this track. Bobby Schwartz once walked out of a league meeting there in protest over the state of the surface.

Having lost the first test 55-52 at Ipswich – despite Shooey's 18-point maximum – the stage was set for a night of high drama at the London track. Shawn Moran had taken over as the captain of the USA after being voted in by his team-mates, and his brother had just returned from a serious shoulder injury to take his place in the side paired with his brother. In front of a large audience, they commenced the evening by getting their team off to a flying start with an opening heat 5-1.

But then in the second race a series of falls delayed its completion. Kelly took a heavy fall in his second outing and was excluded. Then, in heat seven, Kelly crashed again, as did England's Jeremy Doncaster. Doncaster described the third bend as like riding on 'black ice'. Shawn laid down his machine to avoid the fallen Doncaster and he found himself immediately backing into the fence. He emerged clutching his ribs and was very shaken.

With England leading 21-19, Shawn told his team manager John Scott to inform the referee, Frank Ebdon, that they had no intention of carrying on. Ebdon ordered the third and fourth bends to be graded, while Shawn began packing up his equipment. As the debates and concerns were aired, the rain began to fall. The crowd became restless and slow handclaps echoed around the stadium as Ebdon finally persuaded Shawn and the American team to continue. The racing resumed as steady drizzle fell, and the conditions deteriorated to such a degree that the meeting had to be abandoned with a result declared as England 34 USA 36.

But the drama was not over yet. In all the confusion of the night's events, Sam Ermolenko forgot to take his drugs test and he was suspended from all British League competition until a tribunal later in the year. They imposed a ban on the American for fifteen months, but common sense eventually prevailed and after a successful appeal he was allowed to resume his British career in 1988.

Kelly, meanwhile, had problems of a different nature. Along with Jeremy Doncaster of England, he too was required to provide a urine sample for a random test. However, according to Frank Ebdon's report, he had to drink gallons and gallons of water to be able to do the necessary. It was nearly 12.30 a.m. before he could finally make his way home.

America lost the third and final test at Sheffield, 59-49, to lose the series 2-1. Shawn scored 10 points and Kelly 9 on their own British League track.

England v. USA, Cradley, 1984. Shawn leads Michael Lee.

1988 was the sport's Diamond Jubilee year and an international tournament was planned that included the top four nations, England, USA, Denmark and Sweden. They would meet each other once in a conventional match and points would be awarded on a league basis – two for a win, and one for a draw. The top two nations would then meet in the Grand Final later in the season.

In an incident-packed match, America defeated an emerging Sweden 47-43 at Swindon – it was their only victory in the tournament. Inconsistent refereeing resulted in Kelly gesticulating angrily at the referee's box as he completed each lap and the race was not stopped when his partner Sam had crashed on the third bend. An almost identical incident in the previous race had seen the referee stop the race and Kelly, expecting the same decision, had slowed up. Shawn also made a gesture at the referee as he came to the start line for the following heat, questioning the official's sanity!

Denmark and England qualified for the final at King's Lynn, which the Danes won as well, 52-38.

Shawn paired up with Ermolenko in the World Pairs championship and qualified for the final by winning their semi-final in Austria. With the final set for Bradford, a track where both riders had experienced a good deal of success, they were among the favourites.

They met the Danes and England in their first race, and Shawn managed a second behind Hans Nielsen, with Sam in fifth. Gundersen finished last and it looked as though it would be a battle between England and the USA. But while the pair remained in the hunt until the last race, Denmark came back to win another gold and the English pairing of Simon Cross and Kelvin Tatum relegated America to third.

'Both of them had a very giving spirit basically as riders,' said Sam. 'There are a few categories: you either get a rider who demands his position on the track to make sure he can succeed, and then you get a rider who will alternate to see how we go between us, or get a rider who'll say, "Look, I've got the ability and the confidence to take whatever there is, you go for what you want." And that was the Morans. There was a lot of conflict between Shawn, Kelly and myself, because we had the same attitude. It was like, "Well, you take what you want," and a lot of the time it meant that it could be quite difficult. But when we did come up with a game plan they were all for it and went with it.

'But with the brothers, you learnt very quickly, whatever they did it doesn't really matter because they were very capable of natural talents. Kelly was very smart, meaning if there was a quiz, he was very knowledgeable on whatever subject there was. Shawn was so happy and lucky. They didn't really care if they didn't have their space, they just went with it,' Sam recalled.

Just prior to the World Team Cup Final, which had now reverted to its original one-off final and was being held in the USA, America staged an American Cup

Captain Shawn points the way during discussions at Swindon in 1988 with Robert Pfetzing, while Randy Green, Sam Ermolenko and Mike Faria look on.

challenge team event against a Rest of the World side. The Americans won both meetings. The first event was a conventional speedway match at Ascot's South Bay stadium, while the second was a long track event at the legendary Ascot half-mile.

'Ascot South Bay was a bit like Costa Mesa with a little bit of banking,' said Kelly. 'We won both events, but I think the other boys were a bit distracted by our trophy girls in their bikinis. I put up Armando Castagna and Kai Niemi and one or two of the others at my sponsor's house and they just loved it. It had a pool, nice weather and a shop down the road to get more beer; they didn't want to go back to England. They had a great time.'

Among the Rest of the World team was Australian Glyn Taylor who was particularly impressed with Kelly's talents. 'I marvelled at what he could do on a bike,' he said, 'he was just lacking professionalism. I raced in America and beat him on the half-mile at Ascot, but I couldn't dream of beating him on the smaller ones. He was outstanding. I think every rider was in awe of how much talent Kelly had.'

Denmark ruled the roost again in the USA when it came to the World Team Cup Final, winning with the following scoreline: Denmark 44, USA 32, Sweden 22, England 22. Kelly struggled to collect 5 points, while Shawn scored 8 as they claimed a silver medal.

However, America's top-scorer, Sam Ermolenko, made his feelings of disillusionment plain in the press conference when he said that things had to change

Shawn and Lance King in the Long Beach pits before the 1988 World Team Cup Final.

within the team for their glory days to return.

America's hopes for 1989 took an early set-back when Shawn was banned from all World Championship events by the AMA when he failed an alcohol test. John Scott suddenly found himself in a situation where he was not able to select his captain for the World Cup or Pairs.

'I am very disappointed,' he said, 'not only for Shawn, but also America. It will be impossible to replace him in our World Team Cup squad, because he was a rider you could rely on to score 13 or 15 points.'

At the time of the final, he had to select a team without Sam Ermolenko who was sidelined with a broken leg, and Kelly was far from fit, having recently returned from a hand injury. It was America's worst display in the competition – finishing on just 8 points – in which Kelly top-scored at Bradford with 6 and provided the team's only race win. England was victorious, but this triumph was overshadowed by one of the blackest days in the history of the sport when an opening race crash saw Erik Gundersen seriously injured. The incident was so bad that all four riders who were involved in the race had to withdraw from the meeting. Gundersen's injuries were so severe that he was forced to retire from the sport.

'It was bad enough reading about it, but it was even worse being there,' recalled Shawn who was in the US pits. 'Poor Erik, but Simon Cross, Lance and Jimmy Nilsen, they all had to withdraw. It was strange that all four riders were out of the meeting like that. But it was bad for Erik and we all felt for him, because we may have been rivals, but we were all friends as well.

'Erik and Hans were the best during my time,' said Shawn. 'They were incredibly fast and they could ride any surface. They were quick from the gate and they could pass you from the back. If you got behind those guys, you just wondered what you could do to get by them.'

The test series against England returned and America lost 2-1, with the third test at Swindon ending in a massive 75-32 defeat. They were ravaged by injuries to Sam, Kelly, Ronnie Correy and Gary Hicks, and despite the valiant efforts of Lance King with 12 points and Shooey scoring 9, they couldn't prevent their biggest defeat in the history of these two nations doing battle. It even surpassed the USA's whopping 72-36 win over England at Ipswich in 1984.

Following their fourth place in the Cup final, the USA found that they were relegated from Group A and had to qualify for the final for the first time since 1984. Kelly seemed to think that it could be just what the team needed to get them to pull together and regain some lost ground. They travelled to Olching, Germany, for the first round, where they also faced the hosts, Sweden and Australia. They had two meetings to decide the single qualifier for the final in Czechoslovakia, and the combined race points would decide the outcome.

Sweden beat America into second place by just one point in the first round, with Kelly scoring 8 points and his brother failing to score. A month later, it was a different story as Shawn turned in an unbeaten performance to lead America into the final with just a three-point lead over Sweden. Kelly scored 6 points.

Craig Cummings was wielding the spanners for Kelly that year and, as he was racing at Belle Vue – a very small track compared with Pardubice – he needed a powerful engine to be on the pace in Czecho.

'I did the engines for him that year,' said Craig. 'But finances were a bit tight and, obviously, the engine he used for Belle Vue was never going to be powerful enough for Pardubice – which is a massive track. So we did a bit of DIY tuning before we left.'

In the final, they faced the holders England, Denmark and the hosts, Czechoslovakia. Ronnie Correy was dropped to make way for the emerging Billy Hamill, who joined Kelly, Shawn, Sam and Rick Miller, in the reserve spot for his first World Final. As captain, it was a decision that Shooey did not like being a part of.

'I didn't like that part of being the captain,' he said. 'I could see that Ronnie just wasn't going to do it, I had that feeling through the qualifying rounds. I don't know why, but he never did well in World Finals. Billy was going good and it was the right decision, but I did feel bad for Ronnie.'

The Americans were faced with some problems when they arrived for the practice at the big Czech circuit, when Shawn Moran's equipment went astray somewhere between Amsterdam and Prague. Meanwhile, Kelly's leathers had not arrived in time for the practice session and he was eventually seen wearing a pair belonging to Ermolenko – the happy-go-lucky Californian admitted that they were roomy!

The day before the World Team Cup final, the FIM staged a special banquet and also provided a cabaret. Craig Cummings recalled an amusing incident. 'Shawn Moran and Rick Miller were two of the funniest guys together, they were hilarious. They were always trying to get one up on each other with practical jokes. Anyway, at this banquet after the practice, they had a magician come round and he took half-a-dozen watches from people for a magic trick. Kelly wasn't there; he had already gone to bed by this time. Hans Zierk (the celebrated German engine tuner) had an expensive Rolex, Shawn had a swatch, a sort of plastic thing. So the magician does his trick, and when they were handing the watches out at the end, Shawn gets the Rolex and says nothing, like no problem, while Hans Zierk gets the last watch – the swatch. Zierk is jumping up and down and shouting, 'This is not my watch!' The magician's panicking, and half the people had left by this time. Meanwhile, Shawn is just playing it off as if he didn't care. They're all panicking about this Rolex watch and Shawn is sitting there with his hand covering his wrist, and he thought it was the funniest thing. Eventually, after about twenty minutes, he got his watch back.'

When the day of the final came around, Shawn had still not received his equipment and he borrowed a set of leathers from one of the juniors. His bikes however, were already at the track as they had been transported ahead by road.

Kelly was in the first race and finished a distant and disappointing fourth and looked well off the pace. 'He was still a little hung-over from the night before, and he went out for his first race and came last,' recalled Hamill. 'He didn't even want to practise and just wanted to party, but Craig made him do it. John Scott was going to pull him out of his next race, but he begged him to give him another chance.'

'He had an absolutely shocking first race,' agreed Cummings, 'and he came in after the race and he looked at me. I wasn't particularly happy because of what had happened the previous evening. And he said, "You think I'm shit, don't you?" And I said, "No. I know you were shit there." And he said, "Just watch this." And he went out and didn't drop another point. He scored 12 points from four starts. He was not even on the pace in the first one, and then all of a sudden he came to life. I think he was the only guy that won a race from the outside gate, and the track is so wide that you've got cover an extra 30 metres or something like that, just to get across everybody into the first corner. But Kelly made it somehow – unbelievable. His talent really shone through there.'

Unusually for Kelly, he was making the starts, which were absolutely necessary on a track which came in for universal criticism from the riders and their team managers for its slick nature. It was Kelly's first race win of the afternoon that put America back in touch with England and Denmark, and kick-started their assault on the World Team title. After a couple of pointless rides from the struggling Miller and Shawn, Kelly appeared again to put his country back in the running with a heat 9 win over Zdenek Tesar, Kelvin Tatum and Tommy Knudsen. Young Billy Hamill, who was brought in as a replacement for the out-of-touch Miller, kept the pressure on with a second place behind Hans Nielsen and Sam won his next race.

At the interval stage, mainly through the efforts of the Moran brothers, the USA held a slender one-point lead over Denmark, who in turn were one point ahead of England.

Shawn won heat thirteen – the first race after the interval – and then Kelly maintained their lead with his third consecutive race win. Czechoslovakia, although not in the running to challenge the top three were proving to be spoilers, as they took vital points from the front runners. With the final four races to come, America were leading with 30 points, England were second with 27; the Danes' challenge, however, had faltered and they were further back on 24 points, and the Czechs were making their presence felt with 15 points.

The Yanks were thrown into a pressure cooker environment, when Billy Hamill finished fourth behind the winner Antonin Kasper of Czechoslovakia, Kelvin Tatum of England and Denmark's John Jorgensen. Then Simon Wigg put England level with the Americans on 30 points, when Shooey was unable to find a way past the twice British Champion.

With just two races remaining, it was a straight fight between the old enemies – England and the USA. Then enter Kelly Moran. He had already proved to be an inspiration, but he was in such a determined mood that his victory in heat nineteen made sure that his country was in the driving seat for the final race. But, crucially, English racer Jeremy Doncaster was back in third. It was left to the comeback man, Sam Ermolenko, to make sure of the gold in the last heat. The Danish number one, Hans Nielsen, made the start to lead, but 'Sudden Sam' slotted into second and clinched the first place for the stars 'n' stripes.

Speedway Mail left no one with any doubts about the hero of the hour with a headline that read: 'Kelly's Heroes.' The Moran brothers were the stars, and they overcame all the obstacles thrown at them to inspire their team to a memorable performance. Kelly finished as the team's top scorer with 12 points; Sam scored 11, Shawn 10, Billy raced to an important 4 points, while Rick Miller struggled in the slick conditions and failed to score. Cummings' 'DIY tuning' certainly did the trick for Kelly, and it wasn't long before his talents with motorcycle engines would attract even more deserving compliments.

'Kelly and Shawn were an inspiration that day,' said Hamill. 'Shawn was wearing borrowed leathers and had to use borrowed equipment because his went missing in transit. No rider wants to do that in a meeting as important as a World Final.'

'It was my comeback year from my leg injury,' recalled Sam, 'and I just went along for the flow. It was one of those things when it was a nightmare of a deal, but it turned out pretty special. I don't remember all the teases in the pits, but Kelly certainly did come alive.'

It was America's first World Team Cup victory since 1982, and Kelly admitted that it had been such a long time coming that he had forgotten the words to the Star Spangled Banner. The Moran brothers were the central part of the USA's first World Team Cup victory, and now, unwittingly, with the likes of Billy Hamill and Greg Hancock making their presence felt at the higher level, they found themselves at the beginning of a new era. But twelve months later, for various reasons, neither Kelly nor Shawn were selected to defend the title.

Kelly partnered 'Rocket' Ronnie Correy in the 1990 World Pairs championship. They were the two in-form riders at selection time, as they were the two highest-placed Americans in the British League averages. For me at least, it seemed a strange combination. There is no doubt that Correy deserved his chance, but he had yet to really prove himself at the highest level, and Kelly was not a good starter. With six riders in a race, I felt that Kelly needed someone who could get in amongst their opponents on the first bend, and make a few holes in the traffic to leave him with a little less to do. At that stage in his career, I don't think Correy possessed the necessary aggression to be able to do that.

Nonetheless, they qualified for the final when they finished in second place behind Denmark's unbeaten pair of Hans Nielsen and Jan O. Pedersen at Prague, Czechoslovakia. They did well and showed great promise for the final, with Correy scoring 24 points and Kelly supporting him with 20 points.

The final, held at Landshut, Germany, was marred by an opening race accident which left England's Simon Cross with serious back injuries. The six riders in a race format was already unpopular with the riders, and it was the last time that this format was ever used. Cross was charging around the outside of the track in a bid to join his fast-starting partner, Kelvin Tatum, at the front. He had already passed Kelly when New Zealander David Bargh appeared to clip Correy's wheel which seemed to nudge the American into the path of Cross, who then took an innocent-looking fall. But the result of this innocuous fall was an ambulance trip,

Shawn and Kelly pictured with the 1990 World Team Trophy. Their performances inspired America to their second World Team success.

and he was out of the meeting with a career-threatening injury.

The following race saw Todd Wiltshire crash when he was brought down by Hans Nielsen, when the Dane made a rare mistake. However, further back in the field, Germany's Gerd Riss had been struck by a stray bike and lay prostrate on the track – another victim of the much-hated six-man formula. Riss was out of the final too, with a broken ankle. Suddenly, England and Germany were left with one rider each.

The Morans had always been excellent sportsmen. When a rider crashed, team-mate or rival, they were always among the first riders on the scene to check on the fallen rider's health. Cross was a friend to both of them, and it angered Kelly to learn that it took an injury of this nature, and the one sustained by Gerd Riss, before the FIM officials finally came to realise what the riders had been telling them all along – six-man races in such a competitive environment as a World Final were just not safe on most tracks.

Correy won the re-run of the opening race, but Kelly was back in fifth. As the meeting unfolded, it was Denmark and the young Australian pair of Wiltshire and Leigh Adams who emerged as the title challengers. Denmark's experience eventually overcame the youthful zest of the Aussie duo and clinched first place with 43 points – just two points ahead of Australia.

America was never in the hunt. They finished in sixth place with 28 points, with Kelly scoring 13 and Correy 15. Kelly never got to terms with the event and failed to even win a race, and when he was in a decent position, Correy was at the back. When they finally seemed to get it together as a pair, it was too late. They never shined together, and one can only wonder what might have been if Shooey was selected to ride in the final with his brother at last?

Sam Ermolenko took over as the new captain of the USA. He was a consummate professional who had overcome serious leg injuries from a Long Track crash in 1989, to reclaim his place as America's number one. However, it was suggested by insiders that his approach to the captaincy was not welcomed by some of the team.

In 1991, Shawn Moran took out an Auto Cycle Union licence so that he no longer had to make costly trips back to the USA. The ACU refused to allow him to race in the England-USA test series, even though the AMA raised no objections. Kelly, meanwhile, was overlooked when it came to defending the World Team Cup in Denmark. The Danes regained the title on their own circuit and the USA slipped back to third – while Kelly swept to a 15 point maximum to win the prestigious Peter Craven Memorial trophy for the second time.

In the England *v.* USA test series, Kelly was unable to appear in the three tests due to family commitments and mechanical difficulties. The USA lost all three matches, but the young and inexperienced side put in worthy performances in all three tests.

Prior to the 1992 season, Kelly Moran announced that he planned to quit international racing as it was proving too costly. However, he had a change of heart and raced for America in the test series against England. In the programme for the first

Shawn Moran and his mechanic, Jimmy Van Dyke, at Swindon in 1988.

test at Belle Vue, he explained the situation: 'I had enough of travelling all over America and Europe to represent my country, only to find it was costing me money. I decided the days of riding for glory and prestige were over,' he said.

Fortunately, John Scott, the USA team's manager and arguably speedway's ultimate English gentleman, persuaded him to reconsider.

'John contacted me and said that they'd like me to reconsider and ride in the test series against England. We had a long chat and I agreed to change my mind, partly because they asked me and partly because there was no international travel involved. But I looked at the test venues, fancied them, and decided to give it another go.'

He went on record to say that the venues chosen, Belle Vue, Wolverhampton and Swindon, were favourites among the American riders. He thought that racing at these tracks would give them a few extra points before the series had even begun.

The first test at Belle Vue saw America take a series lead with a 60-48 victory. Kelly was paired with Bobby Ott and they scored three 5-1s and never lost a heat. Ott scored an 18-point maximum, while Kelly scored a paid 12 points. It seemed that the decision to bring the experienced Moran back was a shrewd move.

'They were the best team riders around,' said Greg Hancock of the Moran brothers. 'They always looked out for you. When you came out of the start you could guarantee that they were gonna take a look for you, and help you out the best they could to slow anyone up who was chasing you.'

The second test at Wolverhampton, the home track of Ermolenko and Ronnie Correy, saw them clinch the series with a 61-47 victory. It was a solid display from the team, but Kelly was off the pace and failed to score. He struggled with his bikes and was replaced by reserves, Charles Ermolenko and Josh Larsen, after his second ride.

Greg Hancock and his buddy, Billy Hamill, produced a brilliant display of team-riding at Wolverhampton that was likened to the Bruce Penhall/Bobby Schwartz partnership of the early 1980s. Hancock travelled with Kelly to Swindon for the final test, and the ever-cheerful Kelly left a lasting impression on Greg.

'One time, driving in the van, I picked Kelly up from somewhere and we were driving down to Swindon,' he recalled. 'I remember we were coming over a hill and the sun was glaring right at us. It was quite a nice, warm day, but there were so many bugs and stuff on the windows. I remember coming over the hill and not being able to see because of the bugs and stuff. So I cleaned the window with the windscreen wipers and, of course, it smeared a whole bunch. And I remember Kelly said: 'You're no F1 driver are you? You don't clean the windscreen when you're coming over the hill so fast with the sun in your eyes. You just don't do that.' That's something I've never forgot, so every time I clean my windows I think of Kelly.'

With the series wrapped up, England travelled to Swindon in a bid to prevent a whitewash. Sam was not scheduled to appear as he had commitments in Europe, and the captaincy was handed over to Kelly. However, the English management were not happy when Ermolenko arrived at the stadium hoping to ride, as he was unable to travel to his meeting in Poland because of an aircraft malfunction. They became even more irate, when they were told that he would be riding at reserve! This meant that he could be called upon to race at anytime during the match.

Sam's brother, Charles, took a heavy tumble in his opening race and was forced to withdraw. Therefore, Sam appeared to take his place in the team. Without Hamill as well, England put on a battling display but eventually the Americans saw off their challenge and won the encounter 58-50.

As captain, and on his home track, Kelly put in a lot effort but managed just 3 points. Often he looked down on power, but he did feature in some important races with his partner Hancock which contributed to the team's success. It was a great honour for Kelly to walk up as captain of his country to collect the silverware for a test match win and another series victory. In many ways, it was justified that the man they called the 'Jelly Man', the 'Wizard of Balance,' could have the honour of being the captain of his country. After all, before Ermolenko, Hamill and Hancock, on a bleak wet afternoon in Reading, it had been little Kelly with that race win over Gordon Kennett in 1979 who had started his country on their way to international stardom.

'I didn't really think I deserved it,' said Kelly modestly. 'I don't know how it came about. I guess it was because I was racing for Swindon at the time, and they thought that I would know where all the bumps were and all that kind of stuff. But, yeah, it was nice to go up and receive the silver plate for winning the test series. I remember a few of us, including some of the English boys, went to a Mexican restaurant that I found after the meeting and we had a great time.'

That was the last time Kelly raced for his country, as the USA regained the World Team Cup in Sweden that year. A new generation of American riders were emerging, and 'Sudden' Sam was hitting the best form of his distinguished career. A new chapter in the history of American speedway had begun.

Just as it seemed that the name Moran would not be seen in an American race-jacket again, Shawn was set to appear for the USA side in the 1993 test series against England. Once again it was the US manager, John Scott, who displayed all the diplomatic skills of a seasoned politician, to pave the way for Shooey to make a return to the American team.

The USA were weakened by the serious injury to Ronnie Correy and Scott had hoped to use the former US captain in the international side. However, as Shawn was still riding on an ACU licence and not an AMA permit, the Speedway Control Board manager, John Eglese, ruled that Shawn was not eligible to race. The AMA chief, Bill Boyce, had already told Scott that as far as the authorities in America were concerned, Shawn could indeed appear for the USA again. Therefore, John Scott took his case to the FIM, where CCP secretary Anthony Ruberecht overruled the SCB and Moran was free to ride.

At first he was just lined up to ride at the first test at Sheffield, where he had enjoyed so many successful seasons. There was talk of him possibly making a shock return to the World Team Cup squad as well, but this was just the press

John Cook (left) and Billy Hamill pictured with Shawn at the England v. USA test at Wolverhampton in 1993.

rumour mill working overtime.

Shawn admitted that he was in two minds whether to ride because of the previous problems he had had with the AMA. But he said that he 'didn't want to let anyone down.' Sheffield was now competing in what was now called Division Two, so top flight-action was thin on the ground. But the prospect of Shawn Moran making a return to the track where he made his name in a stars 'n' stripes race jacket left the Tigers fans eager with anticipation.

Unfortunately, the match was a victim of Britain's infamous wet weather and his return to Sheffield in international racing was postponed. America retained the World Team Cup at Coventry, when the recently-crowned World Champion, Sam Ermolenko, clinched the title with a final-heat victory.

The first test was now at Arena Essex and the confident Americans defeated England 65-43. Shooey's vehicle broke down en route to the track and he was unable to take his place in the team. The USA, already without Correy, then found that Greg Hancock was ruled out for the rest of the season when he dislocated his elbow.

There was something of an 'old boys' feel about the team that assembled at Wolverhampton for the second match, when Bobby 'Boogaloo' Schwartz flew in from California to help his fellow countrymen. John Cook, who had returned to

British League racing with Poole, also turned out for the team with Shooey. America took an unassailable 2-0 lead in the series when they beat England 58-50. Shawn scored 3 points, which included a paid win in his first outing behind his team-mate, Billy Hamill. The star of the show, however, was undoubtedly 'Cowboy' Cook, who rolled back the years with Schwartz to score 10 points.

The final test was at Sheffield. Schwartz had returned home and Josh Larsen was able to take his place in the final test. America took the lead in the opening heat, but England kept on the pressure throughout the match. Local interest in the match had been good, but Shawn had only scored 1 point from his five starts when he lined up alongside team-mate Larsen, and the English pairing of Simon Cross and Joe Screen, for a last-heat decider. America held a 2-point lead and needed just three points from the last race to secure another win.

Shawn climbed aboard Sam Ermolenko's bike and made his way to the tapes for the final race. Screen and Cross sped out of the gate and the English camp began to celebrate, but Shawn had other ideas. In typical vintage style, he inched by Cross and then picked off Screen and secured the win for America. Shooey had done it. He was a hero for his country again.

That was Shawn Moran's last international race for the USA and he ended his international career in thrilling style. Happily, it ended with him doing what he was always remembered for at the track which was his spiritual racing home: coming through when it mattered, to the delight of the Steel City public.

The likes of Hamill, Hancock, Larsen, and latterly, Chris Manchester, were the new generation of racers who were inspired by the exploits in American race-jackets of the Moran brothers. They had helped put the USA on the international map with their unique and talented style, which ensured that they would never be forgotten.

'They were an inspiration,' agreed Hancock. 'I got to spend some time with them in test matches and stuff, and that was great because they were tremendous team guys. They were some of the best in the sport and you couldn't really beat what they could do. They were so approachable and easy to talk to and they were always there to offer support and always tried to show you the light at the end of the tunnel.'

5

HAVE BIKE, WILL TRAVEL

Life at the top as an international speedway rider is very hectic. As well as racing for a team in the British League, the successful racer can expect to be called upon to race for his country, as well as pursue his own World Championship dreams. They usually accept very lucrative offers to race in open meetings on the European continent and, sometimes, the successful star will race in either, or both, of the Swedish and Polish Leagues. The conventional speedway season runs from late March to late October, but it is quite possible to race all year round.

Australia, New Zealand and South Africa, run their season during Europe's close season, and many of the world's top stars travel to these countries to race. Not only is it a way of earning extra money, but it also keeps the rider race fit and, hopefully, it has a positive effect when they arrive at the tapes for the start of a new campaign in March.

Some riders have travelled to Argentina to race in the close season, while in the late 1970s there was also some racing for the top riders in Kuwait. However, it is usually to the countries in the southern hemisphere that the top stars travel.

Australia and New Zealand have a proud history in speedway racing. It was in Australia where the sport first began to flourish, and when Britain began staging their own racing, the Aussies travelled half-way round the world to show the Poms how it was done. The Kiwis have provided some of the world's most famous riders: Mauger, Briggs, and Ronnie Moore are just a few of the names that have left a big impression on the sport.

Test series between Australia and a touring team from England were common-place, but the Anzacs often faced a Rest of the World side as well. The visiting foreigners might have been just enjoying themselves, but to the local boys it was just as serious as any racing in Europe. They had state and national championships to race for and, on occasion, there was team racing too.

Shawn Moran made his first trip to Australia in the winter of 1980/81, and was the reigning US Long Track Champion when he joined Bobby Schwartz, Dennis Sigalos, John Cook and Denny Pyeatt down under. He had just completed his first full season of British League racing and rode in an American team.

The competition was a Tri-Nations tournament that saw the Yanks face the Aussies and a team from England. However, it had been hoped that the 7-match series would be run as an official test series event, but the governing bodies would not sanction its status. England won the series, but America's best performance came in the second match when they lost to the host nation by just one point.

Shooey experienced his best display when he finished with 9 points. He raced in individual events too, and although he didn't bring home any silverware on his first visit, he showed a lot of promise.

'It was so hot,' Shooey recalled. 'Poor Michael [Lee, England international] passed out with the heat. He was even whiter than usual! It didn't matter if you were from California or not, with all your leathers on it was really hot.'

Australia has a reputation for running speedway meetings on very big tracks. Claremont is especially big as the track is also used for car racing. But while not all the tracks are as big as Claremont, one wouldn't see any tracks the size of the ones in California. It was also common that speedway would form one part of a programme of events, which would also include cars, and sidecar racing.

Shawn was far more experienced when he made his second trip to Oz, and was based at Adelaide. He scored 12 points for a combined Australia/USA team that lost 55-53 to a touring England test team, and then followed that performance by finishing third behind John Boulger and Robert Maxfield, in the South Australian Solo Championship. He teamed up with Boulger to ride in a special best pairs at Adelaide's Speedway Park, but finished second behind the Bruce Penhall and Bobby Schwartz partnership. Shooey scored 14 points and was only defeated by Phil Crump. Boulger scored 5 points for a combined total of 19 points which left them 3 points adrift of the winning pair. Once again, he was joined on the trip by John Cook and Denny Pyeatt.

While he was wintering in Australia, Shawn was often based at Adelaide and would stay with Suzanne O'Malley, who was the race director of Speedway Park. 'He stayed with me on most of his trips into Adelaide,' she said. 'He was always with a mechanic and there were occasions when I had up to twelve of them, Danes, Swedes, English, Americans, Poles you name it, they have been here. But Shawn and Bruce [Penhall] were among my favourites.

'It always amused me that everyone thought he was a 'party animal', but he and I had many quiet moments over a home-cooked roast and a good Aussie wine – he was one of the few that bothered to return the favour when he had the time. Sure I would usually pass him on the way in when I was on my way out (to work) and there were times when he could be with me for a week and I would only see him racing or at an airport (arriving) and again when he left. But one thing about Shawn, he was never any trouble, would always oblige if anyone wanted autographs and was nothing but a thorough gentleman whenever I took him into my own personal circle of friends.'

During his third trip to Australia in the winter of 1982/83, he joined his fellow countryman, Dave DeTemple. DeTemple was a unique rider as he raced with a false leg, but his handicap didn't appear to detract from his ability on a bike. He attracted the attention of British League bosses, but despite being linked with many clubs, he never signed for any of them. Nonetheless, he was a high-spirited individual. On one occasion he joined Shooey in a restaurant in Adelaide, and turned round his false leg and asked people to tie his shoelaces! Another party trick of his was to stick a fork into his leg and then ask someone to take it out … no one ever did!

In an article published in *Speedway Mail*, Shawn recounted an embarrassing moment when the duo was travelling to a meeting together. 'We were driving along in a car with a trailer and two bikes on the back, and suddenly I went round the bend too fast and the trailer came right round, hit the side of the car, dented it, and then sent Dave's bike flyin' across the road! The police came and gave me a bit of aggravation about the whole thing. That was really embarrassing because it was Dave's bike and not mine.'

On another journey with DeTemple, the pair ran out fuel in the middle of the night and were miles from anywhere. They decided to take their bikes off the trailer and ride for three miles to the nearest town. 'We couldn't see each other at all, so what we agreed to do was to drag our footrests on the road so it would set off sparks. When we got to the nearest town, the police couldn't believe it. There we were with no licences, no lights and no brakes, and they let us off!' said Shawn.

However, in his first meeting at Adelaide for his 82-83 campaign, Shawn crashed in his first race. But in the handicap final, he came off the 60-metre line to pass the field and rounded Steve Baker to win the final with inches to spare. In the South Australian Championship, he finished in fifth place with 11 points, behind his Sheffield team-mates Mark Fiora and Baker, with DeTemple in third with 13-points. He was unbeaten in the qualifying races in the Mildura Masters Solo Championship, but lost the sudden death final to local favourite Phil Crump.

A broken leg prevented Shooey from his usual winter trip in 1983/84, but he returned in 1984/85. However, a slightly different schedule was planned as he intended to go to New Zealand as well. But he was denied the chance to race there by his national governing body, the American Motorcycle Association. The AMA advised Moran and his fellow countrymen, Bobby Schwartz and Rick Miller, not to ride in a meeting scheduled for Western Springs, as the New Zealand Auto Cycle Union (NZAU) had informed the AMA that the Springs were running a 'black' track. An administration dispute had arisen between the NZAU and a new organisation, the SCB. Both the AMA and the NZAU were affiliated with the FIM, so if the riders did compete there then they could have jeopardised their own World Championship hopes. Therefore, despite waiting to see if the dispute could be resolved and whether they could race in the planned meetings, the American trio went home without turning a wheel in the 'land of the long white cloud'.

Shawn joined a tour organised by ex-rider Nigel Boocock for the winter of 1985/86. He had just come off his best season ever in Europe, and it showed when he got off to a blistering start. On a massive 630-metre track at Claremont, Perth, he powered away to win the Grand Final after Mick McKeon had fallen. On a smaller 380-metre circuit at Bibra Lake, about 15 miles away from the Perth city centre, he produced a performance that showed the Aussie public why he was called the 'Miracle Worker'. He had won all of his qualifying heats when he lined up in the final against Glyn Taylor, John Jorgensen, and Glenn Doyle. For three laps, it looked as though Taylor would win from the Dane, Jorgensen, who had passed Moran for second place. But then Shooey dived through on the inside of the leading pair to take the honours on the final lap.

Shawn concentrates while he waits for the tapes to rise for another race.

Returning to Claremont, Shawn broke the track record twice as he won the CIG All-Nations Solo Cup with 30 points. Rick Miller was his closest rival in second on 26 points. His unbeaten run was ended at the Speedway Park, Adelaide, by his Tigers team-mate, Peter Carr. But he was at it again in New South Wales, when he took the honours at Broken Hill with a victory in the six-lap final.

Once more, the heat was causing problems for the some of the party. 'We all went to the beach,' said Shawn, 'and Peter Glanz got really bad sunburn. He had something like first degree burns, which was like fire burns you know? God they were bad. When he was fit enough to race, in his first race, at the start, he looped at the gate and landed heavily. It's always a shock when that kind of thing happens, because those bikes are real fast, and it dragged him a bit. He had his leathers on and his skin, which was already peeling, well it was raw after that. Oh God, that must have been painful.

'Mitch Shirra tipped over a go-kart and tore a lot of skin off his arm. We often used to go to the go-kart track when we were racing in Vojens (Denmark), but he did this in Australia. Well you can imagine how painful this could be when you've got your leathers on. Well, his father, Tom – great guy – he made up this medication to put on his arm so he could race, and that was really clever. I don't know what it was, but that was kind of neat.'

After a break of two weeks, the Australians couldn't believe it as the Moran magic continued when he won an individual meeting at Mildura with 14 points – dropping one point to Miller. He broke the track record and also smashed the one-lap record twice. He also blitzed the field at Murray Bridge with a 15-point maximum to win the meeting. In the final, Jorgensen seemed to be heading for a win when Shawn stormed past the Dane on the last corner to take the chequered flag. On Boxing Day night, Shawn won at Newcastle in the Coca Cola International and lowered the track record in the process, as he came from the back to defeat Carr, Mitch Shirra, Miller, Chris Watson and Sean Willmott. Aussie journalist Peter White said of Moran's stunning displays: 'He was far and away the classiest rider on show.'

Shawn top-scored with 18 points to lead a Rest of the World team to an 83-37 victory over Queensland. In an official test against Australia at Brisbane, Shawn scored 11 points as the Rest of the World team turned over the Aussies 58-50. At the Inter Nations Cup, however, Shooey's devastating run of form came to an end when he finished at the back in the final which was won by Denmark's Peter Ravn.

But this seemed to be only a blip as he then won the 10-lap Coca Cola Solo Masters at Liverpool, and was top again as he won the Mildura Masters with a maximum and took both the four and one-lap records. He finished his most successful tour with a cut foot as a result of chain coming loose, and then blew his engine in his last meeting. But there was no doubt that Shawn Moran had wooed the audiences all over Australia with a series of devastating displays. Nigel Boocock began to plan his next tour and Shooey was at the top of his list of riders he wanted to bring back with him.

'It sure beat staying at home for the winter,' said Shawn in his column in

The great Ivan Mauger gives Shawn some advice during a practice session at Sheffield in 1984.

Speedway Mail. 'Racing for twelve months of the year doesn't really bother me. It was a really good tour, plenty of racing and loads of sunshine – what more could an all-American boy ask for?'

Kelly was due to join his brother in Australia for the 1986/87 tour with the Boocock touring party, but a dreadful hotel accident, which left him with severed arteries in his wrist, ended his hopes of racing down under.

The tour got off to a controversial start, when the boss of the Speedway Park at Adelaide cancelled their meeting for 6 December because they had appeared at the rival circuit, North Arm, a week before they were scheduled to race at the Park. Happily, the promoters at North Arm re-booked the troupe, which included Kelvin Tatum, Phil Collins, Rick Miller, Valentino Furlanetto, and Andrew Silver. It was at Murray Bridge, during a weekend off, that Shawn had a taste of four-wheel racing.

'Phil Collins and myself took part in a stock-car race at Murray Bridge,' he revealed. 'We had to start at the back because we never had the necessary qualifications, and we took part in the qualifiers. We had a 10-lap race in one direction and then another in the opposite direction. I can't remember if Phil got to the final but I did, and I finished in 3rd or 4th place. It was a lot of fun and I think I would have liked to have done some more car racing, especially toward the end of my career on motorcycles.'

A violent storm which caused structural damage in Adelaide forced the postponement of their racing engagement in Adelaide. Although it was a largely successful tour, Shawn couldn't repeat his domination of the previous tours. However, he did break the track record at North Arm, and he made a few visits to the podiums at various venues. However, he does recall a frightening incident with the local wildlife when he was travelling with Kelvin Tatum and Darren Boocock.

'We were stuck in traffic, so I pulled the sun visor down and there was this monster spider! Oh God it was big! I have never seen Kelvin run so fast in my life. I just managed to creep out of the car without disturbing it. I thought the thing would fall on me. But Darren eventually got the thing out, but that was a shock for sure.'

It was planned that both Kelly and Shawn would race in South Africa in early 1988, but Shooey preferred to spend his time in Australia and decided not to go. Early in the tour, Shawn won an individual at Broken Hill, but his racing engagements were few when compared to previous years. However, the former Cradley Heath and Leicester rider John McNeil successfully managed to stage an Australia *v.* the Rest of the World match at the Parramatta City Raceway, Sydney, which the Aussies won 60-48. Shawn led the scoring for the ROW with 15 points.

Meanwhile, Kelly had a full programme of racing in South Africa. The country was often in the news in those days as this was the time of the hated apartheid movement. Peter Murray ran the shows at Corobrik, while Buddy Fuller looked after things in Durban.

'I loved it out there,' said Kelly. 'I never saw any of the trouble that we were always hearing about at that time. If I could, I'd liked to have settled there. We had a great time and the promoters there put on a good show –

The spectacular style of Kelly Moran thrilled crowds all over the world.

and the beer was cheap too!'

Along with Kelly in Africa were fellow Americans, Rick Miller and Randy Green, plus BL Stars, Marvyn Cox, Rob Tilbury, Robbie Fuller, Kelvin and Neville Tatum and Charlie McKinna. They took part in a Champion Spark Plugs International Series. They raced at two venues, Corobrik, Johannesburg and King's Park, Durban, and these two tracks required different set-ups as Marvyn Cox explained: 'We used to race on the Friday at Corobrik, Johannesburg, and then on the Saturday at Durban. It was very different at Johannesburg because it was two and half thousand feet above sea level, and it took a long time to get the bike set up properly because of the altitude. Any vehicle in that area, whether it was a car, bike, or anything, didn't run so smooth. So we had to change everything: different jets, carburettor set ups, and run the bikes leaner, a hell of a lot leaner in fact. But the altitude didn't affect the racing. When we used to drive to Durban – which was a six-hour drive – the cars used to get faster and faster. So we had to change everything.'

Kelly was third in the Natal International Challenge with 13 points behind Miller and Kelvin Tatum. The African public saw the track record lowered three times, by Tatum, Kelly and finally, Miller. Then they were showed the ability that Moran possessed which had thrilled the crowds all around the world.

He needed to win his last race to force a run-off with Miller and Tatum, when he fell on the first bend. When he remounted, Miller had nearly completed a lap, while local rider, Nic Floyd was going round the third and fourth bends. Kelly reached some very high speeds and he managed to catch Floyd and pass him on the last corner to take second place.

When Kelly loaned his bike to Randy Green to practise – as his own hadn't arrived – the 'Jelly Man' found he had to borrow machinery as Green seized the engine. This undoubtedly affected his chances in the series, as he had to wait a little while to get a replacement. When he was finally back on his own equipment, he led his team, 'Kelly Moran's Team,' to a four-team tournament victory with a 12-point maximum at Durban.

He again thrilled the crowd in a race described as one of the best ever seen in South Africa. He lined up against Miller and Kelvin Tatum, who were also unbeaten, and the local rider and former BL star, Denzil Kent. The trio from overseas swapped the lead on several occasions until Moran took command. Cox, Alan Simpson and Wayne Couglan were the other members of Kelly's successful team which won the tournament by just one point over Kelvin Tatum's side.

Kelly seemed to go particularly well around the Corobrik track and he shattered the track record on his way to 10 points in another four-team event. Kelly eventually finished third in the individual series with 56 points, behind winner Miller (67 points) and Kelvin Tatum (66 points). His mechanical problems certainly prevented him from making a more serious challenge on the honours. However, Cox recalled a particularly memorable moment: 'He used to share a room with Rob Tilbury. Kelly once said to Rob, "you're never gonna beat me," and Rob said, "I'll beat you before the tour is finished." Kelly said, "even if I have a 30-metre handicap, I could still beat you." Rob said no way – so they had a bet on it. It was at Durban; and when Kelly went up to the line he deliberately touched the tapes so that he would be handicapped the 30 metres. Then he got 3rd, 2nd, and then on the last corner he went round Rob and passed him and beat him. That stood out a mile. He'd said he'd do it, and the following meeting he'd done it and done him up well. He just wanted to prove a point. It wasn't for much money, maybe £5 or £10, but it showed how good a class of rider he was. To come back from 30 metres to win a race – that was pure determination. He was magical, brilliant, he was doing wheelies and coming from behind – he was very good out there.'

However, in between all the racing, the troupe had the opportunity to see the sights of one of the world's most colourful countries. 'We went to the Kruger National Park for a safari,' recalled Kelly. 'We saw all the animals, rhinos, hippos and all that kind of thing. I watch all the nature programmes, and some of the guys were wandering around taking photos, but I stayed in the van – it can be pretty dangerous out there, you know? On one occasion there was this family of baboons and one of them yawned and those front teeth of his were pretty scary. We had all the windows open because it was so hot, and some of the guys threw cookies out for the monkeys, and I suddenly thought, what would we do if one of them got in here? All jump out?'

'Anyway, Kelvin is with me and "Turbo" Tilbury and a few others and we come across this herd of elephants. A car had passed us in the opposite direction, but we didn't think anything of it, because we're all having a good time. I did think he was being silly going so fast. Well, I later found out that that car had upset one of the bull elephants, so when we turned up the elephant was upset and headed straight for us. Well, the guys all panicked and I slammed it in reverse and got outta of there. "Turbo"s' saying, "come on Jelly Man, let's get outta here," so I did. It was a bit scary there for a little while.'

The riders played down the incident, but Tatum would later admit that he was more terrified with Kelly driving in reverse at such a high speed than the angry elephant that eventually turned his attentions elsewhere. They also toured some of the gold mines too which, although Kelly found them interesting, were far less dramatic for them.

Kelly Moran was very popular in South Africa, and *Speedway Mail* carried a photo of one of the banners out there which read: 'The Pocket Rocket, the Jelly Man. If anyone can, the Jelly Man can – Kelly Moran.'

He returned there in 1989, but after winning the first round at Corobrik with a 15-point maximum, he crashed and broke his collarbone. Racing in a pair's event, he locked up in front of David Steen, who was unable to avoid the American and took him down. He missed most of the tour through the injury; but did make a return for the final round.

It was a problematic time for Shooey too. While at home, Shawn leant over to pat a dog, which for some reason lunged at Shooey and tore open his bottom lip. He was rushed to hospital, where stitches were required to close the wound.

Nevertheless, he made his usual winter trip to Australia and raced for the Rest of the World side that defeated the Aussies 45-33. He also finished runner-up to Sam Ermolenko in an individual meeting at Renmark. But he had his revenge on his fellow countryman at the West End Solo Championship at Adelaide, winning the meeting ahead of Simon Wigg and Ermolenko in the fastest time of the night.

Just as there are differences racing in Africa, so it was in Australia too. 'At one stage we had to fit these really big mufflers to the silencers,' recalled Shooey. 'We used to call them suitcases, because they were like mini suitcases when they were fitted to your bike. When you'd put the bike on the stand, if it wasn't balanced right, the weight would make them topple over!'

Kelly finally joined his brother in Australia for the 1989/90 season, where he was due to appear in the Phil Crump Testimonial meeting. Other Americans had also made the trip over earlier in the season, such as Mike Faria and Steve Lucero, while Billy Hamill also took advantage of some close-season racing in readiness for his first British League season commencing in March 1990.

Shooey won the Australian Masters at Mildura, with Hamill finishing runner-up. Kelly appeared with his brother in a scaled-down Australia *v.* the Rest of the World match at Melbourne and he scored 6 points from three rides, with his younger brother scoring one more point. Kelly's best individual performance was a fourth place at the Newcastle International Trackmasters, which was won by the Aussie favourite, Mick Poole. Despite a fourth place with 14 points in the qualifying heats in the West End International at Adelaide, he failed to transfer from the semi-finals and missed the sudden death final, which was won by Hans Nielsen.

'What I remember most was that everything was so far away,' Kelly recalled. 'I mean travelling by road from one venue to another, well it made travelling from track to track in England look like a walk down to a local store!'

However, for the 1990/91 close season, Kelly headed back to Africa where he won the Transvaal Open Championship at Germiston with 13 points, after he defeated England's Richard Knight in a run-off. Once again, he provided some spectacular racing and was joined in the series by future World Champion, Mark Loram.

'The idea was to go out there and put on a good show for the locals,' said Kelly. 'It was by no means a Mickey Mouse show, and there was a lot of endeavour and talent out there.'

A ban imposed by the FIM prevented Shawn from racing down under during that close season, but a combination of injury and impending retirements meant that neither would thrill the crowds during Europe's traditional close season again. Their spectacular style of racing, crowd-pleasing nature and their always approachable and polite manner, were a big hit with the crowds. They left these places with happy memories, and the audiences were left with the thrills of seeing two of the most charismatic and entertaining riders of their era.

6

AN OCEAN APART

Kelly's decision to remain and compete in the USA for 1983 may have been greeted with dismay by British League supporters, but in California his homecoming was greeted with enthusiasm and viewed as a massive boost to US Speedway racing.

John F. LaDouceur, the promoter of the San Bernardino track, said: 'I think with his talent and crowd pleasing style of riding; he will bring more people to our track.'

Following the success of the 1982 World Final which was held at Los Angeles, speedway racing in the USA was attracting more interest than ever before. Having lost America's golden boy, Bruce Penhall, to the television cop show *Chips*, Kelly's charismatic persona was looked upon as an ideal crowd-puller.

It was at the beginning of the new speedway season, that a new speedway magazine was launched in the USA, simply titled *Speedway Magazine*. The publishers chose to emphasise the big news of the return of the 'Wizard of Balance', and it was Kelly who appeared on the front cover of the first issue. The photographer Jim Brown used three different cameras to capture a special action shot of Kelly, which was then blended into a blue sky to make him look as though he was flying through the air.

'They wanted me to hang off the bike like I used to do when I was racing,' Kelly recalled. 'But I couldn't do that for them because it was something that I did naturally when I was racing. You know, it was the racing situation that I was in which caused me to do that. I tried to explain it to them that it wasn't something that I could just do. But they kept on saying, 'Oh no, you gotta do the hanging off the bike thing, it'll be great.' So I think I did about four or five laps for them, and then I got bored. But I think they got what they wanted and I had a nice meal afterwards. It was neat to be on the cover.'

He also had his own column in the magazine, titled *Kelly's Kolumn*, which gave the diminutive star a vehicle to air his views on the stories and races that mattered in the world of speedway.

There were several changes to the Moran brothers' programme for the new season, the most notable of which was a major sponsorship arrangement with the motor vehicle products specialists, STP International.

'STP actually approached me, through KK and Kenny Best,' revealed Kelly. 'They had been dealing with Alan Christian and they approached us about getting involved. As we were racing in the British League, I think they kind of liked the idea of international exposure. But STP, Uno, Arai and all the others, these sponsors were all set up by KK and Kenny.'

The Morans wore distinctive red STP leathers and Rick Salvino looked after the sponsorship in the USA, while Nigel Tubb was the man responsible for their European exposure.

'Up until this point, all speedway sponsorship had been a product-based deal,' explained Tubb. 'But the decision was made to sponsor the Morans on a cash sponsorship, a healthy retainer if you like. It was a world-wide agreement and the first of its kind in the sport. It was ahead of its time, and we had the 'Team STP' concept going ten years or so before the 'Team Exide' thing which was so successful a few years ago with Billy Hamill and Greg Hancock. I know that if we did it now, we would be in the Grand Prix series as 'Team STP'.

Craig Cummings agreed that it was a good deal and product. 'It was a very good sponsorship for both of them; because I don't think there was any sponsorship in the sport like that at the time. They got a reasonable amount of money, not a huge amount, but a sizeable amount. All their leathers were paid for, plus all of the product that we could use and it was a good product too. That was good for the sport as well, as all through that time there was hardly a major sponsor in speedway.'

There was no doubt that they were very grateful for the sponsorship with STP, and they would later be joined by Lance King. Kelly expressed his gratitude in his column and as Nigel Tubb revealed, their arrangement with them was a massive success. 'They were very marketable,' said Tubb. 'They were unique. Not only were they brothers, but they were both very successful riders. It wasn't that one of them was good and the other was average, both of them could win titles left, right and centre. They were excellent ambassadors for the sport and the product. You could take them to meet anyone: from the managing director down to the humble fan. It didn't make any difference, they were always a pleasure to deal with, friendly, humorous, and Kelly could charm the birds out of the trees.

'Once the other riders saw that the Morans were using the product and winning races, they also wanted to use it too. For example, we had a product called AP75, which was our equivalent of WD40, and the riders found that it was significantly better. So STP's reputation on the speedway scene grew. Very soon the various parts wagons around the tracks carried STP's products. Yes, it was a great success and interest in the company was phenomenal.'

But this was not the only change for Kelly, as he set about making a fresh approach to his racing for 1983. He switched from Weslake engines to Godden, and he set his sights on what he wanted to achieve in 1983, as he revealed in his column: 'Talk about winning, what do you think about my kid brother being National Champ? Sorry Shawn, but the next one's mine. I am so excited about '83, I am also riding a Godden for Jim Busby. Shawn and Christian are going so well,' he observed. 'I feel the change at this stage in my career could give me a tremendous boost to my World Championship hopes.'

Both the brothers began the new season by appearing in the US Spring Classic Championship, but it proved to be less than successful for the flamboyant duo. Shooey was in stunning form in the first meeting at Costa Mesa, which he won with an unbeaten score. However, at the second round at San Bernardino, he held a comfortable lead over Bobby Schwartz when he suddenly caught some drive and his front wheel reared up. He was unable to get away from his bike and he was sent, shoulder first, into the crash wall. He had sustained a broken right arm, and a visit to Dr Carlo Biagi was a priority if he was going to be able to ride in the 1983 England *v.* USA test series.

The two round Spring Classic series was won by John Cook on 25 points, and Shawn finished runner-up with 21 points. Kelly, though, struggled in both meetings, with his best performance coming at San Berdoo as he finished way down the field on 10 points. It has to be remembered that Kelly had only spent one full season racing in California, before he headed to the British League.

'The transition from European quarter-mile tracks to the American tracks is such a difficult task, and I guess it showed during the classics. But be patient, I have adjusted to the Godden and have practised as much as possible. I feel confident that you will see my European form very shortly,' he wrote.

Shawn Moran had a plate inserted into his arm and was able to race for Sheffield on 7 April – halving the normal recovery time from six weeks to just three. But his delayed start to the season meant that he had to forfeit his place as the Golden Helmet Match Race Champion. He was the winter holder, but due to the injury he

Sheffield v. Reading 1983. Shawn is on the inside gates alongside Bobby Schwartz (Reading), Reg Wilson and Pierre Brannefors (Reading).

was unable to defend the helmet against Dennis Sigalos. Instead, Siggy and Kenny Carter went head to head for the title – which the latter won.

However, the helmet and some equipment valued at £3,000 were stolen from the premises of Shooey's sponsors shortly before the tapes went up on the new season. Maurice Ducker, who sponsored Moran through his company 'A&E Transport', immediately put out a reward of £1,000 for information leading to the recovery of the helmet. All things considered, it was not a good start to the new season for Shawn.

In his column, *Go For It*, which appeared in the weekly Sheffield programme, he revealed some of the problems he was having with his arm. 'It's sure going to take a few meetings before my arm is fully fit. I had a practice at Scunthorpe and it ached afterwards, and most nights I've woken with pain. It hurt real bad during last week's match with Leicester [his first match of the season when he scored 10-points in their 42-36 win] and I decided it was best not to race in the second half. There's nothing I can do, but hope that time will see a continual improvement.'

Kelly had little time to really settle on the Californian circuits before he packed his bags and headed to England to ride for his country in both the test series and the World Team Cup qualifying round. When it was announced that he would be flying in to compete, Eastbourne were reported to have considered applying for a ban to prevent him from racing in Britain. Bob Dugard, who was still hopeful that Ron Preston would eventually return to ride for the Eagles, was still upset at Kelly's decision to remain at home.

Happily, he did race in England, and it was reported that the rift between Dugard and Moran was resolved. But throughout the season, much to Kelly's annoyance, the sport's press continued to speculate about his plans for 1984.

Sheffield also spent the opening weeks of the season playing the waiting game: not only for Shawn, but for the Kiwi, Wayne Brown. He had delayed his return from New Zealand because of business interests, but eventually it was clear that he would not be returning. The Tigers were facing an uphill struggle from the beginning.

In America, Kelly won his first scratch main at Costa Mesa on 20 May. He did it in typically spectacular fashion by passing Mike Bast on the inside. 'After winning the main at Costa Mesa, I knew all the hard work, uncertainty and verbal abuse from Europe was worth it all,' he wrote in his column. 'To win my first scratch main of the season at Costa Mesa was a great feeling. Even though I started out here in 1977, it still changes you a lot when you race in Europe on the big tracks for five years. Every time I came home, I felt like a Third Division rider. I couldn't ride the small tracks.'

This was followed by another victory, this time in the Fair Derby, and it was clear that he was getting to grips with things at home. He was fast becoming the rider to beat and the competition in the States was intense. John Cook had remained at home too, and riders like Mike Bast, Mike Faria, Alan Christian, John Sandona, Robert Pfetzing and Dubb Ferrell were all tough competitors. As expected, the Californian crowds loved Kelly's entertaining and exciting style of racing, and his approachable nature was a massive hit with the public. There was no doubt that he would be one of the front-runners for the US National Championship in October.

Greg Hancock was one of the top riders racing in junior speedway at the time, and he clearly remembers the exciting style of Kelly Moran.

'He was the "Wizard of Balance" as they called him and the guy was amazing on a motorcycle. He could put the bike anywhere he wanted – he would literally just hang off the thing. Him and John Cook were two riders specifically that could actually come into the corner so hard at Costa Mesa that they would back in and hit the crash wall and ricochet down the straight. There were just those two guys who could do that. Kelly would come in with finesse, like it was no big deal, hit it and would bounce off with his back wheel. He could ride any bike – he was just raw talent.'

Ivan Mauger saw Kelly at his spectacular best in California. 'The best picture I have ever seen in speedway is of Kelly taken at San Bernardino – I was there when it was taken,' he revealed. 'He had passed a couple of guys in a handicap race, and he was up on one wheel and his head and arm were right under his handlebars. He was at full racing speed during that. There were some guys who were good at wheelies, good when they were 30 yards in front, pull on the handlebars and lift up the front wheel. Both the Morans – Kelly in particular – and John Cook, those three guys could do those things at full racing speed. The other guys, who were good at wheelies – the wheelie business was a modern phenomenon – they couldn't do it at full racing speed. They could only do it when they were way out in front or at the back.'

Shawn was given an early opportunity to regain the Golden Helmet title, but he was unable to relieve Carter of the championship and he was beaten in both legs. But the Sheffield number one continued to be a heavy points-scoring machine and was worshipped by the fans.

Ken Carpenter was the track photographer at Sheffield and he was also a long-time fan of the sport, but he always enjoyed watching Shawn race.

'I remember watching Shawn change direction three times in one corner,' recalled the photographer. 'He was weaving through the corner, from the inside to the outside and back again. It was quite incredible to watch. He had so much talent.'

He retained the Denny Pyeatt memorial trophy at Reading with a dominating display on a track which was one of his favourites. He also won the Dusty Haigh Memorial at Halifax and was in good form, which made his elimination from the World Championship not only puzzling, but very disappointing too.

The Tigers team, which included David Bargh, Dave Morton, Reg Wilson, Phil White, Eric Monaghan and Alan Mason, could just about hold their own at Owlerton, but on their travels it was a different story. They lost both their home and away legs in the first round of the Knockout Cup against Coventry, and they found themselves in the lower reaches of the league table.

Shawn's season looked as though it was over when he crashed at Hackney and broke his left leg while he was guesting for Eastbourne – Kelly's old club. He was

153

attempting an outside pass on Hackney's Finn Thomsen, when the report in *Speedway Star* said that he had ran out of track and crashed into the fence. Once again, Shawn headed to Galashiels for the expertise of Dr Carlo Biagi in a bid to save his season.

It was while Shawn was in hospital that Craig Cummings struck up a friendship with the colourful Californian. 'I first met the Moran brothers in the bar at Cradley Heath,' said Craiger. 'I used to help George Hunter, who raced for Wolverhampton, and he used to leave his bikes with me to clean – I think I was still at school then. My family knew Carlo Biagi and he said that they had Shawn Moran there. So we went along to see him and a friendship developed from there. That's how it started and he asked me to come and work for him in 1984.'

An amazing recovery saw the American make an earlier than expected return and he won the World Long Track championship. But the demands of speedway racing were greater than Long Track, and he only had a few outings toward the end of the season.

Glover moved quickly to sign the unsettled John Davis, who had had a falling out with his club, Poole. Davis did well and helped to plug the gap left by the absent Moran.

Kelly qualified for the US Nationals and Shooey missed the British League Riders' Championship in order to return to the States and defend his title. As usual, the championship took place at Costa Mesa on 15 October 1983. This was the title that Kelly had been building up to win when he took to the track at the beginning of the season. Shawn was not the only European-based rider to return, as so too did Dennis Sigalos, who had qualified for his second World Final that year and was top of the averages in Britain.

Kelly appeared in the first race and blasted from the start to defeat Mike Faria, Gene Woods and Buddy Robinson by a wide margin. In his next race, Sigalos and Kelly were level pegging until Moran stormed around the outside to win his second race. For Shooey, he slid off in his opening heat, but was able to restart in the re-run following a tangle between Sam Ermolenko and Alan Christian. But a second chance was not of any use to him and he finished at the back. Any hopes he had of retaining the number one plate were almost over. Shawn did win his second race, and then began to prepare to meet his brother in heat ten.

The elder brother was the only rider in the field who had won his first two races. As the tapes rose, they hit the first corner evenly – if anything Shawn was ahead on the inside – but Kelly found some grip on the outside and powered into the lead. He won, with his brother second. At the interval stage it was all about Kelly, as he was ahead with an unbeaten 9 points. Faria was his nearest challenger with 7 points and then a clutch of riders were on 6 points, Christian, Bast, Brad Oxley and John Sandona.

Shawn Moran passed Steve Lucero to get into second place in heat thirteen, but he couldn't do anything about Faria. Bast had the opportunity to spoil Kelly's party plans in heat fourteen, but he was unable to match his speed from the gate which meant that he needed to collect just two points from his last race to take the title.

Shawn with the Golden Helmet.

The top three at the 1983 US National. From left to right, Mike Faria (second), Kelly (first, and about to pop the champagne) and Dubb Ferrell.

In heat eighteen, Kelly faced John Cook, Sam Ermolenko and Steve Lucero. In a fantastic duel, Cook and Kelly swapped the lead with some tremendous wheel-to-wheel action, which 'Cowboy' Cookie eventually won when he pulled away on the very last bend. It didn't matter, as Kelly was champion and the 9,000-strong crowd greeted a popular winner, who received the traditional bumps for new champions.

Kelly finished with 14 points, second was Faria with 13 and 'Dangerous' Dubb Ferrell came from nowhere to claim third with a last race win over Shawn to finish with 11 points. Shawn was sixth with a total of 9 points, and one had to wonder how his fitness stood up to the confines of Costa Mesa.

Kelly immediately announced his intention to remain in the US for another season, but the sport's press in Britain continued to indicate that now he had won the US National Championship, he would return to Eastbourne. Of course, all this was untrue. 'Let me put the matter to rest once and for all,' he wrote in his column. 'The rumours are totally false. I've always maintained that I definitely wasn't going back to England in 1984 and that I would stay in the United States. This was true before I won the National Championship, and it is true now.'

Speedway Magazine voted Shawn Moran their rider of the year for his courageous effort in becoming America's first World Long Track Champion. He was away in Britain having the pins removed from his broken leg, so Kelly accepted the award on his behalf.

Meanwhile, there were changes afoot at Sheffield. Ray Glover watched his three-year team plan disintegrate before his very eyes in 1983 when Wayne Brown – a £12,500 signing from Berwick – quit the British League. A tug of war developed between the Yorkshire club and Belle Vue over the talents of David Bargh, and Glover saw a season of struggle emerge from the promise of '82. It was also clear that there had been a considerable strain on the club's finances. The Tigers were not the only track to be experiencing this of course, as the sport was beginning to slip into a decline in Britain.

Glover was trying to juggle the finances, when on the eve of the new season he announced that he wanted the Tigers to drop to the National League. Wayne Brown still refused to make a return to England, and the team were placed on the transfer list. Shawn Moran immediately attracted interest from Poole, despite a £35,000 asking price.

Then, local businessman Maurice Ducker stepped forward to take over the Tigers and they remained in the top flight after all. Ducker was also Moran's sponsor, so there was no question that the Tigers' would lose the spectacular American. However, there wasn't much time to assemble a competitive team.

Shawn remained as captain, and he was joined in the team by the experienced Reg Wilson, Dave Morton and Alan Mason. They were the familiar faces, but Ducker then pulled off something of a coup when he signed former World number two, Les Collins from Leicester, who had closed down. Then he snapped up Jan O. Pedersen on loan from Cradley. Martin Hagon also came in too, and suddenly it looked as though the Tigers had the makings of a promising side. The team manager's duties were handed to the former British Champion and England manager, Eric Boocock.

Shawn was hoping for a better season and he started off by scoring a maximum in the Tigers' 42-36 League Cup victory over Newcastle. Reg Wilson found himself paired with Shooey, and he was happy to ride with the American. 'He was brilliant to ride with and he knew exactly where to be. I've seen Shawn go in between two riders and he was no danger to anybody because he was so smooth and safe. He was a magic captain, too,' he said.

Nigel Crabtree was a National League rider with Stoke in 1984, when he 'doubled-up' with the Tigers. He, too, was very impressed with Shooey's approach to the role of captain. 'That American thing came out. There was me going out against some of the top riders in the First Division and Shawn would come over and tell me, 'Come on man, you can win this.' You know you can't. But that's the American way and it does gee you up. When they're patting you on the back, sometimes you can go out and win a race because you feel that you can't let them down. I remember I had trouble with my bike and Shawn strode out with his, and that made me feel such a part of the team.'

Eventually, after long and protracted negotiations, Neil Collins also joined the

Tigers to strengthen them even more – Wilson eventually made way for his arrival and he went on loan to Newcastle. But it was the form of Shawn Moran that was getting everyone excited in the Tigers' den. Around the Sheffield track he was in devastating form, and it wasn't until he was defeated by Swindon's Phil Crump on 24 May that he lost a race to an opponent. Until the arrival of Aussie Crump, only an exclusion for a tape offence in the home match against Cradley dented his unbeaten run. At that point he had just completed a sequence of five matches without a single defeat at the hands of an opponent. Three of these paid maximums came at Wimbledon, Wolverhampton – where he also lowered the track record to 60.00 seconds here – and Halifax.

When he qualified for his first World Final by winning the Intercontinental Final at Vetlanda, Sweden, Shooey became the first Tiger to make the last sixteen since Doug Wyer in 1976. 'Flyer Wyer', however, did not travel to his World Final in Poland as one of the favourites, but Moran did.

'I'm absolutely delighted to have won the Intercontinental Final,' said Shawn in his column in the programme. 'I always felt that I could reach a World Final, which was my only aim. Winning the meeting was an added bonus, and it sure is a nice feeling.'

Such was the interest in the charismatic and flamboyant American racer that the Sheffield skipper made a record. He did a re-working of the 1975 Chris Spedding hit single, *Motorbikin'*, which reached number fourteen in the British charts. Spedding was a guitarist who had most notably played with Roxy Music, and this hit single was his first major solo success. The single was released under the name of 'Shawn Moran and his Pit Crew' – the crew consisting of Steve Gibbons and guitarist Frank White.

'It seemed like a good idea at the time,' said Shawn. 'I was going well and having a good season, when Maurice and the announcer at Sheffield, Jim Kershaw (he was also the DJ at the local radio station Radio Hallam), suggested I do this record. It was felt that it would be good thing to do. I went into the studio and did the recording but it was so boring. I don't know how many times I did this talking, rapping chorus. It was like, 'That's okay, do it again'.'

It was a novelty record and didn't trouble the British charts in any way, but Nigel Tubb recalled that it did generate a favourable amount of local interest. 'There was a lot of interest in the *Motorbikin'* record. It went down well with the Sheffield media in particular, and he did a lot of radio interviews. The record was played quite a lot on the local radio station. It wasn't looked upon as some sportsman who was trying his hand at being a pop star.'

While Shawn was thrilling the British crowds all over the country, Kelly was also enjoying one of his best seasons. As the reigning National Champion, he was the one that everyone else was gunning for, but the man they called, 'The Jelly Man' – because of his habit of getting into trouble – was on the top of his game and the extra pressure was of little consequence to him.

He started slowly in the Spring Classic series, which was won that year by Dennis Sigalos, but finished runner-up to Siggy in the Denny Pyeatt Memorial at Imperial.

Shawn pictured with his record, 'Motorbikin'.

He won the first Scratch Main of the season at Ventura and qualified for the final the following week. In a special match race at the venue – which was popular with the fans and riders because of its location close to the beach – he defeated 'Flyin' Mike Faria. Ventura would prove a happy hunting ground for Kelly in '84. At Costa Mesa, he won his first Scratch main on 11 May, and then the following week he did the double, when he won both the Scratch and Handicap mains. A week later he went to San Bernardino – the Inland Motorcycle Speedway – and won his first Scratch Main there since 1982. He lost a run-off for the first staging of the *Speedway Magazine* Cup to Alan Christian at IMS.

His form was so good that the US selectors could not ignore 'King Kelly's' performances and he was drafted into the World Team Cup squad and qualified for his third World Championship Final. He was winning wherever he went, which included an event which was staged at the Silver Bowl in Las Vegas, Nevada.

Robbie Klima, the president of the NANTO Company, asked Harry Oxley to supply the riders for four speedway meetings. Klima had successfully promoted truck racing events, but never a speedway meeting. Referee, Irwin Moon and announcer John Smith all travelled with the riders to the venue, which included Kelly, Faria Christian, John Sandona, Brad Oxley, and other top names from the Californian scene. However, freak desert thunderstorms forced the cancellation of the first two meetings, but it was perfect weather for the third of the scheduled events. But the surface was in a dreadful condition, and there were more crashes than were normally seen in a meeting for this standard of riders.

'It was so rough that you couldn't slide the bike into the first corner,' recalled Kelly. 'The track was about the size of Wolverhampton, and I let the rest of the riders go into the first turn and then picked them off from the back.'

Towards the end of the meeting, the track began to settle down and Kelly qualified for the final where he met Oxley, Sandona and Craig Shaefer. The in-form US number one won the event and characteristically celebrated with a display of wheelies, but the feeling among the travelling band of riders was that they were glad it was over.

Deservedly, Kelly was receiving a lot of praise and he was a good ambassador for the sport in the USA. In an interview he gave to *Speedway Magazine* before he set off for the World Final, he was happy to be described in such glowing terms for once.

'I think that's a really nice compliment. I had never heard that before and I think it's a neat compliment. I just try to be nice to everybody. I have a much more relaxed attitude now that I'm racing in Southern California. I think I'm a much better person all the more for staying over here and I'm having a great time and I think it shows in my racing.'

Ventura Raceway in northern California, known as the 'Commotion by the Ocean', was a larger track than either Costa Mesa or San Bernardino and was quick with banking. The meetings were staged on Tuesday nights and the track produced such stars as Mike Faria –who was virtually unbeatable around there at times – Bobby Ott and Sam Ermolenko. Kelly really got to grips with the circuit in 1984 and

'King' Kelly leads Sam Ermolenko in California.

teamed up with Faria to win the US Best Pairs Championship. They tied with the Lance King/Robert Pfetzing pairing on 26 points, but Kelly defeated King in a run-off for the title. Later, he also won the Ventura Track Championship and yet, despite all this success, Kelly revealed that he wasn't always getting the attention he expected.

'There was, and I guess there still is, a crossover between surfing and speedway,' he explained. 'Guys would roll up to a meeting with their surfboards strapped to the tops of their vans and their bikes in the back. They really looked the part too, with their blonde hair and everything, and they always attracted the girls. I would think, "Well, I won the event, how come the girls are over there with those guys?" I never did surfing or jet ski, which Cookie and Mitch Shirra used to do. All the girls and the bar were on the beach, you know.'

Speedway was booming in California, but the sport was taken a lot less seriously in the USA than in Europe. It was looked upon as entertainment and attracted its critics in Europe – but the sport there could have done a lot worse than to look at some of California's ideas.

Bobby Ott was a team-mate to the Morans at Belle Vue and he spent longer than most racing in the States before trying his luck in the British League. 'It's more of a meeting place to have a few beers, and hoot at the girls and so on,' said Ott. 'If you did a straw pole at the exit, I doubt that half the crowd would even know who won the main finals. But it's great fun and got me a good start. Riding off handicaps makes you sharp and agile on a bike and makes you able to take a bump or two.'

Bert Harkins also feels that the Southern Californian circuits were an excellent training ground for riders when they decided to move across the Atlantic. 'With the tracks being so small, it meant that no one could get away – which was good. That's why riders like the Morans did so well when they made the trip over to Europe. They were used to turning hard and defending their position, whereas in Britain, once they had the set-up figured out, they could get away. They found it easy.'

Easy or not, Sheffield's season took a setback in June when Jan O. Pedersen crashed and sustained a broken arm and was ruled out for the rest of the season. It was a blow that prevented the team from making a serious assault on the silver-ware that year. They finished in fifth place out of seventeen and equalled their effort of 1982 when Ray Glover declared that he had a team for the future. But with Moran and the Collins brothers in their side, all the signs were that 1985 would be even better.

Shawn raced in the British League Riders' Championship at Belle Vue and finished in fifth place with 11 points. Then he flew to California to participate in the US National Championship.

Bobby Schwartz had won the California State Championship – a title the Moran brothers never managed to win – and registered his intention to win the National for the first time. In the programme, Kelly acknowledged the threat of Schwartz, and also listed Shawn, Faria, and Christian as riders to watch out for.

In heat three, Kelly swept around the outside of Schwartz to open up a lead until the race was stopped, when Dubb Ferrell bit the dust and caused Keith Chrisco to take avoidance action. This time, Schwartz made the start and held off 'King Kelly' all the way to the chequered flag. Shooey broke the tapes in his first race and he was excluded. For the second time, Shawn's opening race had all but ended his chances of victory.

Schwartz was so preoccupied with the presence of Faria that he left the door wide open and found himself back in third behind Alan Christian and Mike Curoso. It turned out to be a costly mistake for 'Boogaloo'. Shawn and Kelly both easily won their second races, and then the defending champion took another victory to lead the pack at the intermission on 8 points. Schwartz won his third – with Shawn at the back – to be in second.

The Morans met in heat fourteen, but it was doubtful that Shooey would give his brother a hard time as even a rostrum place was out of his reach at this stage. It was Faria who pressured the elder Moran brother on the opening lap, but he could only watch as he was fought off and Kelly pulled away to strengthen his grip on the trophy. Schwartz easily won his fourth race too, keeping the pressure on Kelly Moran, while John Sandona won heat sixteen to stake a claim for a podium finish.

Schwartz made another superb gate to win his last race, which left Kelly needing to win his last heat to retain the title. He had to wait until the very last race of the evening to take to the track. He lined up in gate three with Alan Christian alongside him in gate two, and John Sandona on the other side in gate four. Sam Ermolenko made up the quartet by taking up the inside position at the start line.

Kelly and Christian banged handlebars into the first bend, but it was the 'Wizard' who emerged in the lead on the back straight and brought the Costa Mesa crowd to their feet. He took control of the race while it was all happening behind him, with the remaining trio having a virtual war over the minor placings. Sandona took over second, but as they entered the last lap Ermolenko took Christian out – sending him flying in spectacular fashion. The race was stopped and Christian was able to walk back to the pits as 'Sudden Sam' was excluded. As they were on the final the lap, the result stood and Kelly was champion for the second successive year.

A capacity crowd cheered his victory celebrations and he told *Speedway Magazine* 'I sure felt those vibrations in the first corner with Christian. I'm so happy and I will be staying here in 1985.'

Schwartz took the runners-up place with 13 points and Sandona finished third with 11. For Shawn, it was another National disappointment as he finished with 6 points and twelfth place.

With success comes jealously. After one of his best seasons, which included a fourth place in the World Championship and a consistent and scorching domestic year, *Speedway Magazine* put Kelly on the front of their November issue. It was

Kelly in action in the USA in 1984.

clear that the publication had received some criticism from some quarters for their support for the Moran brothers and Kelly in particular – after all, this was his third appearance on the front cover of the monthly magazine. The editor and publisher, Robert Fitzpatrick, answered their critics in his editorial.

'Fourth in the World Final and successfully defending his National title, Kelly has been a fantastic ambassador for the sport internationally, as well as nationally. And, of course, anyone who has seen a race knows that Kelly Moran is 'The People's Choice' – the rider who evokes most crowd response in this country.

'And, yet for all his riding ability and talent, Kelly Moran is much more than just an incredible speedway rider and National Champion. He is a genuine personality whose presence on the speedway scene is something that will contribute to the growth and awareness of our sport in a major way. For that we should be thankful and not be reticent to give credit where credit is due.'

Shortly after claiming his second National title, Kelly represented the sport in the Superbikes championship. This is not to be confused with the now popular road racing discipline in which Carl Fogarty has made his name in Europe. This one-off competition brought together road racers, motocross and dirt-track riders to compete at Carlsbad in a five-lap, two-mile race with a combination of tarmac and motocross surface. It was decided over three heats and a final. Previously, Bruce Penhall and Kenny Carter had both made unsuccessful appearances in the meeting, which was put together largely for TV purposes.

'All the champions in different motorcycle racing fields were represented,' Kelly recalled. 'Shawn couldn't take part when he had the opportunity because he was racing in the British League.

'I rode a Maico 500, a Swedish bike, and it flew man! I was in the first corner first but crashed into the hay bales they had around the track. I closed my eyes when I fell, and when I opened them, there was straw everywhere. I got back on but those guys were gone. People like Jeff Ward and Ricky Johnson, they were in it and we had a lot of fun.'

Cheered on by his father and friends, he managed to complete the course in his second race. American motocross stars dominated the event, and little Kelly could only just about reach the ground with the tips of his toes when he was seated on his machine. The winner was Danny Howerton, after the defending champion, Eddie Lawson, had an engine failure during the final practice lap.

'I remember before the actual event, the day before we had a practice day,' revealed Kelly. 'We were out in the open and I got changed next to Ricky Johnson, who also did Mini Bikes when he was young. I always wore what I call a "goolie protector", you know? Anyway, I had this protector on, and with a clenched fist I punched it and said to Ricky: "You got one of these?" He looked at me and said: "No, I never wear one of those." Anyway, Ricky goes out to practise and does one of those real high jumps of his and lands awkwardly. He comes walking back in like John Wayne and I said to him, "You should have a worn a gooly protector Ricky!" I think he always wore one after that!'

The boom in speedway racing in America was illustrated when two new tracks opened in California for the 1985 season – the 250-yard California Speedway at Carlsbad, which had a pits ranking which depended on where you finished during the meeting to determine where your pit place would be for the following week. The top ten of the 'All Star Pits' were the best places. This was promoted by STP man Rick Salvino and *Speedway Magazine* contributor Paul Heffernan. Kelly was asked to offer his technical advice on laying the new track.

'It was through my sponsors, STP, that they asked me to advise them,' he recollected. 'I thought, well, it's not rocket science you know. But it was bigger than Costa Mesa and about the size of a Reading or Wolverhampton track maybe. It was wide on the corners, but there was no banking. I did that so there would be more racing lines for the riders, and guys like Christian, Faria and Brad Oxley liked it. Going into turn three there were ripples, or bumps, a bit like the first bend at Swindon used to be. A lot of the riders used to try and slide through there, but I used to hang back and freewheel through it – still at speed – because you knew they were going to get into trouble. It was especially so with the handicap racing. We just couldn't iron those bumps out for some reason.

'The funny thing about Carlsbad was that they never had any vendors selling food or T-shirts or anything like that. The people used to bring their own, so when you're on the straightaway you could smell their barbecues and food they would bring. You had all these different aromas as you went round the track.'

The second track to open was Ascot South Bay Stadium, which was smaller than the legendary Ascot half-mile and Ventura, but bigger than Costa Mesa.

This meant that it was possible to race five times a week: Ventura on Tuesday, San Bernardino on Wednesday, Ascot on Thursday, Costa Mesa on Friday and Carlsbad on Sunday. This type of programme meant that a good living could be earned in the US. At this point the rich pickings in the British League were few and far between, and American riders Lance King – who had finished third in the 1984 World Final – Sam Ermolenko and Steve Lucero all returned for a full season.

'Kelly was the only one I really knew because he rode in 1985 in America, and he was like a superstar, National Champion and No.1,' said Sam. 'He just got on a bike and rode – it was a natural raw talent, and watching him ride was so inspirational, because he had such a classy style. So, really in 1985, my strategy was to learn the trade and I was spoiled in Southern California with a lot of different styles. There was John Cook, Alan Christian, Kelly, Mike Faria and Dubb Ferrell – they all had a different style of racing. Kelly had his own style, and he was so friendly on the race track and yet so fast.'

It seemed that Kelly had begun the 1985 season where he left off, when he won the Denny Pyeatt Memorial at the first meeting of the season at El Centro. However, once again he failed to make it count in the Spring Classic series which was run over three rounds that year – Costa Mesa, San Bernardino and Long Beach. However, he then won the Scratch main at the season opener at Ventura. He followed that by winning four mains in a row at Ventura before illness ended his unbeaten run. He won the opening night's Scratch main at Carlsbad, and on 12 May he won both the Scratch and Handicap mains at Ascot. He came off the 60-yard line and earned a standing ovation from the crowd when he won the handicap by inches on the line from David Hancock. Then at the end of May, he swept aside the opposition to win the Bruce Penhall Classic. At this early stage in the season, everyone was asking: 'Who can stop "King Kelly"?'

Billy Hamill was a regular on the junior circuit and as Kelly was a superstar, and a favourite of the young American, he was always hoping to receive some good advice from the National Champion. 'He gave me some great advice once,' Hamill recalled. 'Before his races he always used to watch the third division guys – which are the amateurs who were just starting out. And I asked him why he always did this, and he replied: "To find out where all the bumps are tonight, 'cos they'll find 'em." And it was so true.'

To commemorate his double National wins, a special Kelly Moran pin badge and zipper pull was produced by one of his sponsors, *Knotty Ideas*. It was a nice souvenir and was much sought after by badge collectors.

Shawn returned to Sheffield for his sixth British League campaign. His Tigers team included the Collins duo, Les and Neil, Martin Hagon, Peter Carr (a new signing from Belle Vue), the 1983 European U-21 Champion Steve Baker and the grass-track specialist, Gerald Short. A four-point victory over Belle Vue in their opening match of the season had Shooey very excited about the season ahead, as he explained in his column in *Speedway Mail*: 'It's real great to be in a winning side at last! It was quite a surprise to win at Belle Vue. It was a good team performance as far as the Tigers were concerned, and I loved it! I really can't explain what it feels like to be winning these good matches, but I just couldn't stop smiling!'

When the 1984 BL newcomers, Exeter and Newcastle, withdrew and returned to the National League after just one season back in the top flight, it became clear that British speedway was not in a very healthy condition. Eastbourne also gave up the fight against financial hardship and was joined in the lower league by London's glamour club, Wimbledon, and also Poole. The league had shrunk to just eleven teams and it was clear that there would not be enough meetings for the top riders to earn their money, but the BSPA (British Speedway Promoters' Association) also had to find a way of cutting costs.

They came up with two solutions: the first one was to expand the League Cup competition to include all the teams and it would be run on a league basis. The league championship would then follow in the second half of the season. Their second idea was to scrap the individual second half, which was a controversial decision as the fans felt that they were being short-changed. Nevertheless, this went ahead and was replaced by a six-heat junior match.

'I could never understand why they stopped the second-half individual. It was a lot of fun,' said Kelly. 'We could test machinery, fool around and entertain the crowd with wheelies and stuff. All the riders used to race in it with a fun spirit you know. There were some guys who were a bit of a stick in the mud, but we used to say to them, "Ah come on, so what if your team lost, let's have some fun." The team event, the serious stuff was over, so you could have some fun in the second half. It was good.'

The Sheffield boss, Maurice Ducker, was alarmed by the Tigers losing six league cup fixtures in a row and he immediately blasted the team and warned them that changes were on the way. He was adamant that there would be no room for riders who did not come up to the task. First to go was Short, who made way for another tiny Dane, Sam Nikolajsen, who was signed from Coventry. After a series of disappointing performances, Australian Steve Baker was on his way out of Owlerton and was replaced by another Danish rider and former U-21 champion, Alf Busk.

'You've got to have a good team to attract the public and a very flamboyant rider like Shawn Moran helps sell speedway,' explained Ducker.

The Tigers started off their league campaign with six successive victories, with away wins at Cradley and Swindon. They were showing their teeth at last and were unlucky to be eliminated from the Knockout Cup by Reading. Suddenly they were top of the league, but defeats at Ipswich and Belle Vue disturbed their momentum and let their rivals close the gap.

Shawn was enjoying the best season of his British League career. He won the Overseas and Intercontinental Finals and qualified for his second World Final. Shooey also won the Northern Riders' Championship and was top of the averages for a large part of the season, eventually finishing runner-up to Hans Nielsen of Oxford.

The Golden Helmet was also revamped and was now run on a weekly basis, with the holder meeting the opposing team's top rider. This system took away some of the prestige of the competition, but it opened it up to a lot more riders. Shawn challenged for the helmet eight times and won six of them. I especially recall one glorious performance at Swindon when he defeated the holder, Bo Petersen. I had a bet with a colleague at work that Shooey would win and, to show his class, he went on to score a maximum as the Tigers won the match 41-37. He successfully defended the helmet against Reading's Jan Anderson (twice) and Hans Nielsen, before losing it to Tommy Knudsen. Earlier in the season he had taken the helmet off Petersen at Sheffield, and defended it against John Davis, before losing it to the reigning World Champion, Erik Gundersen.

'It was satisfactory for me to work with Shawn in 1985, because he had such a fantastic season everywhere,' said Cummings. 'He was in every World Championship right to the death. His domestic form was fantastic and I think it was one of his best years. He was pretty much unstoppable and he was flowing everywhere he went.'

Shawn also dabbled with a new engine, the Phil Pratt engine called the PPT 500. Previously, Pratt had tuned some of his engines but, as Cummings revealed, he proved difficult to work with when they used his own power plant.

'It was a very good engine and Shawn broke the Sheffield track record on that engine. But he was difficult to work with. If anything went wrong, it was always our fault. If a rocker arm broke it was always something that we were supposed to have done, it was never anything wrong with the engine. In the end we used the Italian GM, which is a good engine and is still being used at the top now.'

Shooey's brilliant season was also good for STP too, as Nigel Tubb explained:

'Shawn was always looking for ways of pushing the STP product. At the 1984 Overseas Final, he was fined because he put STP stickers on his helmet colour. He was the first to do that and, although he was fined, it gave us a lot of exposure. At the Golden Hammer individual at Cradley, he covered his leathers with STP stickers. They were all interlocked like chain mail and that was another picture which gave us even more exposure,' Tubb said.

'Then there were the competitions in *Speedway Mail* and *Speedway Star* which we held. It was things like, "What does STP stand for?" Shawn and I found some of those entries interesting! And then there was another which asked the readers to write in with the most unusual place they had seen an STP sticker – and that was even more interesting! Even now, over fifteen years since the sponsorship ended, I still see some of those stickers around various tracks – on pit supports and terracing. It was very successful.

'Interest in the company was phenomenal. STP was the best-known sponsor in speedway. On my own initiative, I did a survey among speedway supporters to name a well-known sponsor in the sport. Almost every one said STP. It was a tremendous success.'

While the 'Miracle Worker' was blitzing the opposition in England, Kelly's season in the USA came to a shuddering halt in a crash at Carlsbad. Rich Sweaney got into trouble on the second lap and Randy Blevins was left with nowhere to go except to crash into him. Kelly was also close behind as he was making up ground in the handicap main, and had no time to avoid the fallen pair. He lay on the track for fifteen minutes before he was put in a neck brace. But he was able to walk under his own steam to the waiting ambulance. He sustained an injury to the cartilage in his ribs and broke a bone in his foot.

This injury was a culmination of a run of bad luck that began in the American Final, when a fall in a run-off for the final qualifying spot ended his World Championship hopes. This was followed by a victory in the *Speedway Magazine* Cup, but a scorer's error meant that the win was taken away and handed to Alan Christian. His injury prevented him from appearing for the USA team in the World Team Cup final that year. No sooner had he recovered from the injuries sustained at Carlsbad, when he developed a case of bursitis on his elbow, and he was ruled out of the Californian State Championship at IMS.

'1985 was my worst year ever,' Kelly reflected in his column. 'I try not to think about it. We missed 71 races out of 120, and I missed six weeks. Everything that could have possibly happened did: 'flu, accidents, injuries, machinery – everything.'

Despite his problems, Kelly was still among the favourites for his third successive US National Championship. He had missed a large chunk of the season and could only finish third in his first outing behind Bobby Ott and Brad Oxley. If he was to retain the title for a third time, and to keep it in the family for four years, he had to win his second race. However, the fast-starting Mike Faria and Robert Pfetzing kept Kelly back in third and his championship hopes were over. He won his third outing, but finished down the order on 6 points. It was a long-overdue victory for Alan Christian, the original STP man, with Schwartz second and Faria third.

'It was kind of neat to win the Nationals and keep it in the family for three years,' reflected Kelly. 'When we started out, it was the Bast brothers who were winning it all the time and they were like the superstars. So for us to do a similar thing, well, it was cool. It's nice to win but we didn't go over the top about it like some sportsmen do – you know, crying and all that kind of stuff. For Shawn and myself, it was like, "Oh, we got gold, that's cool." It's nice to think that what we accomplished will be in the history books for as long as they keep them. That's neat.'

Sheffield relinquished their grip on the top of the British League, and they were not alone in failing to have an answer for an Oxford team who dominated the league programme, by losing just three matches. They also won the Knockout Cup and the Midland Cup, with only Coventry denying them the Grand Slam when they won the League Cup. The Tigers could take some pride in being one of the three teams to defeat the Cheetahs, and they finished runners-up in the league. But their only silverware for that year was their Northern Trophy win over Belle Vue, which came during the opening weeks of the new season.

It may have been the club's best result in the league since 1973 – when they were runners-up to Reading – but it was clear that it wasn't good enough for Maurice Ducker. Their skipper had experienced the best season of his career, but he needed consistent support. The Collins brothers, who never gave less than their best, had not provided the support that was required – especially away from home.

Shawn's prolific season attracted praise from all quarters. In a series in *Speedway Mail*, entitled 'The Entertainers,' its uncredited author says of Shooey: 'Shawn Moran does work very hard at his racing. He doesn't just get on a bike and go. But equally he has all the abundance of natural talent that no amount of time or effort could reproduce. It's this talent that ensures he knows the right lines to take and talent that puts him in the top handful of riders in the world today. It is this that marks him out, even in a select little band, as something special.'

The times were tough for British speedway. For the first time since 1981, the World Final returned to Britain, and was held for the first time at the unfashionable Odsal Stadium, Bradford. During World Final week, *Speedway Mail's* preview edition carried a story asking all loyal British supporters to support their World Final at Bradford, because of low ticket sales. Happily, a massive crowd assembled on the day to witness Erik Gundersen's second world title success. But if proof were needed that the sport in Britain was in decline, then that story was it.

As the New Year dawned, rumours began to circulate that Kelly Moran was planning to return to the British League. His fans had heard it all before, but this time it seemed that it could be true. The 'Jelly Man' could not return to Eastbourne as they had joined the National League, so where would he race? The answer was Sheffield.

'It was such hard year [1985] that during a six-month period, every time I crashed I seemed to hurt myself. I remember that on the day of the Nationals, something didn't feel right,' said Kelly. 'I was going for the treble, and I was thinking, 'I wonder what the track will be like? Oh, it don't matter, I like that track.' I decided to take a ride on my mountain bike to the beach to relax, and I travelled along a route which was like a dry river bed. It didn't matter which way you went, east or west, you could get to the beach. I was pedalling away, and along this particular stretch the track drops away to the side. So if you're looking at a clock: twelve o'clock is straight ahead, but it falls away at two o'clock, and when you take the two o'clock route it gives you a good adrenalin rush. But this time I buckled the back wheel. I didn't hurt myself, but it was like, "Oh man." I got the feeling that something was trying to tell me something. I don't think it was long after that I started to feel that I wanted to go back to England to race. I always got along well with my brother on and off the track, and I thought it would be cool to ride with Shawn at Sheffield.'

Bob Dugard put a £25,000 price tag on his wayward star, but was quoted as saying that he was ready to negotiate, and thought that it was a fair price for a rider who would be a big draw for any club.

'We lost money when Kelly decided to stay home in the States, but in saying that, nothing would give me greater pleasure than to see him back here for another season. As well as being popular with the supporters, Kelly would also prove to be a prolific points scorer. The kid's a natural, and could well become World Champion.'

And so, with just over a fortnight to go before the start of the 1986 season, Kelly Moran agreed to join his brother at Sheffield. Ducker was clearly delighted, and with two of the most naturally talented riders in the world in his team, it seemed that major trophies were set to come to Yorkshire at last.

7

PAIR-FECT

Just as Kelly Moran's return to America had caused much excitement and anticipation, so his return to Britain would attract similar interest. *Speedway
Magazine* in the USA was obviously disappointed with his decision to race in
the British League again, but admitted that California's loss was Britain's gain.

His arrival was not without its controversy, however. Sheffield's boss, Maurice
Ducker, successfully appealed to the Speedway Control Board to have his
starting average reduced from 9.62 to an assessed figure of 7.50. He argued that
in view of his three-year absence from the British League and his injury lay off,
the figure with which he finished his last season with Eastbourne was not a
realistic one.

Originally, his request was refused by the British Speedway Promoters'
Association, but the SCB upheld his appeal – much to the disgust of his rivals.
They felt that the three-time World Finalist and double US National Champion,
would make a mockery of that average which was, without doubt, artificially
low.

Ducker admitted that it took 'a lot of wrangling', to get Kelly to return to the
BL. His brother, the captain of the Tigers, had also played a negotiating role in
the deal. 'I have to admit that I did a lot of persuading, but in the end he had
to make up his own mind for himself,' wrote Shawn in his column in *Speedway
Mail*. 'It will do Sheffield a lot of good too, because in the all the years I have
been riding here, we haven't really had another eight-point plus rider. Kelly's
easily capable of that and a lot more besides.'

Shawn had indicated that if he didn't win the 1985 World Championship, he
would have to consider his future in Britain. He was obviously encouraged by
the big bucks that were available to earn in the USA at this time, and was
looking beyond the glory of medals.

'Money and happiness are by far the most important things and I'm pretty
sure I could be happier and make more money if I stayed in the States,' he
wrote in his column. 'Hell, some of the top guys are averaging over $1,500 a
week, which means that some weeks they're making more than that.'

But, thankfully, he did return to form the league's most spectacular
spearhead. Not everyone felt that signing two charismatic brothers for the same
team was a good idea. Given their hell-raising reputations, critics predicted that
the club would be taking on more than they could handle. Kelly responded to
these critics when he was interviewed in *Speedway Mail*. 'Some say there are

pros and cons about riding in the same team as your brother – especially one where he has become something of an idol. But the way I see it is, if he's happy enough to be here after five or six years, then it can't be all bad.

'As long as I'm getting the results, I don't think anyone should be interested in how I lead my life. We all do things wrong when we're growing up, and who's to say I haven't, or that I'm not a reformed character? I'm still going to party that's for sure! Over here the big thing is to hang out in the pubs all the time, and I'm going to want to avoid that,' he said. 'I guess I'll be watching a lot more videos this season. Back home you can go to the beach, but I guess the North Sea this time of the year is out of the question! That's not my idea of fun at all! But I really needed those three years at home. It was a real break for me, and there's no pressure on you at all except from yourself.'

Les Collins was the man to make way for Kelly and the rest of side was Peter Carr, Neil Collins, Martin Hagon, Tony Forward and Peter McNamara. The former British Champion and ex-England boss Eric Boocock was the team manager.

'They were great lads to have in a team, and we had some laughs you wouldn't believe,' he recollected. 'I think they were the most talented people that have ever been in speedway. It's fair to say that Kelly had more natural talent than Shawn, but he liked a drink more than Shawn and took it less seriously. But they're as bad as you let 'em. I had no problems with them really – they were great kids.'

However, before heading to England, Kelly took part in the Spring Classic series in the States. This was one series that never seemed to be a good one for him. But this time he got off to an encouraging start when he finished second to Bobby Schwartz at the first round in Costa Mesa with 13 points. Shawn was further down the order with 5 points. The second round at San Bernardino was almost postponed because of the bad weather, but the track staff did a wonderful job to get the meeting on. It was won by Sam Ermolenko with 12 points and Kelly came fourth with 11 points. Shooey struggled again with just 4. With one round left, Kelly led with 24 points; Lance King was second on 23 points and then came Ermolenko and Alan Christian on 21 points. The last round, however, was washed out by heavy rain and Kelly was eventually declared the winner.

In his last column for *Speedway Magazine*, he wrote of his decision to race at Sheffield for 1986: 'The best racing in the world for experience is there. When you race the same guys day in day out, you don't seem to learn anymore. But when you get the chance to get around the country racing different tracks and different riders, that's when you get the experience and you start learning different things. There are five or six riders in this country who've beaten everybody else – we've even beaten ourselves. I'd rather start getting back on climbing up the ladder, rather than stay on the lower rungs.'

It was planned that Kelly would move into the house next door to his brother in Sheffield. These houses had many visitors during their stay at this address,

Sheffield 1986. From left to right, standing: Eric Boocock (team manager), Peter Carr, David Walsh, Martin Hagon, Maurice Ducker, Neil Collins. Kneeling: Peter McNamara and Kelly. The captain, Shawn, is on his bike.

and among them was Sam Ermolenko.

'I remember going over to Shawn and Kelly's houses in Sheffield. That was kind of cool I thought, because they were living next door to each other. They had two different styles of mechanic-ing and ways of taking care of their equipment and stuff. That was a kind of education.'

A bumper crowd packed into the Sheffield stadium for the first match of the new season, against Bradford on 27 March 1986. The Tigers were obviously rusty and were slow from start and lost 42-36. Shawn scored 7 and Kelly 4 points. It was a disappointing start, but it would take Sheffield's new signing a little while to get back into the groove after three years in the USA – and he also had the new Italian GM motor to get used to.

The following week, Shooey suffered two engine failures as Belle Vue came away with a 43-35 win. Kelly scored 5 points, but most importantly he secured his first race win in his opening ride. This may have been a settling-in period for the new team, but their League Cup hopes were in tatters. A win at Wolverhampton, which saw Shawn top-score with his first maximum of the new season, gave the team fresh hope in the cup. Kelly was struggling with a lack of power and could only score 3 points after spluttering to a halt in his first race.

But then they faced Coventry in the Challenge Cup. They won the first leg at

Owlerton stadium 41-37 and Kelly was beginning to show glimpses of his true form. In the second leg two days later, the Tigers roared into the final with a 46-32 victory. On a difficult track made slippery and treacherous by rain, Kelly adapted to the conditions and scored 9 points, with Shawn on 8. It would be a feature of the Sheffield teams over the next three years that they would adapt better to the less than perfect conditions, as it gave them a level playing field against their fast-starting opponents. For if there is one thing that you knew about the Tigers side, then that was that none of them were particularly consistent out of the gate and they had to do it from the back.

This meeting was the turning point for Kelly, who then began to display the kind of form that made him one of the most exciting riders in the world. He was having problems getting used to the British League. After three years in California, he had forgotten how cold Britain's spring season could be. Boocock commented that when he watched him get ready to race, it looked as though he was preparing to race in the Antarctic.

There had been many changes since he last raced regularly here in 1982. The league had shrunk considerably since he left, which meant that he wasn't racing as often as he would have liked. Riders were no longer allowed to touch the tapes, and it was compulsory that all riders had to use the Barum tyre in BL competition – this was a controversial move among the riders which was designed to cut costs, as the Barum was said to be cheaper than

Kelly checks on the Tigers' progress with Maurice Ducker and Eric Boocock.

the preferred Dunlops, Carlisles, or Pirellis.

'That won't bother me at all,' Kelly said of the new tape rule in *Speedway Mail*. 'I don't know how to roll at the start! I guess some people could have trouble with it and I think it would be better to fine people than exclude them. That way the fans don't suffer by not seeing all of the riders.

'The only thing I'm disappointed about is the lack of meetings,' he admitted. 'Sure I'm getting a lot of guest bookings, but they should be a bonus on top of my Sheffield commitments rather than a way of making up earnings. Hell, as I remember it, we were racing three or four times a week a few years back.'

However, the guest bookings were an essential part in getting him back into the groove of British racing. As he was on a low average, he was a popular choice and an effective one too. He scored 13 points for King's Lynn at Swindon, 8 at Wolves for Bradford, 11 for Bradford at home to Reading, 10 for Wolves at home to Ipswich, 7 for Bradford at Coventry – where Shawn was also on guest duty for the Dukes and scored 11 – and a paid maximum (9+3) for Reading at home to Wolves.

However, it was on a wet evening at Swindon when not only did Kelly show that he was back to his world-class best, but the Moran brothers illustrated all their talent and ability. This was the first display at club level of their unique on-track understanding.

The date was 31 May, and they arrived at Swindon to find the Wiltshire side enjoying an encouraging start to their new season, with Kai Niemi providing good support for their high-scoring Aussie, Phil Crump. The Robins had not lost a League Cup match at home. About an hour before the start, the rain poured down and it didn't stop until almost a quarter of an hour before the start of the match. Many people stayed away that evening because of the inclement weather and it was one of the poorest crowds of the year – but the stay-away fans missed a classic. The track looked heavy after the soaking, but there were no signs of the match being postponed.

Shawn Moran won the first race in a quick time, and to prove that the surface was just to his liking, he passed Crump. Kelly won his first race too, and in the fastest time of the night. Swindon established a two-point lead, but it was the Morans who kept the Tigers in touch with race wins. Shooey was introduced as a tactical substitute when Sheffield slipped to six points behind, and won the race, with his team-mate in third, to bring them within four points of the Robins.

Kelly came from the back to sweep around Jimmy Nilsen to take another race win in the next race. Captain Shawn kept the momentum going by winning heat eleven, despite Niemi putting him under pressure.

With one heat to go, Swindon was ahead 38-34. The best the Tigers could hope for was a draw, and to do this they needed their two riders to finish in first and second places to obtain maximum points. They were optimistic about the chances of achieving this as the Moran brothers were unbeaten as they came to the line to face the Robins duo of Kai Niemi and Mitch Shirra. What followed

Shawn in thrilling style for the Tigers at Swindon.

were four pulsating laps, and it was a crying shame that only a small crowd would witness this classic race.

As the tapes rose it was a rush to the first bend, but it was Kelly who emerged ahead on the back straight, and immediately he looked for his brother. He slowed up the pursuing Shirra and Niemi, and Shooey moved alongside for that all-important 5-1. But the Robins pair were not going to give up easily. Kelly appeared to have the speed to stay ahead, and he was displaying all his tremendous track craft to look out for his brother and dictate the pace of the race. For the full duration of this duel, there was barely anything between the competitors. Just as Niemi thought he may have found a gap and squeezed into it, Kelly would block the move and allow his brother to move up alongside. But Niemi was beginning to get the measure of Shawn as they entered the final lap.

He took up the outside run which was where the grip was and, although Kelly had control of the race, he worked out that he could use the extra grip to find a way by the Tigers skipper and get the all important second place to give Swindon the win. As they entered the final two bends, Niemi followed Kelly on the outside, and as they came off the last turn, and to the delight of the Robins' supporters, Niemi looked to have the speed to get by Shooey to take second place at the chequered flag. However, he didn't reckon on Kelly's wily track craft. He was well aware of the Swindon rider's efforts, as he had been for the entire race. Just as he approached the finish line, he slowed up enough to make Niemi hesitate for a split second. This was enough to allow Shawn to grab second by inches on the line, and earned the Tigers a spectacular draw.

The crowd were astounded at what they had just witnessed. It was doubtful whether they would see such a magnificent display of team riding and track craft again for many years. In all my years of watching speedway I have never seen anything before, or since, to equal that for both drama and skill. It was clear that the Moran brothers were more than a match for anyone on their day.

'They were nearly twins on the track,' said Boocock. 'Many times they would leave it until the last minute. They were both very aware of what the other was doing, so Kelly would have a crack, and if he was going to get past then Shawn would wait. Sometimes you'd think, "well, they're not going to do this", and then one would make a move and the other would go at the same time. They were very good, but it got a bit hairy sometimes. They were always too much aware of one or another, 'cos they were not only racing as a pair, but also for the team. But I had no problems with them.'

The match at Swindon was Kelly's first maximum for Sheffield and the team seemed to have turned the corner. But then a series of disasters struck the club – punctuated by a success for the team – which ruined a promising season.

During the very next meeting at Oxford, Captain Shawn locked up in front of Per Sorensen, and fell. But Sorensen was unable to avoid the fallen American and he ploughed into him and Shooey sustained a broken ankle. Despite this, the Tigers won three matches in succession until the second bombshell hit the club.

At the end of June, Maurice Ducker announced that Sheffield would close unless someone could come along with £250,000 to pay for the licence and riders. He was quoted as saying that he was losing £500 per week, but the final straw came when Coventry's riders complained about the state of the track. They protested and at one stage threatened to walk out, even though the track had a new top dressing. Ducker decided that enough was enough, and made the announcement.

However, a meeting was called between the controlling companies after the weekend and appeals from supporters and his riders persuaded Ducker to carry on. Assurances from the stadium owners and pledges from fans seemed to be enough for him to withdraw the threat of closure. The Tigers were back in business.

The team responded in the best way they could, by defeating Oxford in the first leg of the Challenge Cup Final with a 45-33 win. With Shawn still missing through injury, Les Collins returned to score 8 points in his place, while Kelly scored 7 points. The question was: would a twelve-point cushion be enough to take to Cowley for the second leg? Former Tiger, Jan O. Pedersen, was booked in as a replacement for Shooey and he led the scoring with 11 points. Neil Collins and Kelly put in a sterling display to hang on to the Cheetahs' tails and do enough to win their first major trophy since 1974. They lost by ten points on the night – 44-34 – but they did enough to ensure the trophy came to Yorkshire.

Their victory was all the more remarkable since, as the season unfolded,

Oxford dominated the league by winning every match, thereby successfully defending their league title. However, the champagne had hardly stopped flowing when the third problem hit Sheffield and their season was all but over.

Kelly Moran was racing in Poland when an off-track accident in a hotel ended his season, and only the quick thinking of fellow rider Chris Morton saved his life. Kelly tripped and put his left arm through a plate glass window and severed the arteries in his wrist.

'There's no way he'll race again this season,' wrote Shawn in his column. 'His arm injury is bad – really bad. But the last thing we want to worry about now is riding. I'm just thankful that he's alive to tell the tale.'

Shooey was able to make a track return for Sheffield and they raced on using guests to cover for Kelly. They battled to the semi-finals of the Knockout Cup, but found that Oxford were in no mood to let any silverware slip from their grasp and the Tigers were eliminated. Sheffield eventually finished in sixth place out of eleven teams, but they could rightly point at the injuries which had denied them a higher place at the end of the season.

Shawn Moran had a mixed season, but finished third in the British League Riders' Championship with 11 points. Unfortunately, injury ended his World Championship hopes. He finished in sixth place in the British League Averages and was a model of consistency for the Tigers. He returned to America and finished second in the California State Championship behind the winner, Bobby Ott and Bobby Schwartz. It was the closest that either of the brothers ever came to winning that championship. In the absence of Kelly, Neil Collins paired up with the Tigers number one in the British Open Pairs, and they finished third with 18 points (Shawn 11 and Neil, 7). Since the meeting was held at Sheffield, it was definitely a case of the one that got away for the Morans. Shooey ended the season on a high note, winning the Golden Helmet by defeating Hans Nielsen at Sheffield. Kelly had made an unsuccessful challenge against Ipswich's Jeremy Doncaster at Foxhall Heath earlier in the season.

For Kelly, it was a disappointing end to his return to British racing, but Ducker revealed in an end of season report that crowds had increased at Sheffield. Things looked better for 1987. The team remained largely the same for the new season.

A local rider, Sean Wilson, had received several rides at senior level in '86 and he was pencilled in from the start for the new campaign. Other new faces were Ian 'Egon' Stead, and Adrian Stevens. It was a young side, with an average age of just twenty-one, and they had secured a major sponsorship with NSF (National Smokeless Fuels).

Meanwhile, Wolverhampton had signed their second American. Ronnie Correy arrived at Monmore Green for his debut season in the British League, and he revealed in an interview he gave to *Speedway Mail* that the boom in American Speedway was over. 'Things are changing over there. It's not as successful as it used to be, and this year they have altered the division system and the prize money,' he said. 'Even I don't know exactly what's going on.

Kelly Moran in Sheffield colours in 1986.

Although you hear people saying that there is a lot of money to be made in California, I don't think that's true any more.'

There were some doubts whether Kelly's wrist would have healed sufficiently, and he raced during the opening weeks of the season with a special guard to protect the tender wrist from flying shale. But the brothers started 1987 in fine form during Peter Collins' farewell meeting at Belle Vue.

The meeting attracted a lot press interest as Bruce Penhall came out of retirement to race in a series of special match races against Collins. The American won all three. The meeting was run over the traditional 20-heat format; only the top six scorers would then meet in a sudden death six-lap final. Each race winner would receive a prize, however, and the Morans regularly collected prizes that afternoon. Shawn was second with 12 points and Kelly also qualified for the final in fourth place with 10 points – his opening race win was just 0.04 outside the track record.

'I could get to like this,' said Kelly as he stepped up for his third prize that afternoon. 'It sure is a mighty fine way of making sure no one let's up until the chequered flag comes down.'

In the final, it was Shawn who led from the start to take first place overall, but all of the finalists received a microwave oven. But it was a good start to the new season for the brothers.

Sheffield started well, and the Moran brothers' experience was useful in helping the younger riders make their mark in the top flight. Peter Carr was paired with Kelly and they produced some match-winning performances, and Sean Wilson often found himself riding alongside Shawn as the season progressed.

'They taught me so much,' said Wilson, who went on to be one of Sheffield's best riders, and led them to championship success in 1999. 'They were so good to me and helped as much as they could. They'd always help me, and made sure I was right and helped me to talk to people and that. It wasn't, 'do this or do that' or tell me what gearing or engine to use. You'd just learn by watching 'em.

'To ride with Shooey was great as he used to look after me in every race. When we went into a corner he'd just move me a little bit and then put me back to where I should be – he had so much good control. I mean we had 5-1s over Hans Nielsen a couple of times and things like that, which is great when you're sixteen or seventeen, as he used to ride with so much skill. They were chalk and cheese really. They're not the same, they're two different people. But they were incredible riders and fabulous team men.'

Peter Carr had similar memories of racing with Kelly: 'Kelly was probably the better rider, but Shawn was the faster rider,' he reflected. 'Around Sheffield, I could stay alongside Kelly. But when we went to the smaller tracks you could just see how good he was there. I'd be struggling to stay alongside him and he was just taking it easy when you looked at him. On the bigger tracks he was fast, but I could keep up with him. He would always leave me room and look for me.

So would Shawn. They were both unbelievable how they could ride every track. When they used to have second halves, they were both scared of me doing a dive under 'em. They used to say, the both of them, "don't dive under me."

'Oh God, yeah, Pete was the King of the Divers,' Kelly recalled. 'He'd just dive up on the inside, and it used to be like, "Hey Pete, look at the helmet colour, man, I'm in your team".'

Adrian Stevens once revealed in a profile that the Morans were the riders he would like most like to model himself on. 'They look so at ease when they are racing. Super showmen and real crowd pleasers,' he said. 'Prior to joining Sheffield I had heard all these great things about them, but they were far better than I envisaged.'

The Tigers started well in their League Cup campaign, and went seven matches without a defeat, which included victories at King's Lynn, Reading and Hackney. Their win at King's Lynn was with a whopping 50-27 score line, and the Morans both left the track with maximums against their names. It was at Swindon where the in-form Tigers' unbeaten run was brought to end, losing 45-33.

The Moran brothers' form throughout the year was worthy of their reputations – in fact it was one of Kelly's best seasons racing in Britain. But once again injuries ruined the Tigers' year. Kelly crashed and suffered a nasty shoulder injury, which ended his World Championship aspirations, and kept him out of action for a month. Then Shawn also missed part of August, when he sustained a shoulder injury.

These injuries, combined with inconsistency from the bottom four riders, meant that Sheffield again ended the season without any silverware. Ducker was frustrated and blasted his riders, saying that Neil Collins was the only rider to give the team 100 per cent at all times. It was obviously a heat-of-the-moment outburst, as his top four riders, the Morans, Collins and Carr were not only a match for most of their rivals, but they often surpassed their opponents. Unfortunately, it was the inexperience of their tail end riders that let them down. Ducker even admitted this later in *Speedway Star*. But Ducker put all the team on the transfer list – with the exception of Collins. Kelly took exception to the remark that only Collins was giving everything all the time.

'Hell! If it hadn't been for Shawn, Sheffield would have closed years ago. I just can't see how they can print that,' he said. 'The first I heard about it was when a very good friend of mine called me and asked me why I wanted a transfer? I told him that I never asked for a transfer and then he told me to look on teletext. I did, and it told me that we were all on the transfer list at Sheffield.'

Finally, Kelly made his long overdue debut in the British League Riders' Championship and put in a steady performance to finish in third place with 11 points – after he defeated Kelvin Tatum in a run-off. The meeting was won by Hans Nielsen, but poor Shawn experienced his worst BLRC when he was unable to sort out his mechanical difficulties and failed to score. It had been a good year for Kelly despite the disappointment of his world title exit, and he was involved in the confusion of the Golden Helmet.

Once again this helmet had gone missing during the winter, so when Simon Wigg defeated Shawn for the helmet, he was pictured wearing the Czechoslovakian Golden Helmet he won in 1986. The situation became farcical as the match races continued despite the absence of the helmet. Kelly made an unsuccessful challenge against the holder, Jeremy Doncaster, at Ipswich. Swindon's Mitch Shirra was the holder of the non-existent title when Sheffield came to Swindon. Kelly was nominated as the challenger, but as he got ready the encounter was called off. Nobody seemed to know what was happening – least of all the riders – and the competition was suspended. Whatever happened to helmet? Nobody knows.

For Shooey, his highlight of the season was a third place in the World Long Track championship, but his form for the Tigers continued to be consistently good. As the season came to an end, rumours began to circulate that he wanted to leave Sheffield.

It was announced that Shawn believed he had become stale at the Tigers' den and felt that he needed a change. Ducker, although disappointed, could see his point, but a £30,000 asking price made many clubs think twice. Reading, though, were installed as favourites for his signature.

'Shawn and I both feel that a move could do him good, for he has not gained the success this year that he would have liked,' Ducker told *Speedway Mail*.

It was widely believed that Shawn could have earned a lot more money if he hadn't been so loyal to the Tigers. Ducker was both his promoter and his sponsor at one point, and some felt that the two interests clashed. Reg Wilson believed that neither of the Morans got the financial rewards that their talents deserved, as was illustrated by this recollection from the former Sheffield star. 'There was a picture of Hans Nielsen's home in *Speedway Star*, and I said to Shawn, "why haven't you got something like that or an equivalent to that?" They couldn't manage the business side of things and that let them down. It's happened to others; they've had loads of ability on a bike, but if you haven't got that business sense, then it's not enough to carry on. The ability can only do so much.'

'The two interests were conflicting interests,' believed Cummings. 'Because if Shawn had ridden for another team, I'm sure he would have earned a lot more money.'

The 1988 season was the Diamond Jubilee year for British Speedway, and many clubs had special meetings planned to celebrate. The BSPA organised a special international tournament between England, Denmark, America and Sweden. But with just weeks to go, it looked as though Shawn would not be racing in Britain. Perhaps the asking price was too much, but Shawn had not managed to get fixed up elsewhere. He had his bags packed in preparation for a full season in the USA, when a last-minute deal was struck and Shawn agreed to pull on the Tigers race jacket once again.

'I had no grumbles with the club, promoters or the fans,' said Shawn. 'I just

Shawn (left) and Kelly get their heads together before the start of another important race for Sheffield.

felt that I needed a change of scenery. It was something that I thought about for a long time. But there were very few clubs that were able to meet Sheffield's demands. I think Reading were the only possibility with a swap deal involving Mitch Shirra. In the end I was left with a choice of either remaining at home or coming back to Sheffield.'

In spite of all the frustrations, threats and transfer moves, the Tigers team for 1988 had a familiar feel to it. After all, Shawn was back with his brother. Peter Carr, Neil Collins, Sean Wilson, and Ian Stead also returned. But the season began with the Italian, Valentino Furlanetto, and Gordon Whittaker both making their debuts for the Tigers.

However, team manager Eric Boocock faced injury problems immediately when Collins was unfit to start the new season as he had not fully recovered from an injured wrist he sustained at the end of 1987. Peter Carr crashed heavily in Australia and sustained leg and foot injuries, which also forced him to miss the start.

The League Cup competition which, in various formats, had formed the opening half of the season since 1981, was scrapped. Hackney had withdrawn from the top flight and this meant that only eleven clubs now operated in the British League – unofficially viewed as a 'Super League' – and the participating teams now met each other twice in official home and away league fixtures. It meant that the serious business of league competition started straightaway, which was bad news for the Sheffield Tigers.

They got off to the worst possible start by managing just two draws in the first eight league matches. By the time Collins and Carr did return – and it was widely believed that the latter returned too early in June, while Collins made it back in May – any league and cup hopes they may have once had were over. They would be playing catch up for the remainder of the season and Ducker ringed the changes throughout a tough season.

Throughout it all, however, the Moran brothers continued to give the club solid and spectacular service. This was in spite of their early elimination from the World Championship at the American Final.

Former World Finalist and England international Paul Thorp was a regular visitor to Sheffield, when commitments allowed, and he struck up a friendship with the Morans – especially Kelly.

'We used to live about an hour away from each other across the Pennines,' he recalled. 'I used to go to Sheffield when I could to watch the racing. I got to know Kelly very well and we just hit it off. They were both really nice guys. They'd always put themselves out to help, but they didn't have that attitude that some Americans had. Some of them didn't, or wouldn't, mix with the English lads. But the Morans weren't like that.

'They were both so talented and had loads of natural ability on a bike. They were very quick. Even if you were in front, if you looked round they would be there – on your shoulder. They could pass you at any time and anywhere, and that's what made them so popular with everyone, because they were so exciting to watch. When they did make the start they were gone, because they were so quick. We all took it for granted that they had so much natural talent.

'I remember once I watched Kelly race into the first turn and it looked as though he was going to fall off. It was like, "Oh he's fallen off, he's gone." But he came out of the turn in front! He had just incredible balance – it was unbelievable.'

Kelly reverted to a Weslake engine in 1988, as he had agreed a good sponsorship deal with Bill Davies of Antig-Weslake. This seemed a strange decision when most of the world's top riders were mounted on GM and winning races.

'This happened through Darren Boocock,' said Kelly. 'He told me that Bill would do free engine tune ups and he wouldn't make a big deal out of it if we blew an engine. And I thought that was a big saving right there. The Weslake was a good engine and I liked it, and Bill helped a lot of the other Sheffield boys as well. It was a good deal.'

Shawn and Kelly teamed up to represent Sheffield in the British Open Pairs Championship at Reading. Dark clouds threatened all afternoon, but the rain held off. The weather had been particularly wet leading up to this event and Shawn had missed a lot of racing through postponements. The track was heavy and grippy, but this proved to be a good thing for some of the racers in the field.

Every British League team was represented, and it was a marathon of racing entertainment run over twenty-five heats in front of a noisy crowd. There were two groups of four teams and one group of three, and the scoring was on a 4-3-2-0 basis. Therefore, a pair that finished second and third would score more points than the race winner. It was a scoring system that was designed to ensure that the best pair would win. Shawn fought a lone battle in 1987 when he won all of his races, but his partner, Peter Carr – who was brought in to replace the injured Kelly – failed to score, and they failed to progress beyond the group qualifying stages.

The line-up was correctly considered to be superior to the World Pairs Final, which was held at Bradford later that year. Sheffield was in Group B and faced Wolverhampton, the hosts Reading, and Belle Vue. The Tigers pair was unbeaten in their group and only Mike Faria of Belle Vue seriously troubled them. The familiar system off Kelly on the outside and Shawn on the inside produced the goods. Kelly particularly seemed to relish the outside as he was able to take full advantage of the grip on the outside gates to blast around the traffic on the first bend. Even the fast-starting Jan Andersson of Reading had no answer to the American duo's track craft.

Sheffield were joined in the final stages by Cradley Heath, the reigning champions, Oxford, and the highest-scoring second place teams, Reading and Coventry. The Morans continued their unbeaten form by defeating the Coventry pair of Kelvin Tatum and Tommy Knudsen. Then they faced the Oxford pairing of Hans Nielsen and Marvyn Cox. Nielsen made the start and moved over to block Kelly's expected charge around the outside; and Cox took third after Shooey retired from the race to inflict the Americans first defeat of the afternoon.

Reading's Andersson split the Oxford pair in heat twenty-two, while the Moran brothers got back to winning ways by holding off the persistent Cradley pair of Erik Gundersen and Jan O. Pedersen. With two heats remaining, Sheffield and Oxford were level with 17 points each.

Around the terraces, it was clear that the neutrals and the Reading fans preferred a Sheffield win due to the local rivalry. Furthermore, the Morans, Shooey in particular, were very popular at the Smallmead Stadium. Kelvin Tatum of Coventry crashed and was excluded when they faced the Oxford pair. In the re-run, Nielsen and Cox made light work of defeating the lone Bee, Tommy Knudsen.

And so, after twenty-four races, Kelly and Shawn found themselves facing Reading. Nothing less than a first and second place would do to force a run-off for the title. As the tapes rose, Kelly stormed around the outside and Shawn joined him at the front. But on the last lap, Andersson regained second by slipping through on the inside of Shawn, which was enough to end the Tigers' hopes. It was a disappointment for the Morans, and they must have rued Shawn's retirement when they faced Oxford.

However, the enforced inactivity for Shooey through so many meetings being postponed – Kelly managed to beat the weather with some guest appearances to keep his hand in – cost them first place. He later revealed that, after seven races – the most they would expect in a league match was six – his arms were so tired that he couldn't hang on anymore.

'For some reason, I always had problems with my arms,' said Shooey. 'They would ache if I hadn't raced for a while. I don't know why, but sometimes they would get really tired. Usually it would get better as the meeting went on, but if I hadn't raced for a bit because of the weather or whatever, it was like, "Oh God," you know? They would really hurt and I would have problems hanging on. It wasn't a big problem, after a match or two they were okay, but I couldn't really do anything about it. It was just one of those things.'

The matches for the league campaign in 1988 were extended to fifteen heats, with the final race being a nominated rider's heat. The team manager's could nominate their own riders to contest the final heat, and this resulted in many appearances for the Moran brothers.

A month after the British Open, Sheffield returned to Reading to contest a league match, and the public were left with no doubt that they were unlucky not to win the Open. The Tigers trailed 31-23 after ten heats, but the Morans inspired a memorable victory. They were paired together three times in the closing stages and won all three, which included the last-heat decider which they had to win to clinch the match. The Reading guest Jan O. Pedersen had no answer to them as they had everywhere covered, although he did come close to splitting the American pair. In the bar afterwards, there was much talk about how good the Morans were that night.

Similar performances were repeated around the country.

'Shawn and Kelly were great in heats thirteen and fifteen,' recalled Carr. 'They would miss the start and pass people lap after lap. At places like Ipswich, the small tracks, I couldn't believe how they used to get round.'

In the individual tournaments, Kelly enjoyed one of his better years. He won the Peter Craven Memorial at the new Belle Vue track, was runner-up to his brother in the Denny Pyeatt Memorial at Reading, and was also runner-up to Poland's Andrzej Huszcza in a *JMS All Stars* meeting in Poland. He finished third in the BCA Classic at Swindon, the Coalite Classic at Bradford and the Littlechild Trophy at King's Lynn. He also did well in Belle Vue's Diamond Jubilee meeting, but missed out in the sudden death, six men and six laps final. There were many special meetings that were put on to celebrate the sport's diamond jubilee, and Sheffield staged their own Diamond Jubilee Championship.

It was a one-off meeting, and among the sport's top stars to take part were Simon Cross, Chris Morton, Paul Thorp, Mike Faria, Mitch Shirra and John Jorgensen. All these riders performed well around the quick Owlerton circuit. It was a unique event as there were twelve five-man qualifying races using a 7-5-3-2-1 scoring system. The top eight scorers from the qualifying heats were seeded to the Grand Final which would be run over 10 laps. They were joined by the two winners of the repêchage races in heats thirteen and fifteen.

The eight top scorers then raced in a one-lap timed trial, where the fastest rider would score 10 points, the second fastest 9 points and so on. The riders' positions on the grid were decided by their qualifying scores, and they were 3 2 3 2, set 10 metres apart. It was a complicated format, but it was one which had been used regularly in Australia.

Kelly qualified for the final with 19 points, and was joint top scorer with Simon Cross. During the one-lap dash, he posted the fourth fastest time of 17.80 seconds, with the New Zealander, Shirra, the quickest with 17.48.

The 'Jelly Man' started in the middle of the front row for the 10-lap final, with Shirra on the inside and Cross on his outside. He made the start and held off a determined challenge from Morton – who started from the second row – to win the Grand Final and the meeting. His winning time was 2 minutes 41.6 seconds.

'The one-lap dash was actually over three laps,' Kelly recalled. 'It was timed from the moment that you started the second lap, so that you were at full racing speed. So you had one lap to get up to speed, do your full lap and then a slow down lap.

'I remember talking to Bobby Schwartz about the ten-lap final, and he raced in the sixteen-lapper they used to have at Ipswich. Bobby was a very clever guy, he worked out that if he fitted an old fuel tank to his machine – like one from an old 2-valve bike or something like that – the tank would be big enough to carry the fuel without the need for a second tank. Apparently the fuel tanks on the older bikes were bigger. Anyway, I told him about this ten-lap race we had planned at Sheffield, and we worked out how much fuel I would need.

'Basically, we had to fill the tank right up to the neck. Now I only ever used to do two practice starts before the race, so when I went into the final I had to wait for the other guys to form up behind me. So I leaned my bike over to keep the clutch cool, and I was worried that the fuel would spill out! But boy was it a long race! I was really glad to see the chequered flag at the end as I was so tired – it was a long way man! Paul [Thorp] he pulled onto the infield as he just couldn't go on any further, he just couldn't do it.'

The STP sponsorship came to end during 1988, and it was a successful arrangement that had lasted for five years.

'It was no fault of the Morans themselves that the STP sponsorship came to an end,' said Nigel Tubb. 'The company was bought out and one of the first things the new owners did was to slash the budget for advertising and sponsorship by half. For example, the Indy Car project, or Champ Cars as it's now called, had its sponsorship reduced to a small sticker on the wing. The only exception was the NASCAR driver, Richard Petty, whose STP-sponsored No.43 race car was so famous,' he explained.

Both the brothers made it to the British League Riders' Championship, which was held at Belle Vue's new Kirkmanshulme Lane circuit. This had proved a particular favourite with the two Americans, and they were expected to do well. On this occasion, however, Kelly could only score 5 points, while Shooey was fifth with 10. Denmark filled the top three places, and Jan O. Pedersen emerged as the winner.

It had been a long hard season for Sheffield and Ducker rang the changes – partly because of injuries, and partly because he was disappointed with the side's lack of success. At one point, the Tigers were joined by a third American, Randy Green, but he hardly had time to settle before he was hit by the Sheffield injury jinx when he dislocated his shoulder in Germany. In the end, the team did well to finish halfway up the table in sixth place, but it was still a long way from where both Ducker and Boocock wanted the team to be.

Changes were inevitable this time and it appeared that Kelly Moran was definitely leaving. Belle Vue were linked with the 'Jelly Man', but he stated that he did not want to leave the Tigers. As for Shawn, he seemed likely to stay as he was set for a testimonial in 1989. However, there were rumours toward the end of the season that the stadium would not be available for speedway, and this turned out to be true.

In February 1989, Maurice Ducker announced that he was pulling the plug after losing £28,000 during 1988. The Tigers' promotion had had a row with the stadium owners over a rent increase and the relocation of the pits. As Eric Boocock revealed, they had had enough. 'We were paying a lot of rent and we had arguments with the stadium – not particularly bad arguments, but the same old ones. We had a team ready to go in February, but we fell out with the landlords again, and we said, "well stick it!". And that's how we all fell out.

'We had some exciting racers, but we didn't have a team of starters,' said Eric. 'Peter Carr has never made a start, Neil and Les Collins, they've made one start to this day. Shawn and Kelly, on their day were very good starters, but they were

Kelly Moran, 1988 Diamond Jubilee champion at Sheffield.

hit and miss. When they were good, they were good; when they were off, they were off. We were selling entertainment and the crowds went up a lot, even though we weren't particularly successful. I mean, how do you judge a successful team? By the results you get? Sometimes you don't. We were very attractive visitors everywhere we went, because the Moran brothers and the rest put the effort in. We all like to win more, but we can't all be winners. But they were good days – really good days.'

Sean Wilson also remembers those days fondly: 'The team was great, absolutely fabulous. Everybody was totally opposite and had a different character. It was a super place to do my apprenticeship; I couldn't have wished to start at a better time with two better riders – I still think that. To see them on a bike; they were just talent and they looked so smart in their STP suits. They were great ambassadors for the sport and enjoyed life fully.'

'I was the oldest in the team,' recalls Kelly. 'We all got along fine with each other on and off the track. Maurice was okay, although he would sometimes talk to the press or the fans before the riders. And that was unprofessional. The track wasn't always up to our standard. It would suit the visitors more than us and we used to say to him, 'why don't you put more dirt down, Maurice?' He would tell us about certain things that were supposed to happen, and they never did. But I don't think it was easy for him, as the landlords of the stadium at that time were not the best to talk to.'

It was an end of an era. Three exciting years that were very much a roller-coaster ride for all connected with the club. But it is a time which is looked back upon with great fondness by the Sheffield faithful.

The Belle Vue Aces are the most famous speedway club in the world. Some of the world's most famous names have pulled on the Aces' body colour: Jack Parker, Peter Craven, Mauger, Collins, Morton and many more. In 1989, Kelly and Shawn were the latest names to join this illustrious list when they moved to the Aces pack for a reported fee of around £50,000. It was the 'Jelly Man' who signed first, and it seemed that it was only a matter of time before he put pen to paper, as he was continually linked with a move to the Manchester club. But Shooey followed when it became clear that a rescue bid to keep Sheffield running would not be successful.

Belle Vue had only spent the one season at the Greyhound Stadium at Kirkmanshulme Lane. They had to find an alternative venue when their Hyde Road Stadium was sold off by Stuart Bamforth for housing at the end of the 1987 season. It was former World Champion and Aces' star Peter Collins who formed a consortium of local businessmen, John Perrin, Don Bowes and Norman Smith, to fund the Aces' move to the Greyhound Stadium.

Collins later admitted that he never intended to include both of the Morans in his original team plans, as he wanted a more balanced side. However, when Shawn became available, they quickly signed the younger Moran. Happily, Belle Vue agreed to run Shawn's testimonial following the unfortunate closure of Sheffield, and he became the first American in the history of the British League

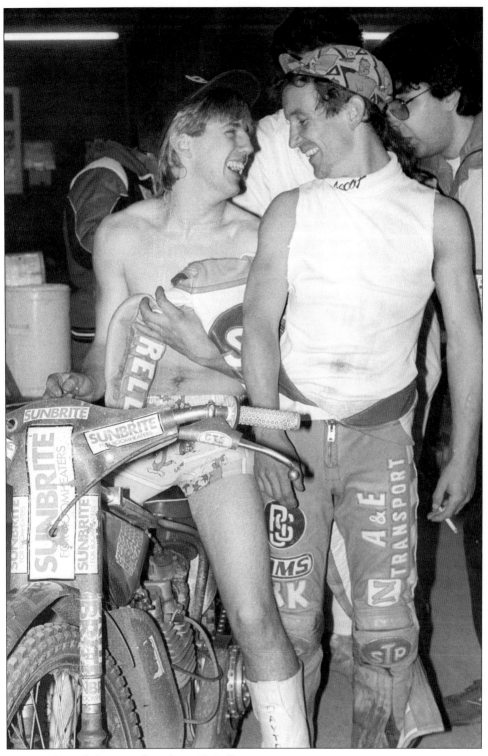

Sean Wilson (left) enjoys a joke with Kelly.

to be awarded a benefit year for his services to the sport.

In a column he wrote for the short-lived publication, *Tracksport Today*, Shawn expressed his gratitude to Belle Vue. 'I must thank the Belle Vue management and the powers that be for letting me still have my testimonial even though Sheffield has closed. It really did look as though I was going to miss out, but now everything is looking good.'

From the outset, the move rejuvenated Shawn's form. He had wanted to leave Sheffield, and now that he had, his career took on a new lease of life. In his first six Gold Cup matches, he scored three maximums and was never below double figure scores. He scored back-to-back maximums in the Aces home and away victories over Coventry. At one point he was top of the league's averages with a figure in excess of 11 points. 'The Miracle Worker' was indeed back.

Meanwhile, Kelly started off reasonably well too and also scored his first maximum for the club in their home win over Coventry. But it was a week later when he showed the Aces fans what a talent he was when he passed Hans Nielsen from the back as he raced to 16 points. Cheekily, he wheeled over the finish line and then looked back at the Dane, as he had just copied what

Shawn's testimonial line-up at Belle Vue in 1989. From left to right, back row: Dennis Sigalos, Gary Hicks, John Cook, Phil Collins, Les Collins, Kelvin Tatum, Peter Collins, Hans Nielsen, Graham Jones, Bobby Schwartz, Chris Morton. Front row: Paul Dugard, Greg Hancock, Robert Pfetzing, Sean Wilson, Neil Collins, Shawn Moran, Erik Gunderson, Martin Dugard, Kelly Moran, Ronnie Correy.

his rival did on a regular basis.

Speaking in *Speedway Mail*, Peter Collins was very happy with the way his team was shaping up. 'It has all come together nicely and we have a great team spirit. A lot of that is down to the Moran brothers. They have so much charisma and somehow it seems to be rubbing off on their colleagues. They are much more outgoing as a group.'

However, by June, Collins had quit as one of the promoting team as he didn't agree with some of decisions that were being taken. Smith had already stepped down, and Collins found himself in the minority when it came to making decisions. This left Perrin and Bowes in sole charge of the Aces team, although the former Belle Vue rider still had shares in the company.

As well as the flamboyant Morans, the team consisted of Chris Morton as the captain, Danish international Peter Ravn, the former Tiger Gordon Whittaker, Paul Smith and the young Joe Screen. By the end of May, however, both Smith and Whittaker had made way for another promising English lad, Carl Stonehewer.

To underline what brilliant form Shooey was in, he won the Peter Craven Memorial Trophy at Belle Vue with a 15-point maximum. As the defending champion, his brother scored 9 points to finish in fifth place. Ronnie Correy took second with Sam Ermolenko in third. However, it was the teenager, Joe Screen, who caught everybody's attention with a brilliant 12 points to take fourth place. This was indeed a remarkable performance among such a strong line-up of world class riders. He was just sixteen years old and was benefiting from the help and advice from Collins.

'He was so fast,' recalled Shawn. 'He was a bit like Kelly was when he was at that age. They used to call him the "Screen Machine", and he was so quick.'

For Shooey's testimonial, a galaxy of track stars assembled to honour the likeable American, including Danish World Champions, Hans Nielsen and Erik Gundersen. Dennis Sigalos came out of retirement to race in the meeting, and Bobby Schwartz also returned to Britain to participate in his big day. Phil Collins and John Cook also came over from the USA – Cook was not able to race in the actual meeting because he didn't have a valid licence. They were joined by another American, Gary Hicks. There was much interest in Hicks, as the Aces were planning to bring him over until the Morans became available. He was the grandson of former World Champion Jack Milne.

'I want people to really enjoy themselves because I've enjoyed my ten years in the BL,' Shawn said in his column. 'I hope there will be plenty of Sheffield fans able to make the journey, because I want them to share in my big day.'

However, the build-up to his testimonial day was not without its setbacks. He took a heavy tumble in Belle Vue's first home defeat of the season at the hands of Oxford, injuring his arm. Then, following a positive alcohol test in a World Long Track qualifying round, it was announced that the AMA had banned the in-form American from all World Championship events for the remainder of the year. He appealed against the decision, but the ban remained in place. If it

Belle Vue Aces, 1989. From left to right, back row: Kelly Moran, Chris Morton, Shawn Moran. Front row: Joe Screen, Peter Ravn, Gordon Whittaker, Paul Smith.

wasn't enough that he was punished by the AMA, for some reason the Speedway Control Board in the British League also saw fit to impose a seven-day ban from BL racing and fine him £200. The ban took effect from 1 August.

'They said I brought the sport into disrepute, but I still think it has nothing to do with them. Normally they only test three riders and I was the fourth to be tested at that meeting. Now I am the first to be punished twice for one offence,' said Shawn.

It was a warm sunny day when Shawn Moran's testimonial took place at Belle Vue on Sunday 28 May 1989. The racing format was a four-team tournament, and a healthy crowd assembled to pay tribute to the popular Californian. It was a successful day and there was also a wheelie competition among other things, which was won by Robert Pfetzing.

The day was marred by an injury sustained by his brother in heat three. He clashed with Ronnie Correy on the first bend and took an innocent-looking tumble. However, he withdrew from the rest of the meeting and it later transpired that he had broken his finger.

The injury ended his World Championship hopes and kept him out of action for three months. Eric Boocock was surprised that Kelly was still out of action when the England-USA test series came round. He told him that when his brother, Nigel, had broken his finger, he was back in action within weeks. As Kelly was frustrated to be out of action for so long, he keenly enquired as to how he came to be back on track so quickly? He had it amputated, came the reply!

'When it shattered, they took the three biggest pieces and screwed them together,' said Kelly. 'The hospital decided to put an aluminium brace on to immobilize it altogether, because the screws have moved. And they warned me that any further movement would mean amputation or a permanently dead finger. I didn't fancy losing a limb.'

After much wrangling over a work permit, Hicks took his place in the Aces' team and he immediately set about showing his potential. He wasn't the only American with a famous family connection to try his luck in the British League. Bart Bast was the cousin of the famous Bast brothers, Mike and Steve, and he was struggling to get to grips with British racing at Swindon when he was paired with Shooey in a pairs meeting at the Robins' track.

The pairing finished second behind another American duo from Wolverhampton, Robert Pfetzing and Ronnie Correy. The experienced Moran shepherded the young Bast around for two confidence-boosting 5-1 results. Bast was so impressed by the help and advice he received that he was moved to pay tribute to Shooey's team-riding, and was quoted in *Speedway Star* as wishing that his team-mates at Swindon would exercise the same kind of consideration to help him in his debut season!

Shawn enjoyed one of his best British seasons and he qualified for the British

Shawn (left) is about to make his move on Hans Nielsen during heat twenty of the 1989 British League Riders' Championship.

The top three at the British League Riders' Championship. From left to right: Hans Nielsen, Shawn Moran, Brian Karger.

League Riders' Championship for the eighth time. The meeting built up to an exciting climax, even though the slick track produced little passing. Shawn entered the final race with an unbeaten score of 12 points and was joined in the race by Hans Nielsen, who had won the world title that year for the third time and was also unbeaten.

Nielsen characteristically shot from the gate and into the lead, but as he moved out to look for the grip to power clear, the Belle Vue number one hooked underneath the Dane and took over at the front. Nielsen pressured the Californian for four laps, but Shooey would not be denied and he became the first American to win the British League Riders' Championship. With an unbeaten score against a field which is rightly looked upon as being superior in quality to that of any World Final, Shawn could only wonder what he might have achieved that year but for the ban from the World Championship. It was the icing on the cake of a good domestic season for the Aces, as he was the undisputed number one.

'He was brilliant and thoroughly deserved it,' enthused promoter John Perrin. 'He has been superb all year and kept himself motivated despite the disappointment of being banned from the World Championship.'

Meanwhile, Kelly returned in late August, but then damaged his hand in a

Shawn receives the traditional bumps after he had become the first American to win the British League Riders' Championship.

garage door and missed another week of action. When he did return, he was not fully fit but he contributed some good points returns for the Manchester club.

Unfortunately, the final weeks of his debut campaign for the Aces were blighted by controversy. Belle Vue were due to race at National League, Rye House, in an Inter-League challenge match. Boss, John Perrin, was furious when Kelly did not arrive for the match – which they lost 49-46. He was seen heading for Sweden instead with former Hackney favourite, Roland Danno.

He was fined £500 for his non-arrival by the Aces' management team, and a further £100 by the meeting referee, Will Hunter. An angry Perrin said in *Speedway Mail:* 'He has been reported to the BSPA and he will not be riding for Belle Vue again this year. The non-appearance of Kelly Moran cost us the match.'

However, a week later, Kelly was back in action for the Aces and Perrin was happy enough with his apology and was quoted as saying: 'He informed me that he intends to do his best for Belle Vue and that's good enough for me.'

'I was never contracted to do that meeting,' said Kelly. 'I told John that I'd let him know if I was going to do it four days before the match. Promoters are bit like boxing promoters as they think they own you, and he got the wrong end of the stick. I did go to Sweden with Roland, but when I got there I sure wished I hadn't – it was freezing cold and snowing.'

But this was not quite the end of his troubled times. There was a heavy security in Kelly's pit area at Belle Vue, and it transpired that there was a media reporter from the tabloid press harassing the American for a story.

'That bloke came in to specifically hound Kelly,' said Perrin, 'so we wouldn't let him in unless he paid his admission. We don't need publicity like that. The matter was an internal one between Kelly and Belle Vue. As far as I know he didn't come in during the meeting either,' he explained to *Speedway Mail.*

Nevertheless, this reporter still ran an inaccurate story in *The People*, which did little to enhance his reputation. But happily the incident was forgotten, and Kelly got on with what he did best – riding a 500cc, brakeless, speedway bike.

Belle Vue finished fourth in the league, and it was announced that both of the Morans were in the Aces' plans for 1990.

'What I'd like to say publicly is how much they did for Belle Vue,' said Perrin. 'They certainly put bums on seats as well as scoring points wherever they went.'

The British League had shrunk even further to just nine clubs when the 1990 season had got under way. With Britain staging the World Final at Bradford that year, there was much optimism within the BL, although there was a growing feeling that something had to be done.

Belle Vue signed a third American, Bobby Ott, which was an unpopular move with some fans as he came in as a replacement for his fellow American, Gary Hicks. Hicks was a victim of his own success as his average was too high and he moved to King's Lynn for what turned out to be an unhappy year. Mike Lewthwaite and Richard Musson both fought for the last team place.

Shawn and Kelly before Shawn's testimonial.

Shawn signed to ride in the Swedish League for Rospiggarna in the Swedish Elite League. It was a way of filling up his season as the BL had shrunk so much. Speedway in Sweden was experiencing a revival, and other top stars raced in the league which included Simon Wigg, Kelvin Tatum, and Hans Nielsen. Shawn raced alongside the former World Ice Speedway Champion, Erik Stenlund, Mikael Teurnberg and the Norwegian, Einar Kyllingstad.

'It was good as we raced on Tuesdays and Thursdays only,' recalled Shawn. 'Bengt Jansson was the man who set it up and I was a bit like the new kid on the block.'

Shooey did well and finished with an average of 10.19, but his club could only finish in sixth place out of eight teams. He had a good year at international level too, but in Britain his form slumped. He lacked consistency and lost his number one spot to his brother. A number of injuries, such as bruising and concussion, continued to interrupt his season and prevented him from getting into a rhythm.

He also had another disagreement with the AMA when he refused to return to America on his compulsory rider return. He said that he was losing money to return home for just one week, and his team-mate Ott had already been given a one-week ban for his refusal to go back.

'It didn't benefit me any more,' said Shawn. 'To make money you had to get into the scratch and handicap finals, and it was hard to do that because I wasn't used to the small tracks. The local guys race the same track every week, and

Kelly explains a point to his Belle Vue team-mate Nigel Leaver, while John Perrin listens.

obviously they were going to do better.'

He had to write a letter to the AMA to explain his situation. However, in a cynical move by the AMA, they chose to impose the ban after the American team had competed in the World Team Cup – which they won.

Kelly had Craig Cummings as his mechanic in the pits, who had returned to Britain after spending a few years as a mechanic to Bobby Schwartz. 'It was a question of finance,' said Craig. 'He couldn't really afford a full-time mechanic as he was riding in one league only. He had a new house, was married and had a daughter; I think it was tough for him. That was the way it was. We didn't fall out about it, and we made it to the end of the year. I had known him for a long time, and we had been friends for a long, long time. But working for him was enlightening to say the least!

'Nothing bothers him. It was like, "it's in the history books, oh well, let's go and have a pint." That was his attitude. He raced to make enough money to enjoy his life – which was what he did, basically.'

Nevertheless, Kelly enjoyed a better season for Belle Vue in 1990. He produced some wonderful racing and finished third in the Skol Masters at Oxford. In an impressive performance at Wolverhampton in a Gold Cup clash where he scored 12 points, he crashed spectacularly in the final heat. When the announcer asked him if he was okay following his trip into the Wolves safety fence, he replied: 'Yeah, I landed on my head. I'm always okay if I land on my head!'

He qualified for his third British League Riders' Final and put in a determined display to finish runner-up to Hans Nielsen with 12 points. He defeated Ronnie Correy in a run-off, and was by far the most exciting rider on view. Shawn, as defending champion, finished ninth on 7 points, but he failed to score in his last two rides.

Unfortunately, it was a frustrating year for the club's management. They had proved that the team was capable of demolishing their opposition, but time and again, the side's inconsistency let them down. A sequence of six league matches without a defeat put the Aces in a position to challenge for the league championship, which they hadn't won since 1982. But they could only manage to win three of their last eight matches.

But in the Knockout Cup, the Aces were involved in a controversial semi-final with Reading, when after they did all the hard work of overhauling the Racers, they were thrown out by the Speedway Control Board. Reading had protested about the Aces' use of rider replacement for Peter Ravn, as the Danish rider had put in a transfer request. Shawn was quoted as saying, 'All that work for nothing.'

In the end they finished third in the league, but there was much bitterness within the Aces club over a year which had promised much but delivered little. John Perrin faced criticism from the fans and many felt that drastic

1990 British League Riders Championship. From left to right: Ronnie Correy (third), Hans Nielsen (first), Kelly Moran (second).

All action Ace – Kelly racing for Belle Vue.

changes were needed.

Eastbourne announced their intention to return to the top flight and immediately Kelly was linked with a move back to the Sussex club. A provisional team was announced which included Kelly as their number one, and also included a future World Champion in Tony Rickardsson. But internal politics meant that the Eagles did not return to the BL, and in fact they closed altogether!

There were sweeping changes to the structure of British Speedway that saw the two leagues amalgamate into a first and second division with promotion and relegation. The bottom club from the first division would be relegated and replaced by the top team in the second for the following season. Therefore, it seemed that Eastbourne's plans to rejoin the BL in its old format jeopardised these plans, and they were the unfortunate victims. Happily, they were back in business again by 1992.

Shawn Moran faced a winter of uncertainty following a positive drugs sample he provided at the 1990 Overseas Final. The FIM suspended him from international competition until 27 April 1991, and was stripped of his runners-up position in the World Final. This meant that he would miss the first six weeks of the new season. Therefore, he decided to take out a British Auto Cycle Union licence so that he wouldn't have to make compulsory returns to the US to race and, in doing so, he believed that he would be able to begin his third season with the Aces without missing their opening matches.

However, a minefield of red tape seemed to stand in his way. The British Auto Cycle Union refused to issue him with a licence, even though the world governing body – the FIM – the BSPA and the SCB all raised no objection. This latest controversy blew up just weeks before the club's opening match of the new season. John Perrin did his level best to sort it out and public opinion was definitely with the popular American – as it had been throughout this unfortunate saga. Understandably, Shawn was becoming frustrated and disillusioned by the whole episode. 'I'm really tired of it,' he said. 'They're really dragging me around and I don't know why. The FIM don't mind me riding nor does the SCB. And the ACU raised no objections before. Right now I feel like going home and forgetting about speedway. I'll work for a friend in the States and pack it all in.'

The ACU maintained that they would not issue Shooey with a licence until the FIM ban had expired. The authorities' hard line approach to the issue of drugs in speedway racing went a bit over the top when a top National League rider also faced a possible ban for taking an over-the-counter cold remedy, Night Nurse. Consequently, it was not surprising that the ACU were being rigid with their policies. They eventually conceded that they would review the situation if the Speedway Control Board and the British Speedway Promoters' Association indicated by letter that they had no objections to Moran riding.

Eventually, common sense prevailed and Shawn was issued with a licence and was free to start the British season in Belle Vue's first official fixture. But all the hassles and bureaucratic nonsense had taken their toll, and he announced that he would make 1991 his last year as he planned to quit the sport at the end of the season.

Through it all, John Thomas, the chairman of the Glossop and District Speedway Supporters Club, staged a benefit evening for the injured Joe Owen – a team-mate of the Morans at Hull – and former Aces' favourite, Alan Wilkinson. Shooey was singled out by Thomas for a special mention, when he donated a pair of his leathers for the auction which raised £100. 'It's typical of him. He may not be the World No.2 in the eyes of the FIM – but he is No.1. with us!'

Kelly also returned to Belle Vue for his third season in the Aces colours, even though he was linked with a move to Berwick. John Perrin told *Speedway Mail*: 'Before people ask "why Kelly Moran?", I'll tell you. After looking through the riders available, I could see only two, Kelvin Tatum and Marvyn Cox, of anything like the same calibre. With Tatum priced at £28,000 and Cox at over £20,000, my answer to the people who asked the question is, "why not Kelly Moran?"'

They were joined in the team by their former team-mate at Sheffield, Neil Collins, Joe Screen, Carl Stonehewer, Nigel Leaver and Max Schofield. Shawn was made captain of Belle Vue following the retirement of Chris Morton. As the opening fixture, a special farewell meeting was staged at Kirky Lane for their long-serving rider.

But the nightmare of the last few months was not over yet for Shawn: after he won his first race and then followed Ronnie Correy home for a 5-1, a stone hit him under his right eye while watching the racing in between heats. He was forced to withdraw from the rest of the meeting, which saw many old stars make a return to the track, such as Eric Broadbelt, Jim McMillan, Tom Owen, Geoff Pusey, and Paul Tyrer.

By now, both of the Moran brothers were experienced campaigners and the young riders in the team often looked to them for advice and guidance. Joe Screen went on record to say that he enjoyed racing with Kelly and Shawn as they always looked out for him on and off the track. Carl Stonehewer was finding his feet at Belle Vue in 1991 and he recalled that they were great team members. 'They were brilliant blokes – the both of them. Kelly was a flat out party animal, but he was 100 per cent with the young lads. They looked after us superbly and I learned a lot from them.'

Meanwhile, Sheffield had reopened in the second division. Cliff Carr, who was the uncle to former Tiger Peter, lined up Belle Vue as the club's first opponents in a special challenge match that brought the Morans and Neil Collins back to Owlerton for one night. Half an hour before the scheduled start time, the stadium's reduced 2,400 capacity was full. In a close-fought match, the honours were even as the encounter finished as a 45-45 draw; Shawn top-scored with 12-points, while Kelly and Collins scored 9-points each.

Shooey alerted the magazine, *Speedway Now*, about a serious crash at a practice session at Bradford, when a young junior rider, Alan Askew, sustained severe spinal injuries. As a result he was left paralysed from the waist down and was taken to Pinderfields Hospital for treatment – which was the same medical

Joe Screen (left) and Shawn.

establishment that treated three-times World Champion, Erik Gundersen.

'Andrew is in good spirits,' said Shooey. 'In fact, Mr Bear from Bradford brought a strip-o-gram with him, so that cheered everyone up!'

In many ways it was a case of 'as you were', as the Aces team continued to be frustratingly inconsistent. They lost too many matches away from home and once again dipped out of the Knockout Cup at the semi-final stage – this time to Bradford. They finished fourth in the league again, despite several changes to the side's lower end throughout the season.

Shawn experienced a troubled season and he crashed and broke his collarbone twice – once while riding in the Swedish League, and again at Belle Vue. His form in Britain improved, but it was clear that his enthusiasm for racing was not there. Then in September, he returned from a racing trip in Sweden and told Perrin that he had quit. He simply said that he didn't want to ride anymore.

His decision caught everyone by surprise – including his brother. Amazingly, a week later, Shooey was back for Belle Vue and helped them to defeat Eastbourne with 7 points and was paired with his brother for his first two races. He said that he raced because he wanted to see how he felt about the sport, but admitted that his attitude was not what it should be for speedway. He raced again at Wolverhampton, where he produced a lacklustre performance to finish with 4 points, and admitted that it was best if he stopped riding. Perrin said that it was obvious that he was doing no one any favours and it was hoped that a winter away from the sport would rekindle his enthusiasm for racing. His retirement meant that he was withdrawn from the British League Riders' Championship and was replaced by his brother.

It was a similar season for Kelly to the one he experienced in 1990. His individual highlight was winning the Peter Craven Memorial Trophy for the second time at Belle Vue with a maximum, and he said that it was to show the people who left him out of America's World Team Cup team. He also won a pairs meeting at Sheffield with Neil Evitts. It was a unique event as all the pairs were brothers – except Shawn's retirement meant that the only non-family union in the line-up won the meeting! His average only dropped slightly, and at Reading, the fans could only stand and applaud as he rounded the Racers' pairing of Jan Andersson and Mitch Shirra in one spectacular swoop as they tried to block him out. But his season ended painfully when Ronnie Correy piled into the back of him and he sustained another broken collarbone, a punctured lung and three broken ribs. This ruled him out of the BLRC and his place was taken by Joe Screen.

During the winter, Shawn Moran caught his boss by surprise when he announced that he wanted to race again. As the new season approached, it seemed that the Moran brothers would be racing together at Belle Vue after all. Another American, Bobby Ott, also returned along with Joe Screen, Carl Stonehewer, the new Australian signing, Jason Lyons, and Richard Musson. However, after appearing at the club's press and practice day, he had a dispute over terms with John Perrin and he was transfer-listed. On the eve of their

Kelly leads his brother, Shawn, while Swindon's Andrew Silver tries to split the Americans.

opening match against Oxford, it appeared that what Shooey wanted was quite different to what the Aces were prepared to give. To add further to Perrin's headache, Stonehewer missed the start of the season when he broke his collarbone while practising.

Kelly top-scored with 13 points as Belle Vue defeated the Cheetahs, 49-41, while Shawn said that he wanted to race for the Aces and was waiting for the outspoken Perrin to get in touch to negotiate. Instead, Perrin plunged into the transfer market and signed the promising Dane, Frede Schott from Edinburgh. At this early stage in the season, it seemed that Shooey would find it hard to get fixed up elsewhere.

The Aces' Gold Cup campaign was a disappointment. After their win at home to Oxford, another six matches passed before they collected their second victory of the season. It was clear that John Perrin would not be happy with their start to the 1992 season, and with his former captain on the sidelines, it seemed only a matter of time before changes were made.

The man to make way for Shawn was Kelly! The elder of the Moran brothers had experienced a slow start to the season, and had struggled at times. However, Shawn would not ride for the club unless his older brother was fixed up elsewhere, even though it was only Poole that had shown an interest in a loan deal. Therefore, Kelly raced his last meeting for Belle Vue at Oxford where he scored 3 points as they lost 51-39. That night, he was informed that he would be riding for Swindon as from the following day.

Swindon had finished bottom of the league in 1991, but had managed to avoid relegation on a technicality. John Davis had crashed and had broken his leg and was ruled out for the rest of the season. The Robins boss, Ron Byford, had hoped to bring back Peter Nahlin, but he couldn't agree terms with the Swede and snapped up Kelly instead.

He made his debut for Swindon on 30 April 1992, in a Knockout Cup match against Wolverhampton. He got off to the worst possible start as he retired from his first race with engine failure, and eventually finished with 3 points as Swindon lost 47-43.

'It upset me a little to be transferred to Swindon like that,' said Kelly. 'It was just like you said: John came up to me and said, 'You're riding at Swindon tomorrow.' I never understood it, as I thought I was doing okay for Belle Vue. I know I had my disagreements with John, but we got along fine. I never had any problems over contracts – once it was done, then that was it. But I could be outspoken; I wasn't like some of them who would walk away with his tail between his legs. So we clashed a bit, but I thought "oh well, I like the Swindon track".'

In the club's programme notes, the club was pleased with their signing: 'Kelly was very disappointed with his debut as a Robin last week, but we can be patient while he settles in because on his day he can beat the best riders in the world. Hopefully he will have sorted out his machine problems, and tonight we shall see the 'real Kelly' in action, which is one of the most thrilling sights in speedway.'

Among Kelly's team-mates at Swindon was the up-and-coming Australian,

Mitch Shirra (left) talks with Kelly at Swindon in 1992.

Leigh Adams, Mitch Shirra, Jimmy Nilsen, Dean Standing and Justin Elkins. Such was the ruling with regard to English riders, that the Robins signed the inexperienced, but very promising Steve Masters from Eastbourne.

'I joined Swindon around the same time as Kelly – he was a hero of mine,' Masters recalled. 'I was very green and inexperienced when I raced for Swindon then. I was pitted next to Mitch Shirra, who was always positive about his racing. And because Kelly was such a hero of mine, I latched onto him. He was always helpful and along with Mitch, I was never short of advice or guidance.

'The First Division in those days was really tough – especially for someone who was as inexperienced as I was. Kelly was at the end of his career when he came to Swindon. He had some problems, but he was quiet and he got on with his racing.

'I heard all sorts of stories of Kelly doing some pretty amazing things around Eastbourne – he was a legend. They were both so talented. No one could hang off the bike like them. It couldn't be done now, because the bikes are so different to when they raced.'

The day after Kelly had made his debut for Swindon, Shawn made his return to the Aces fold and scored 7 points as they won their last Gold Cup match at home to Bradford. Then, on 8 May, they found themselves in opposition in Britain for the first time since 1982, when the Robins travelled to Belle Vue for a league match.

Swindon had defeated Eastbourne the night before, and Kelly had scored a paid 11 points. The Robins were determined to avoid relegation this time, and made the trip north to Belle Vue with a useful team. However, despite another paid-11 score from a fired-up Kelly, Swindon lost 56-34, and during the battle of the Morans, it was Kelly who won both encounters.

Indeed, it looked as though the Robins were set for a promising campaign, and their new American signing was showing signs of returning to form. That was until they travelled to Poole in another Gold Cup encounter. Kelly was riding well and things seemed set for a 5-1 with captain Shirra, when the chain on his bike snapped and caused the engine to seize. The American was flipped over the handlebars and he broke his right collarbone.

'When he broke his collarbone at Poole, that was a big blow,' believes Masters. 'He was just beginning to get his form back when that happened. It was a shame.'

Just twelve days later, Kelly made a track return in the Bank Holiday clash with Cradley Heath. It was common to stage home and away meetings on a Bank Holiday, and it was usually one match in the morning and then the return in the evening. The fact that the American returned to the track so quickly was amazing enough, but to race in two matches in one day was really quite brave.

However, it transpired that Kelly was pressured into making an early return by the Robins' management, just so that he could ride in the minimum number of races – two – during each encounter. This meant that it would put a little less strain on the side, by not having to replace him with a rider of far less ability.

Swindon v. Poole, 1992. Jimmy Nilsen of Swindon leads his team-mate Kelly, while Poole's Tony Langdon brings up the rear.

At this time, he had been wearing new leathers, which had yet to be worn in. This meant that movement could be restricted as the material is stiff, and when you ride a speedway bike you need to be relaxed and comfortable. This would not be a problem for a fully fit rider, but to one who had recently broken his collarbone which had not yet healed properly, the tight confines of a new leather suit can put unnecessary and painful pressure on the injury. Therefore, he borrowed an old set from Cradley's Greg Hancock.

In the morning match at Cradley, which Swindon lost, Kelly retired from his opening race and was then excluded from his second race for a tape offence. When it came to the evening meeting, he managed a third place in his opening race and then finished at the back in his second, as the Robins took a narrow two-point victory. It was clear that he was far from fit, and by the time he raced in the evening meeting at Swindon, he was just about hanging onto his bike. The track doctor was called to the pits and he was withdrawn from the rest of the meeting under orders from the doctor. Consequently, he was ruled out of Swindon's next match – which they lost – and fate allowed him another week to recover as their home fixture against Bradford was postponed because of wet weather.

The home and away Bank Holiday meetings was a new experience for Masters, and the experienced duo of Moran and Shirra left him with a lasting memory. 'I learnt how to drive fast,' he said. 'We had been racing at Cradley in the morning and as it was a bank holiday, we had the return at Swindon in the evening. Mitch had seized an engine in the morning match, so we dropped by his place to pick up another for the evening. That didn't leave us much time to get to Swindon. I was only twenty-one and new, so I followed Kelly and Mitch. Well, they went like the wind! They went through roadworks, red lights and everything! There is always a few seconds from the lights turning red before the traffic in the opposite direction gets the green, and they were taking full advantage of it. It was pretty scary to keep up, but we made it on time.'

Shawn, meanwhile, was taking his time to get back in the groove, but a paid maximum at Eastbourne was followed by a full maximum at King's Lynn a week later. That signalled that 'The Miracle Worker' was back. Indeed he had some fine displays and finished in second place in the club's averages to Joe Screen. He was back to something like his best form, and won over the supporters who felt let down by his indecision at the end of 1991, and the eve of season contract dispute with John Perrin.

The first major trophy since Perrin took charge also headed to the Manchester club, when they won the First Division Four Team Championship held at Peterborough. Shawn was a joint top-scorer with 7 points. Swindon also qualified for the finals with a series of confident qualifying round performances. But they were handicapped by the absence of the in-form Leigh Adams, and a controversial tapes exclusion for Shirra – followed by a lengthy protest from the Kiwi – and finished in fourth place. Kelly scored a hard-earned three points, but

Shawn in discussion with his Australian team-mate at Belle Vue, Jason Lyons.

Shirra took no further part in the meeting.

The Aces finished in fifth place in the league and once again they were knocked out of the cup, at the semi-final stage, by Bradford. But for Kelly and Swindon, it was a different story.

When he moved to the Robins, the mechanic who had started the season with him could not make the weekly Thursday trip from his Northern base to Swindon. So he had to find another mechanic. He agreed a deal with Rodney Young, a former mechanic to Ronnie Correy, to help him out.

This combination seemed to work as the American began returning to the kind of form that had helped him to make his name. He scored 14 points and passed former Robin, Peter Nahlin, to clinch a draw in the last heat decider against Eastbourne. When Belle Vue came to the Abbey Stadium, Kelly scored 15 points and he swooped round the outside of his brother to take the win and end his hopes of a maximum. He also scored 12 points at Oxford, with only an unfortunate exclusion and a retirement preventing him from scoring more. But suddenly, and without any warning, Young failed to turn up. 'I don't know what happened. I thought we had a deal, but he just didn't turn up,' recalled Kelly.

Meanwhile, the Swindon team were struggling. Despite the solid look of the side, and the talent contained within its members, injuries, inconsistency and bad luck all conspired to ensure that they were facing the embarrassment of relegation again. The track came in for criticism from the riders, while the riders and management came in for even more criticism from the terraces. The atmosphere at the club was not good, as valuable points were dropped as the team's confidence slipped away a bit more with every defeat.

'All of the Swindon teams I have been in over the years have just fallen short,' said Masters. 'Yes, we had a lot of talent in the side, but it just didn't happen. The fans got on our backs. It didn't worry me too much because I was so inexperienced back then, but it did upset the team. I know Mitch and Ron Byford took a lot of stick and they got quite upset by it.'

'Tom Shirra worked on the track,' recalled Kelly. 'And that caused arguments between Mitch and his dad. It was like "Oh God" you know, because that wasn't good. There were so many bumps on the track and we used to say to Tom, "You gotta do something about the first corner." Ron Byford was a nice guy, but it just wasn't working out.'

In the end, it came down to one match at home to Poole. There was a lot of needle between the two clubs over a BSPA Cup clash earlier in the season, when Leigh Adams had defeated Marvyn Cox in a run-off after the two sides had drawn. Adams' victory should have put his side into the final, but Poole protested that the race should not have taken place and, instead, a replay should have been held. Poole's appeal was successful. The re-staging took place at Poole and Swindon were eliminated. There was more than just personal pride at stake, as the Robins also had a score to settle.

The week before, Kelly had scored double figures while guesting at Arena Essex and Mitch had also performed well in the same fixture. Their confidence was high as they believed that they had solved their mechanical problems. However, in heat three, Kelly was following his team-mate Nilsen home for a 5-1 when he seized his engine. He jumped on Adams' spare bike, but struggled on an unfamiliar machine and scored 3 points as Swindon lost 47-43 and were eventually relegated.

'I am just too light for the bike,' said Kelly. 'I knew I had the power to catch the riders, but I was not heavy enough to put weight on the back wheel to pick up grip to get by. We tried adjusting sprockets, but I found every time I came out of the corners I was spinning badly.'

He had experienced the worst season of his career, and yet despite his dip in form, he was still an excellent ambassador for the sport. In a July edition of the Swindon programme, a letter of praise from Judith A. Shields, an English teacher at Ecclesfield School was published about the happy-go-lucky Californian . Kelly and his wife, Lorna, agreed to be interviewed about their lives in speedway by the class for a special assignment.

'The visit was a great success and, although I have already done so person-ally, I would be pleased if somewhere in your programme you could make a public thank you on behalf of the children of form 8E,' she wrote. 'Kelly made himself a few more fans as a result of this visit and it is a pity that Swindon is too far for us to come and support him.'

Swindon's last match of the season ended in a 50-40 defeat at Bradford. The Robins never looked like they would win and Kelly contributed just 2 points, and they were condemned to the cellar position and relegation to Division Two. The match took place on 17 October 1992, and it was the last time that Kelly would race professionally. Kelly's British career had ended similarly to the way in which he had first arrived. There was no big press announcement; in fact his decision to retire was reported by just a few lines at the bottom of an article stating that he wouldn't be returning to Britain in 1993.

During his final season, there were several glimpses of the old Kelly, but it seemed that his heart wasn't really in it anymore. His best individual perfor-mance was a third place in the Super Pink Classic at Swindon. However, he appeared to be tired of all the politics that come with racing in Britain. The smile and the approachable, happy-go-lucky image were still very much in evidence, but there was something about his demeanour that suggested that he wasn't enjoying his speedway as much as he once had. Perhaps racing for a struggling team didn't help, and he confessed after a good night that it was nice to be cheered for once. On one particular occasion, he apologised for cutting our conversation short, and with an air of resignation he said that he had to take a random drugs and alcohol test.

'It's supposed to be random,' he said, 'but I can tell you now that Mitch and myself are always tested.' Therefore, when the news came through that he would not be returning it wasn't a total surprise.

'It was a combination of things,' said Kelly. 'It was a tough season at Swindon. I just couldn't get the set-up right. I would go to one of the away tracks and do

The view that many riders would get of Shooey, this time at Belle Vue in 1993.

okay, and I would think that I got it figured out, but then I'd come back to Swindon and I would be struggling again. I just couldn't get going. It didn't matter what I did, I just couldn't do it. I got along okay with Ron Byford and the rest of the guys, so there was no problem there. I just began to wonder if something was trying to tell me something. I was still pretty upset by the way the Belle Vue thing came about and I just decided that it was time to do something else.'

Shawn Moran was made captain of Belle Vue again for the 1993 season, and it turned out to be a successful year for the Aces. Very few changes were made to the basic structure of the team, but the format for league racing was changed during the winter. A match was now run over eighteen heats, and the number of riders in the team was increased from seven to eight. Screen, Ott, Lyons, Stonehewer and Schott all returned, and were joined by Jon Armstrong and Peter Scully.

The bottom end of the side was changed throughout the season, with Paul Smith and Max Schofield eventually filling the positions. The Canadian Shawn Venables had a short spell in an Aces race jacket before an injury ended his run in the team, and then Mike Lewthwaite had a brief run before the preferred Smith and Schofield made the positions their own. But it was another stormy year for the club.

A rigid pay structure had been agreed upon during the winter by the BSPA, and many of the riders were having problems making their racing pay. The Belle Vue riders were not happy and Perrin once blasted the side by saying that if he gave in to their demands, then Belle Vue Speedway would close within a week.

However, the Aces team continued to hold their own on their home track, but were not picking up wins on their travels. But by the time August came along, the team's prospects began to look better. They won at Ipswich, Cradley and Coventry, as well as progressing to the semi-final stages of the Knockout Cup, when they defeated Wolverhampton. However, they may have climbed to third place in the league table, but they were still 13 points adrift of the leaders and reigning champions, Wolves, and 5 points behind second-placed Eastbourne.

Then, in the final race at Bradford, Shooey produced a captain's performance to team up with Jason Lyons and score a 5-1 to give them an important draw. It was at this point, with matches in hand, that a serious assault on the league title didn't seem quite so unlikely. Even Perrin felt that his side had a genuine chance.

But following a narrow victory over Reading, Perrin quit as team manager after another disagreement with his riders. His co-promoter, Don Bowes, took over the managerial duties, but once again the Aces were knocked out of the cup at the semi-final stage – this time by Arena Essex. While this was a disappointment, they were at least now free to concentrate on the league.

Wolves' stranglehold at the top began to slip following injuries to their American duo of Sam Ermolenko and Ronnie Correy. The Aces won six matches in succession as they closed in on Wolves at the top.

The league championship would be decided in one night of high drama on 25 October 1993, when Belle Vue travelled to Wolverhampton. It was simple – the Aces had to win to be crowned League Champions. It was the same scenario as the Coventry *v.* Hull showdown in 1979.

There was never more than three points separating the sides throughout the match. With the three races to go, Wolves were leading 46-43. Shawn won the next race and Max Schofield took third and put the Aces to within one point of the title. Joe Screen won the penultimate race ahead of Mikael Karlsson, but Stonehewer took third and with one race left, the Aces held a slender one-point lead. Bobby Ott and Lyons faced the Wolves duo of Peter Karlsson and Henka Gustafsson, who was deputising for the injured Ermolenko. Ott made the start and was away, but his partner, Lyons, slotted in behind. He was passed by the Wolves pairing, but he held them up long enough to allow 'Showtime' Bobby Ott to clinch the club's first league championship title for eleven years.

John Perrin sat at home and watched television as his side pulled off a dramatic victory. Howes telephoned his partner to inform him of the win.

Shawn scored a valuable 6 points in the meeting but, unbeknown to most of the people who were crammed into Monmore Green that evening, he was in a lot of pain, having broken a front tooth before the match, exposing a nerve. 'Before the match, I went to a fish shop with my mechanic, Gordon Hemmingway, when I broke my tooth while eating,' he explained. 'Oh God it hurt. When I took the trophy, I couldn't smile properly, well I did, but I wasn't a pretty sight you know. I talked funny too. I wasn't nervous at all; I never really got nervous for those kinds of meetings, even the World Finals. But Bobby pulled it out of the bag when it mattered, didn't he? It's always nice to win and it was good to finish at the top that year.'

Shawn enjoyed a quite successful year and ended it by finishing runner-up in the Northern Riders' Championship at Sheffield. His experience was a boost for the younger riders in the team, and his cool head often helped turn matches. His average had slipped and he was fourth in the team's averages at the end of the season. However, he still scored double figures in 17 of the club's 48 official fixtures, and he finished with three paid maximums. It was clear that he wasn't the force in the top flight that he had once been, but he only scored less than six points on one occasion.

Despite the success, there were doubts about the future of Belle Vue. They were paying a very high rent to use the facilities at Kirkmanshulme Lane – reportedly the highest rent for any speedway team in the country. With promotion and relegation scrapped, it seemed that Belle Vue would apply to join the Second Division to reduce costs. But in the end, they did remain in the top league to defend their title.

As John Perrin began assembling a team, it seemed unlikely that Shooey would be included. In February 1994, the news was first announced that he might switch to the Second Division and ride for Sheffield. A major stumbling block was the conversion of his First Division average, which was a massive 11.76! As good as he still was, it seemed unlikely that he would be able to maintain that figure.

Negotiations were held up while Perrin made sure that he had the side that he wanted; ironically, it was his signing of a new star from America, Chris Manchester, which meant that Shawn was free to rejoin the Tigers. Sheffield's management duo of Neil Machin and Tim Lucking were delighted with their signing and predicted big things for the club.

Shawn scored 10 points during his return to Owlerton, but he couldn't prevent Sheffield losing to Long Eaton, 49-47. They lost the return 59-37, with Shooey top scoring with 11 points. This was followed by a heavy 64-32 defeat at Middlesbrough and Shawn fell while leading heat seven. Despite finishing with 9 points, this match would have a significant effect on the career of Shawn Moran and the remainder of Sheffield's campaign.

The Tigers suffered another thrashing at Peterborough, 65-31, and had yet to win a match. Shawn scored just 3 points in this match. There were concerns about the Tigers' poor start to the season, but everyone was confident that it was only a matter of time before their American signing would begin to show the kind of form that was expected of him.

They lost 58-38 at Swindon, and Shawn crashed in his first race and withdrew from the meeting with an ankle injury. But no one could guess what effect these tumbles were having on the American, as he scored just 16 points in the Tigers' three defeats at the hands of Scottish rivals, Glasgow and Edinburgh. Machin blasted his side after another defeat at the hands of Swindon at home, in which Shawn scored 9 points.

Shawn seemingly returned to form in the Tigers' home fixture against Oxford when he scored 11 points, but they still lost to the Cheetahs. But then, faced with travelling to Newcastle, Shooey stunned everyone when he announced that he had quit!

Predictably, the Sheffield management were upset by his decision and Machin went on record to say that he wouldn't employ any more riders over the age of thirty! Shawn said that he didn't want any more injuries, and he was quoted as saying that if a rider ran underneath him, he would be the first to pull out. He was frank and honest about the fear of hitting the safety fence.

'It was nothing specific; I just didn't want to get hurt anymore. I guess it built up over a season or so,' explained Shawn. 'I would get worried about racing. You know, when you're racing, you find yourself in situations – situations you've got to try and get out of. And sometimes you can't always do that. When I sit and think about some of the conditions we used to race in, oh man! The promoters used to put pressure on you to race. It didn't worry me as a young guy, but it did later. As I said, it was no one thing – it was a combination of things towards the end.'

The Belle Vue boss, John Perrin, gave an indication that Shawn had changed as a rider when he looked back over a troubled, but successful 1993 season. 'He has still got it, but he isn't as good as he was. He's a bit safety first now, but generally speaking he did his job.'

Shawn regretted letting down the club and its supporters, and he never planned it that way. He wanted to do it, but he just couldn't. The last thing that he wanted to be was a danger to someone else, and as a much of a blow as it was to Sheffield, it was undoubtedly the right decision.

His former team-mate, Sean Wilson, recalled a conversation he had with Shawn after he was recovering from a back injury. 'When I did my back and everything, and I was trying to race again, he had just quit. I never asked him why, and we were talking one day and he said, "as much as you want to ride Sean, I don't." And it was as blunt as that.'

Reg Wilson could understand how it came about and recalled his own retirement for comparison. 'You still think you can do it, but part of you won't let you. I know when I finished, because you don't know anything else and you've been doing it for that many years, you don't know any different. You think it's going to go on forever, but it doesn't, it comes to a stop. Shawn admitted it, he had lost his bottle. You can't knock him for that. He thought he could do it, but he couldn't. He was fantastic – one of Sheffield's best.'

There were no second thoughts during the winter this time. Per Jonsson, who defeated Shawn to win the 1990 World Championship in a run-off, crashed badly and sustained injuries of such severity that he was paralysed. Shawn admits that he thought about Per, and Erik Gundersen, who also suffered bad injuries in pursuit of speedway glory.

It was fitting that his last competitive speedway meeting should be at Sheffield –

One of the last pictures taken of Shawn on parade for Sheffield during his brief return in 1994.

a club where he was worshipped and where he had enjoyed some of his most successful seasons. It was the end of an era, as the sport was changing. The riders of the likes of the Moran brothers are a one-off. Some say that we will never see their like again …

'They were in speedway at the right time,' said Eric Boocock. 'They couldn't do it today; even at Second Division you have to be 100 per cent committed. But in those days it was still a bit of fun, and they really enjoyed it. I don't think they have any regrets about doing it. When Shawn won the Long Track with a broken leg, that was a bit brave because they're going a bit quick there. And I'll always remember the 1990 World Team Cup. Kelly had been out the night before and he was absolutely out of it – really bad. But after he got a last in his first ride, he was unbelievable.'

Opinion is divided about the level of success they achieved, and perhaps should have achieved. Sadly, some will tell you that they wasted their talent, which is not the way to look at them. But most people agree that they had a unique talent and they were genuine people, and genuine speedway stars.

'They should have gone a heck of a lot further than they did,' agrees Greg Hancock. 'Maybe that was all they wanted to do though. They had their sights set, and they knew what they wanted to do and they did it. So what we saw was what they wanted. So I think the best we can do is to remember them for the great years they gave us, the great racing, the achievements and inspiration they were to themselves, the fans and to us – the other riders.'

'I never met a person who didn't like them,' said Cummings. 'They are the nicest people you could ever meet. Even Kenny Carter liked them and he hated Americans, but Kelly and Shawn were like his buddies.'

Kelly and Shawn Moran may have been superstars in the world of speedway, but you could walk up to them and talk to them as normal people. They were great ambassadors for the sport, and perhaps the promoters and authorities of the time missed the point when they tried to get them to conform. During the mid-1980s, there was more press interest in the Moran brothers than that of Danish World Champions, Erik Gundersen and Hans Nielsen, but the powers that be didn't know how to handle it. They did things their way and for the most part it worked, and sometimes it didn't. But as they would say, that's racing.

EPILOGUE

The year after Shawn retired, speedway racing began to change. The old one-off World Final was scrapped, and it was replaced by a Grand Prix series, which has proved to be a great success. It has improved the image of the sport and brought it up to a new level of professionalism.

Speedway in America continues to survive in California, but it is a far cry from the boom period of the early 1980s, and it has never managed to establish itself in other parts of the country. The exploits of Billy Hamill and Greg Hancock have continued to ensure that the country remains on the speedway map, and another generation of riders are emerging to take their place.

Kelly and Shawn Moran now lead a quieter life in the deserts of Southern California, where they renovate apartment buildings. They have only sat on a speedway bike once or twice since they retired. Kelly appeared in an 'old timers' race at Costa Mesa, and they both had a taste of Hamill's lay down bike, which left them with varying opinions. Would they like to be involved with the sport again?

'No,' says Shawn firmly. 'I'm happy to sit in the stands with a beer and relax. I enjoyed it and it was a lot of fun. When I was racing I never thought it would end because I was having such a good time, but I do regret not looking after the business side of things a bit better. I do miss all the guys; I think about them and wonder what they're doing all the time. That was the best thing about it, being with all the other riders and meeting people, it was a lot of fun and I had some great times. But no, I don't think I would want to be involved anymore.'

'I don't think the authorities would have me, because I was too outspoken' believed Kelly. 'People sometimes say to me, 'why don't you be the US team manager, you'd be great, Jelly Man.' But it just wouldn't happen. I'd love to be team manager of say Poland – that would be cool! I would like to think that I could still help with my experience. I don't go to speedway here, they've got five-man races to try and get the people in and the AMA were never interested in it. I don't regret anything and I do miss everyone in England – there are so many people to thank, that it would fill a book in itself. But Shawn and I would like to say thanks to all our sponsors, friends and supporters – we had a great time when we were racing. We were very lucky to see the world like we did.'

If they were to have their time over again, I believe that their natural ability would see them compete at the highest level. The history books will show that they made their mark upon the sport but, as I'm sure most people will agree, they were much more than just professional speedway riders.

RACING RECORDS

KELLY MORAN

Born: 21 September 1960, Lakewood, California, USA

BRITISH LEAGUE CAREER AVERAGES:

Year/Club	Matches	Rides	1sts	2nds	3rds	Unplac.	Points	Bonus Pts	Total Pts	Cal. Match Ave.	Maximums Full	Paid
1978 Hull	26	109	23	27	31	28	154	37	191	7.01	-	-
1979 Hull	39	153	55	57	16	25	295	29	324	8.47	2	7
1980 Birmingham	22	101	35	36	15	15	192	16	208	8.24	-	2
1981 Eastbourne	30	135	80	35	7	13	317	5	322	9.54	9	-
1982 Eastbourne	35	146	76	38	18	14	322	29	351	9.62	7	2
1986 Sheffield	21	90	39	29	12	10	187	10	197	8.75	1	1
1987 Sheffield	38	159	73	48	24	14	339	28	367	9.23	6	3
1988 Sheffield	41	207	82	71.5	35.5	18	424.5	24	448.5	8.66	2	4
1989 Belle Vue	24	106	40	30	19	17	199	15	214	8.07	2	-
1990 Belle Vue	39	184	64	67	30	23	356	31	387	8.41	-	-
1991 Belle Vue	41	203	70	76	30	27	392	28	420	8.28	1	2
1992 Belle Vue	10	41	6	12	13	10	55	4	59	5.75	-	-
1992 Swindon	25	113	22	25	36	30	152	20	172	6.08	-	-
Career Totals	391	1747	665	551.5	286.5	244	3384.5	276	3660.5	8.38	30	21
	Matches	Rides	1sts	2nds	3rds	Unplac.	Points	Pts Bonus	Pts Total	Cal Ave.	Full	Paid

The above statistics cover all official league and cup matches.
Calculated Match Average (Cal. Match Ave.) is the total points divided by the number
of rides multiplied by four.

WORLD CHAMPIONSHIP:

1979 Katowice, Poland	11 points	4th
1982 Los Angeles, USA	11 points	4th
1984 Gothenburg, Sweden	11 points	4th

BRITISH LEAGUE RIDERS' CHAMPIONSHIP:

1987	11 points	3rd
1988	5 points	12th
1990	12 points	2nd
1991	Qualified but was unable to compete due to injury.	

OTHER MAJOR HONOURS:

1982 and 1990 World Team Cup Champion, runner-up in 1988, and third 1983, 1984, and 1987. 1986 World Pairs runner-up, and third in 1987 (with Sam Ermolenko) and 1990 World Pairs Finalist (with Ronnie Correy). US National Champion in 1983 and 1984, US Best Pairs Champion 1984 (with Mike Faria), 1984 Ventura Track Champion, 1985 Bruce Penhall Classic Champion, US Spring Classic Champion 1986 and Challenge Cup winner with Sheffield in 1986.

Appearances for the USA: 57

SHAWN MORAN

Born: 19 November 1961, Lakewood, California, USA

BRITISH LEAGUE CAREER AVERAGES:

Year/Club	Matches	Rides	1sts	2nds	3rds	Unplac.	Points	Bonus Pts	Total Pts	Cal. Match Ave.	Maximums Full	Paid
1980 Hull	29	128	28	33	29	38	179	28	207	6.46	-	1
1980 Sheffield	6	21	8	3	3	7	33	3	36	6.86	-	1
1981 Sheffield	24	107	51	30	13	13	226	7	233	8.71	5	1
1982 Sheffield	34	155	84	40	20	11	352	18	370	9.55	3	1
1983 Sheffield	26	120	54	42	16	8	262	21	283	9.43	1	2
1984 Sheffield	39	170	106	36	14	14	404	22	426	10.02	6	5
1985 Sheffield	38	165	94	58	7	6	405	24	429	10.40	4	9
1986 Sheffield	35	153	71	54	16	12	337	32	369	9.65	4	4
1987 Sheffield	43	180	86	64	14	16	400	26	426	9.47	4	5
1988 Sheffield	39	199	106	56	19	18	449	24	473	9.50	3	3
1989 Belle Vue	30	143	74	41	15	13	319	27	346	9.68	3	5
1990 Belle Vue	28	134	43	43	23	25	238	30	268	8.00	1	2
1991 Belle Vue	27	122	42	39	23	18	227	36	263	8.62	-	2
1992 Belle Vue	30	130	57	32	24	17	259	29	288	8.86	1	3
1993 Belle Vue	48	250	72	71	54	53	412	62	474	7.58	-	3
1994 Sheffield	10	46	11	10	15	10	68	5	73	6.35	-	-
Career Totals	486	2223	987	652	305	279	4570	394	4964	8.93	35	47
	Matches	Rides	1sts	2nds	3rds	Unplac.	Points	Pts Bonus	Pts Total	Cal Ave.	Full	Paid

WORLD CHAMPIONSHIP:

1984 Gothenburg, Sweden   7 points   8th
1985 Bradford, England   10 points   5th
1990 Bradford, England   13 points   2nd

BRITISH LEAGUE RIDERS' CHAMPIONSHIP:

1981	13 points	3rd
1982	14 points	2nd
1984	11 points	5th
1985	11 points	5th
1986	11 points	3rd
1987	0 points	16th
1988	10 points	5th
1989	15 points	1st
1990	7 points	9th

OTHER MAJOR HONOURS:

World Long Track Champion 1983 and third in 1987. World Team Champion 1982 and 1990, runner-up 1985, 1986 and 1988, and third in 1984 and 1987. Third in the 1985 World Pairs Championship (with Bobby Schwartz) and 1988 (with Sam Ermolenko), and World Pairs Finalist in 1984 (with Schwartz). European Under-21 Champion in 1981 and Finalist in 1980. US National Champion in 1982, and American Champion in 1986 and 1990. US Long Track Champion in 1979 and 1980. Intercontinental Champion in 1984, 1985 and 1990, and Overseas Champion in 1985. British League Championship winner with Belle Vue in 1993, and Four Team Championship winner with Belle Vue in 1992.

Appearances for the USA: 76

SWEDISH ELITE LEAGUE CAREER AVERAGES:

Year/Club	Matches	Rides	Points	Bonus Points	Total Points	Cal. Match Ave.	Maximums Full	Paid
1990 Rospiggarna	10	31	73	6	79	10.19	-	1
1991 Rospiggarna	6	26	38	8	46	7.08	-	1
Career Totals	16	57	111	14	125	8.77	-	2

RESULTS AS A PAIR

Below is a statistical look at Kelly and Shawn's results as a pair when they raced together in the British League from 1986 to 1991.

Year/Club	Races	5-1	4-2	3-3	2-4	1-5	Points For	Points Against	Race Ave.
1986 Sheffield	7	2	1	2	1	1	23	19	3.28
1987 Sheffield	25	9	2	8	2	4	85	65	3.40
1988 Sheffield	43	17	6	13	1	6	156	102	3.62
1989 Belle Vue	4	1	1	2	0	0	15	9	3.75
1990 Belle Vue	36	16	4	5	8	3	130	86	3.61
1991 Belle Vue	26	10	2	9	1	4	91	65	3.50
Totals	141	55	16	39	13	18	500	346	3.55

Race Average is calculated by the number of 'points for' divided by the number of races.